THE LOST PARADIS

The
LOST PARADISE

the Jesuit Republic
in South America

PHILIP CARAMAN

You bade the Red Man rise like the Red Clay
Of God's great Adam in his human right,
Till trailed the snake of trade, our own time's blight,
And man lost Paradise in Paraguay.

'To the Jesuits', G. K. CHESTERTON

DORSET PRESS
New York

ISBN 0-88029-494-9

Printed in the United States of America

M 9 8 7 6 5 4 3 2 1

Contents

List of Maps

Acknowledgements

In preparing this book I have incurred many debts of gratitude in a number of countries. I should name first Lorenzo Reynal of Buenos Aires. Landing with him at Santo Angel in the Brazilian province of Rio Grande do Sul, I was able to visit San Miguel and San Juan among the fateful Reductions of the east bank of the Uruguay. On another flight with him I saw San Ignacio Miní, Loreto, Santa Ana and Candelaria in the Argentine province of Misiones and also the Reductions of Jesús and Trinidad across the river in Paraguay. Again thanks to him, I was able to follow in reverse at a low altitude for a hundred and twenty miles the route down the upper Paraná taken by Montoya from the Falls of Guairá to the Iguazú. A visit to the Chiquitos missions was also made possible through his kindness. Cloud conditions ruled out a landing at San Javier and Concepción, but from San Ignacio we were able to travel through the bush to San Miguel, San Rafael and Santa Ana and then fly on to San José. At Asunción I was greatly helped by Brian MacDermot, then British Ambassador to Paraguay. As well as arranging for me to meet León Cadogan, who had intimate knowledge of Guaraní customs and folk-lore, he drove me to see the six Paraguay Reductions which I had not visited from the Argentine. Also in Asunción I became indebted to Padre Bartolomé Meliá, who introduced me to a group of primitive Guaraní, untouched by Christianity or, except in their dress, by western civilization, and living as in the days of the Jesuit pioneers in the forest to the east of Coronel Oviedo. It was only after I had exhausted my film that they started playing a ball game described by Ruiz de Montoya in his *Conquista Espiritual*. From Salta in the north of Argentina, Padre Haas took me to the valley of the lower Andes occupied by the Calchaquí at the time of the Conquest. The American Jesuits at Salta and their South American brethren at Buenos Aires, Santa Fe, Córdoba, Asunción and Santa Cruz de la Sierra

9

made me most welcome in their houses. In particular, I am grateful to Padre Ricardo O'Farrell, the Jesuit Provincial of the Argentine, whose guest I was for three months. I must mention also Pepe del Carrill, Argentinian Consul-General in London at the time of my visit to South America, for many introductions to his friends there. I can only thank them collectively for their kindness to me.

In my work in archives and libraries I contracted a further series of debts: to Edmond Lamalle, Keeper of the Jesuit Archives in Rome, and to Ernest Burrus there, for guidance in the early stages of my reading; in London, to Francis Courtney, who made my work much easier by kindly lending me all the books on Paraguay, including Pastells's six volumes, from the library of Heythrop College; to Dr Magnus Mörner, Director of the Ibero-American Institute of Stockholm; and most of all to the late Guillermo Furlong. Almost every day over many weeks in Buenos Aires he answered my questions on a subject he has studied for the greater part of a long life-time; he also introduced me to the National Archives, where his help was invaluable.

For most valuable criticism of the typescript I must again thank Brian MacDermot, particularly for corrections on points of geography; Professor Leandro Tormo of the Instituto Santo Toribio, Madrid, who at great sacrifice of his time examined every paragraph with an expert eye; and finally to John Tranmar and the late Terence Corrigan: both read the book with meticulous attention and gave me useful criticisms of a more general character.

I owe the photographs to many different sources, but especially to the late Felix Plattner, who allowed me to choose any illustrations I wanted from his two books listed in the bibliography; to Bridget Astor, who joined me at Jujuy and flew on to take the photographs of the Chiquitos; and to Alan MacDermot for the pictures of the Guaira Falls. For the maps I am indebted to Anne McGrail, who with great patience drew them under my direction.

Most of the writing I did in ideal conditions at Marchmont, the home of Sir Robert and Lady McEwen. To them both I owe the most extensive debt of all.

P. C.

Introduction

From the end of the seventeenth century there has been a continuous flow of books on the Jesuit Republic of Paraguay. Unlike the Portuguese Jesuits in Abyssinia or the Italians under Ricci in China, the work of the Spaniards in central South America has fascinated a great diversity of scholars, ethnologists, gold-diggers, social theorists, explorers, Utopia seekers and others. In the eighteenth century, the subject haunted the French philosophers, who admired in the Jesuit state a perfectly regulated society. In the early nineteenth century romanticists saw in it 'the loveliest days of a new-born Christianity', and at the end of the century the pioneers of the Labour movement believed they had found there a pattern for British socialism.

In whatever way the achievement of the Jesuits in colonial Paraguay is regarded, it was certainly unique. In a remote region that has now largely been reclaimed by sub-tropical forest, they created not just a new society, but a vigorous civilization comparable with that of the Incas. Today its monuments are slowly being restored, as stone after stone is recovered from the overgrowth of sinuous trees and set in its place to form ruins in some ways as impressive as Machu Picchu.

In *Candide* Voltaire's hero visits the Jesuits in Paraguay. Cynical and insincere, Voltaire uses the priests to illustrate the evils of witchcraft and avarice. They grow rich on the sweated labour of the Indians, and while they wage a colonial war against Spain and Portugal, at home they continue to provide confessors to the sovereigns of those countries. But in his *Essai sur Moeurs*, published twenty-two years later,[1] his position is changed. He now sees in the Republic a triumph of humanity capable of expiating the crimes of the *conquistadores*. These Jesuits were men who never gave way to depression. He likened their government to the ancient rule of Lacedaemonia. 'Everything was held in common. . . . Though neighbouring on Peru, they knew nothing of gold or silver.' As it was obedience to the laws of Lycurgus that made a Spartan, the essence of a Paraguayan was obedience to the Jesuits. This was the nearest comparison he could devise. The Jesuits were at once the founders of the state, its lawgivers, pontiffs and sovereigns.

D'Alembert approached Paraguay from a slightly different angle. Although for him the Jesuits were 'halfbreeds of the Pope', he considered that they had established an authoritative monarchy, grounded on persuasion and sweetness of government. In their towns all the needs of nature were recognized and satisfied.[2] Montesquieu is more generous. The Jesuits, according to him, brought the Indians happiness and made them work; they were the first in the regions of South America to have united religion with humanity; in fact, they healed one of the greatest wounds men have inflicted on men. At the same time Montesquieu emphasizes the communism of the Republic: 'Money was proscribed and trade practised by the towns rather than by the townspeople.'[3] Raynal, the ex-Jesuit and encyclopedist, is more interested in the colonial aspect of the experiment. 'When in 1768 the missions were taken from the hands of the Jesuits, they had reached a degree of civilization perhaps as high as the new nations could reach and certainly greater than anything existing in the new world.'[4]

In Britain the Jesuit Republic became known through the works of three popular writers. William Robertson, the Scottish historian and champion of Liberalism, and one of the first writers after Gibbon to embrace a great sweep of events even in his works on particular subjects, was also attracted by the organization of the Jesuits. In his *History of Charles V*, published in 1770 and highly commended by Voltaire, he gave vivid descriptions of the aboriginal societies in the new world. Against this background he praises the Jesuits for contributing most to the good of the human species. In particular, he admired the equality among the members of the community, and the ordered society in which recent savages were made to work not just for themselves but for the public good. In this way almost all the passions that disturbed the peace and made men unhappy were extinguished. Robertson found it 'difficult to conceive how this regime did not fulfil an extraordinary perfection'.

Robertson made many errors of fact which were corrected by Robert Southey, the English poet and historian, both in his verse poem, *A Tale of Paraguay* (1820), and in his three-volume *History of Brazil* (1810–19). Inspired by an incident in the *History of the Abipones*, an enchanting book by the Czech Jesuit, Martin Dobrizhoffer, and translated by Sara Coleridge, *A Tale of Paraguay* is perhaps the best of his long poetic works. Southey found in the life of the Jesuits the three ingredients of a successful missionary, fervent zeal, abandonment of everything in pursuit of the object, and faith in their mission. While Southey defended the Order against its detractors, he gave the lead to modern Jesuit critics of the Republic by faulting it for its despotic regime which kept the Indians *in statu pupillari.*

In this century English interest in the subject has been stimulated mainly by two works, Cunninghame Graham's *A Vanished Arcadia* (1901) and the play of S. Hochwalder, *The Strong are Lonely (Sur la Terre comme au Ciel)*, which was staged in the fifties both in Paris and London.

Cunninghame Graham's book still has value. He knew the Guaraní, who were brought by the Jesuits from the forest into towns, and for many years lived among them. Moreover, he was nearer in time to the memory of the Jesuits than any other writer. 'I myself', he writes in his Introduction, 'five and twenty years ago have often met in the deserted missions men who spoke regretfully of the Jesuit times, who cherished all the customs left by the company, and though they spoke at second hand, repeating the stories they had heard in youth, kept the illusion that the missions in the Jesuits' time had been a paradise.' As one of the founders of the Labour party,

Cunninghame Graham was attracted, not without reason, by what appeared to him the perfect harmony of the ideal socialist state. Hochwalder seizes on two disparate crises, confuses his story by telescoping them, and sacrifices dramatic impact by departing from the facts.

In this new presentation of an old subject, I have tried to make use of the most important work done mainly by Spaniards and South Americans since the appearance of *A Vanished Arcadia*. Most recent studies are concerned with the economic structure of the Reductions. In a general book I have given this aspect only a section. Against the background of colonial South American history I have tried to tell the whole story of the Republic, its foundation, early failures and eventual success. The period covers just over a hundred and fifty years from the establishment of the first towns in 1611 to the deportation of the Jesuits from South America in 1768. The last phases of the story fuse with the broader history of Europe, where the Jesuits were expelled in turn from Portugal, France and Spain and finally in 1773 totally suppressed as a religious order by Pope Clement XIV.

The term Paraguay in a secular sense is used here for the vast area administered under the Viceroyalty of Peru from Asunción. It included parts of Bolivia, the entire Chaco and, until it was lost to Brazil, the province of Guairá. The Jesuits used the term, Paraguay, in a different sense, to denote the geographical limits of their own administrative unit which they termed a 'province': it included not only the Paraguay of the civil governors, but the entire Argentine, all Uruguay and the Brazilian Province of Rio Grande do Sul. The work of the Jesuit 'province' of Paraguay defines the limits of this book. In writing of the Jesuits it has, of course, been impossible to avoid altogether their peculiar terms or the peculiar use they gave to terms. To make it easier for the reader to become familiar with them, a list of these terms is given.

Today the principal interest of a study of this kind lies perhaps in the treatment of a primitive people and its preparation to take its place in a more developed society. Most criticism of the Jesuit system in Paraguay does not take account of the fact that the experiment was incomplete when it was brought to an abrupt end. But even so, where it did take root, an aboriginal population and culture were preserved; where it was cut short, as in Patagonia and the Chaco, whole tribes were exterminated. There is no doubt that, had the Jesuits been allowed to remain, both the history and map of South America would be different today. Entire regions marked blank on the modern maps, two hundred years ago formed part of their Republic, where travellers could go without fear and at each stage of their journey find peaceful villages policed by Indian officers. The Upper Amazon, the Chaco, the tropical forest of eastern Bolivia, today for the most part *terrae incognitae*, were then populous territories. The towns fell into final ruin in the course of the long wars of the nineteenth century.

But this is a minor tragedy compared with the loss of missionary expertise, which was not recovered even by the Jesuits after the Order was restored in the nineteenth century. Their system of segregation of Indian from Spaniard, which would today be condemned as a species of apartheid, undoubtedly saved the Indian until he had attained maturity. Possibly it was more a policy of parallel development, worked out in minute and practical detail, that was never again formulated, although as late as 1940 it was hit on accidentally but never put into practice by the Rhodesian Government. A hundred years earlier it might have prevented the Aboriginals of Australia from becoming a very reduced and depressed minority.

But it is for the reader to draw what conclusion he will. I have tried merely to tell the story.

Marchmont – Tisbury P.C.
September 1970–April 1973

Calendar of Events

1511 Solis discovers the Río de la Plata.

1526 Sebastian Cabot sails up Río de la Plata as far as confluence of Río Paraguay and Río Pilcomayo.

1535 Pedro de Mendoza founds Buenos Aires.

1537 Asunción founded. Buenos Aires abandoned.

1542 Alvar Núñez Cabeza de Vaca, appointed Governor, reaches Asunción.

1543 Cabeza de Vaca deposed by Irala.

1550 First Jesuits land in South America (Salvador de Bahia).

1557 Irala dies.

1575 Fra Luis de Bolaños reaches Asunción and preaches to Guaraní.

1580 Buenos Aires refounded.

1587 Jesuits from Brazil reach La Plata estuary.

1587–99 Itinerant Jesuits work among Guaraní, mainly in Guairá.

1602 Jesuit conference at Salta: decision to abandon Paraguay.

1603 Synod of Asunción under Martín Ignacio de Loyola, who protests to Jesuit General.

1607 Diego de Torres appointed Provincial of Chile-Paraguay.

1609 Cataldino and Maceta leave Asunción for Guairá.
Griffi and González cross into Chaco and preach to Guaycurú.
Lorenzana and de Martín go south from Asunción towards the Paraná.

1610 Loreto founded on banks of Paranapanema.
Ignacio Guazú founded north of Paraná.
1615 Guaycurú mission abandoned.
1616 First Flemish Jesuits reach Paraguay.
1621 González enters the province of Tape.
1628 González, with two companions, slain in Tape.
1629 First incursion of Mamelucos into Guairá.
1631 Evacuation of Guairá.
First Itatín mission founded.
1632 San Miguel, first Reduction east of Uruguay, founded.
1636 Mamelucos attack Tape Reductions.
1638 Osorio enters Chaco from Jujuy.
1639 All Tape Reductions withdrawn across Uruguay.
April. Osorio and Ripario murdered in the Chaco.
1641 March. Mamelucos defeated at Mbororé.
Juan Pastor crosses the Chaco to preach to Abipones.
1642 Last attack of Mamelucos defeated.
Cárdenas takes over administration of diocese of Asunción.
1647 Cárdenas becomes Governor of Asunción.
1650 Cárdenas leaves Asunción.
1687 San Nicolás, the first of 'seven' Reductions, moved to east bank of Uruguay.
1691 José de Arce founds San Ignacio in Chiquitos.
1697 San José (Chiquitos) founded.
1732 San Javier for Mocobíes founded from Santa Fe.
1740 Concepción for Pampas Indians founded.
1746 Quiroga and Cardiel explore coast of Patagonia.
1747 Rosario for Abipones founded.
1750 January. Boundary Treaty signed in Madrid.
1751 April. Jesuit conference at San Miguel.
1752 Altamirano lands at Montevideo.
1753 February. Encounter between Guaraní troops and Spanish-Portuguese forces at San Tecla.
Pampas Reductions abandoned.
San Joaquín refounded at present site.
1754 November. Armistice between Guaraní and Spanish-Portuguese forces.
1756 February. Battle of Caaibaté.

November. Cevallos arrives in Buenos Aires.
1757   Pombal's *Short Relation* published.
1760   Belén for Guaycurú founded.
        Sánchez Labrador travels from Belén to Corazón in Chiquitos.
1761   Boundary Treaty rescinded.
1763   San Pedro for Mocobíes (last Reduction) founded.
1766   March. Anti-Jesuit riots in Madrid.
1767   April. Jesuits suppressed in Spain.
        July. Jesuits suppressed in South American colleges.
1768   May–August. Jesuits removed from Reductions.
1773   July. Clement XIV suppresses Jesuits.

Note : the dates given for the foundation of the Guaraní Reductions are taken from Pablo Hernández, *Organización Social.* Del Techo and some contemporary Jesuit documents, e.g. Annual Letters, give dates that differ by a year, occasionally by more. The divergence is explained by the method of dating. The earlier date usually records the feast day on which a cross was erected among a group of Indians, the later date is that given in official documents issued by the Governor of Asunción or Buenos Aires, authorizing the Jesuits to establish an Indian township.

THE LOST PARADISE

I

The Scene

Seen from the air, Nuestra Señora Santa María de la Asunción, as it was called by its founder, Juan de Salazar de Espinoza, on 15 August 1537, appears the ideal site for a capital city in central South America.

Asunción, as it soon came to be known, lies at the confluence of the Paraguay and Pilcomayo rivers. Like a serpent, the Paraguay encircles on three sides a group of small hills, making the position a natural fortress, protected by a wide expanse of water. A lagoon, joined to the river by a broad channel, forms a fine anchorage. From the high ground above, a panoramic view extends across the river to the south, west and east. Only to the north did the settlement need artificial defences. From almost any eminence within the city a Spanish sentry could spot the approach of hostile Indians from the seemingly endless and empty Chaco: its leagues of swamp, scrub and forest were never controlled in Spanish imperial times, nor for more than a century later.

In 1526, eleven years before the foundation of Asunción, Sebastian Cabot had sailed up the river Plata to the Paraguay: his object was to discover a passage from the Atlantic to the mines of Peru and of Bolivia, then known as the province of Charcas, or to the mines rumoured to exist in Paraguay. The estuary of the Plata was to become the gateway to El Dorado: it would also avoid the arduous and costly journey via Cartagena and the Isthmus of Panama to Lima and Santiago de Chile.

Confident that silver, if not gold, was to be found at the headwaters of the river, Sebastian Cabot renamed the estuary La Plata: it had previously been called Río de Solís after the

Spanish navigator who had discovered it in 1511. On his way Cabot had stopped at Santa Catarina, where he had heard that the Indians of the sierra wore silver crowns and gold pendants; he was shown some examples, but was not told that the gold in fact had been seized by the Guaraní Indians in the fifteenth century in raids across the Chaco on the southern frontiers of the Inca empire.

Sailing up the Paraná, Cabot built a fort at Espiritu Santo near the present city of Santa Fe; he then continued up the Paraguay to the Pilcomayo: the headwaters lay another thousand miles away. Cabot returned without gold and without making a settlement. In 1552 he founded in England the Muscovy Company: its purpose was to find the north-east passage and open the Russian market to England: this also had been the aim of his 1526 expedition, but he had been diverted to South America by rumours of silver.*

In 1535 a third expedition, this time under Pedro de Mendoza, a courtier of Charles V, reached the Plata estuary and pitched camp on its southern shore at a place its leader called Santa María de Buenos Aires, in gratitude to Our Lady for a safe passage across the Atlantic. The site could scarcely have been more ill-chosen: the waters were too shallow for a good anchorage, and it was exposed to the *pamperos*, the strong south-west gales, as well as to attacks from some of the fiercest of South American Indians.

Besieged here, Pedro de Mendoza escaped up the Paraná and constructed a fort at Corpus Christi, close to Cabot's old fort at Espíritu Santo. Only five hundred of the 2,630 men who had sailed with him reached this point, but the Indians here were more friendly: he abandoned his horses there and they became the ancestors of the great herds that were to rove modern Argentina from the Chaco to Patagonia.†

* Sebastian's father, John Cabot, the Genoese explorer, starting from Bristol, was the first to discover the coast of North America on 24 June 1497. On his return he was given ten pounds and the rank of Admiral by Henry VII.

† Some now question this common theory: they point out that Cabot's map (1526) is decorated with an engraving of a horse, and argue from this that horses existed in South America before the coming of the conquistadores.

From Corpus Christi Pedro de Mendoza sent his lieutenant, Juan de Ayolas, to explore the river. He was never seen again. Mendoza waited a year, then set out for Spain, dying insane on the way. His cousin, Gonzalo de Mendoza, mounted a fresh expedition the next year. With Domingo de Irala, he reached a point near Fuerte Olimpo three hundred miles above Asunción on the Paraguay. Search parties failed to find Ayolas. On the return voyage Mendoza's companion, Juan de Espinoza, attracted by the site of Asunción, founded a settlement there on 15 August 1537.

The small Spanish detachment that had been left at Buenos Aires, tired of fighting the Pampas Indians, abandoned the town and set out for Asunción.

From Fuerte Olimpo Irala maintained a fitful search for Ayolas. Eventually he returned to Asunción, where he ousted his rivals and got himself elected first Governor of the town.

Its original inhabitants were heterogeneous : Espinoza's men and Irala's, the remnants of the Buenos Aires garrison, the crew and passengers of an Italian ship driven by foul weather off its course for Peru to shelter in the Río de la Plata. Like the colonists of the coast of Brazil, the settlers at Asunción were strongly attracted by the fine features of the Guaraní women and readily took them as wives or mistresses : one early writer noted : 'The women generally are virtuous, beautiful and of gentle disposition'.[1] The marriages made for peace, particularly when the bride was the daughter of a *cacique*. With their strong sense of family, the Indians felt obliged to assist or at least not to molest their newly-acquired relatives. Usually their grandchildren and always their great-grandchildren were reckoned Spaniards. From this stock the Jesuits drew many of their most enterprising priests.

At this time the Guaraní people were to be found not merely in the neighbourhood of Asunción but in a vast area of South America stretching from the Guyanas south to the Plata estuary. To the first settlers they were known as the 'Indians of the islands', for they occupied also the numerous islands of the rivers Paraná and Paraguay. The greatest number of them lived on the eastern banks of these rivers and their tributaries, as well as in the provinces of Guairá to the north-east of Asunción and Tape to the south-east. Yapeyú on the Uruguay marked the border between them and the Charrua. But scattered among the Guaraní were tribes like the Guayakí with a different language and culture. The Chiquitos in the province of Charcas were another branch of the Guaraní family. In Brazil they were mostly enslaved, killed, or lost their identity through later intermarriage with the African Negro: the only relic of them today in Brazil is linguistic, in the Guaraní words now established in the Portuguese language spoken there.

In spite of their name, which meant warrior, the Guaraní were a peaceful race, at least by comparison with the savage tribes of the Chaco; nevertheless they were independent in temperament, with no recognizable laws, living in a freedom restricted merely by the need to form a sort of society in time of war. Then they chose a cacique or chieftain: only men of singular valour were appointed: the greater their reputation for heroic exploits, the more subjects they attracted to themselves. A general council of caciques decided on war or peace and elected war leaders. Usually the rank of cacique was hereditary.

However, real power in these communities, which the Jesuits were to gather into their towns, lay often, not with the cacique, but with the shaman or witchdoctor. In Guaraní medicine, sickness was caused by the entry of an alien object into the body, and it was the shaman's business to extract this object, which frequently he himself had inserted in the healing process. Chants accompanied his labour; other chants of his might cause the patient to die. Influential shamans claimed control over natural phenomena, and on their death the bones of these men were preserved as relics and hung in special hammocks in the huts of their successors. On occasion, from the sixteenth to the twentieth century, a shaman would rise up among the Guaraní, stir them to revolt, proclaiming the end of Spanish rule and the beginning of a golden age. At such times a tribe would leave its territory in search of the Land without Evil. Here lived the mother of their chief deity and creator, Nandeuvuçú, the great Father, himself residing in the dark region infested with bats and lit only by the glimmer of his chest. *Mate*, the drink prepared from the Paraguayan tree, is hardly mentioned in the early accounts of the country : it seems to have been used as a magic herb only by the shamans.

The first conquistadores reported that the Guaraní were a kindly people, but doubted how far they might be trusted. As today, when they can still be found in their primitive state, they lived in small groups in jungle clearings or on the river banks where the forest came down to the water. Unlike the Indians in the remnants of the Inca empire, they had no stone buildings. 'Their dwellings', writes Muratori, basing himself on the writings of the early Jesuits,*

> were wretched huts raised in the woods and made of the boughs of trees and bamboos put together without order, whose entrance is usually so narrow that they must creep to go in. When . . . asked the reason for so odd a contrivance, their answer is that they cannot otherwise be well guarded against flies, gnats and insects . . . or be sheltered from the darts and arrows their enemies would not fail to send among them through the entrances of their huts were they higher or larger. A little earthenware makes up the whole of their moveables.

All the Guaraní tribes cultivated pumpkins, mandioca and sweet potatoes. The digging stick was their only agricultural instrument, but they depended largely on fishing and hunting for their main livelihood. After five or six years they considered their fields exhausted and moved on. Their principal concern was to choose a territory that was well stocked with wild animals, which they caught mainly with traps and snares.

The Guaraní were cannibals, but they restricted their victims to their more heroic enemies taken in war : by eating their flesh they believed that they would acquire their valour.

* L. Muratori, *A Relation of the Missions of Paraguay* (London, 1759), p. 23. Apart from the *Commentarios* of Alvar Núñez Cabeza de Vaca, the only sources of information on the primitive Guaraní at the time of the Conquest are Jesuit writers, principally the anonymous authors of the Annual Letters, Ruiz de Montoya's *Conquista Espiritual* and the material incorporated into del Techo's *Historia*.

For this reason the less brave were allowed to live. Until they were killed, the victims were treated generously and given wives. As the ceremonial slaughter proceeded, small boys dipped their hands in the prisoner's blood while they were instructed in their duties as warriors. According to one Jesuit writer, when the dead man's flesh was served up in the form of fritters, each participant in the feast assumed a new name.[2]

Physically, the Guaraní resembled most South American Indians: olive in complexion, as fair as or fairer than the Spaniard, thick-set, well-proportioned, nimble, average in height, with large heads and little body hair. To the European they appeared reserved: they seldom looked a stranger in the eye. They were reckoned to number several million.

Friars of St Francis had sailed up the Paraguay with the founding Fathers of Asunción; others from Spain had landed in 1541 at Santa Catarina in Brazil with Alvar Núñez Cabeza de Vaca, who had been appointed by Charles V to succeed Irala as Governor, and in the course of five months had made their way with him across country occupied mainly by Guaraní to Asunción. In his concern for Indian welfare, Cabeza de Vaca was among the most enlightened of the conquistadores. During his two-thousand-mile march not a single Guaraní suffered any injustice. Consequently they came out of their forest huts to meet the Spaniards with garlands and provisions. Frightened of their horses, they brought for them chickens and honey.

Asunción was reached on 2 March 1542, almost five years after its foundation. But neither then nor after the establishment in 1550 of a bishopric there with jurisdiction over the entire La Plata region, was the systematic evangelization of the Guaraní attempted. Many of the Indians in the area around Asunción had become Christians but without any instruction: one priest, leading a vagabond life, had baptized many adults: he had persuaded them that they needed only to submit to baptism: later there was confusion when Indians claimed that they were Christian because, on entering a church at the time of the asperges, some drops of water had fallen on their heads. Their idea of God remained more consonant with their myths than with Christianity.

Cabeza de Vaca's arrival split Asunción into two factions. The first settlers resented and actively obstructed his enlightened policy towards the Indians, which had the backing of the Church. The turmoil was made worse by the constant attacks of the savage Guaycurú from the Chaco across the Río Paraguay. To save Asunción, Cabeza de Vaca was forced to mount a punitive expedition against them. On his return to Asunción in April 1543 he was deposed by Irala, whom he had left as interim Governor, was imprisoned and eventually despatched to Madrid.

Cabeza de Vaca had based his policy on the principle that the Guaraní should not be harassed, but rather enticed from their nomadic life into permanent settlements where they could be effectively Christianized. It was his defence of Guaraní women, in particular, which had brought him the unpopularity which Irala had been quick to exploit for his own ends: often Spaniards living on small ranches near Asunción surrounded themselves with harems of ten to thirty Guaraní women who, with their relatives, formed small colonies.

Irala himself died in 1557. An ambitious Basque soldier of fortune, he had stamped much of his character on Paraguay: his policies were inspired by a search for gold which his successors maintained for two centuries. With 350 Spaniards and 2,000 impressed Guaraní, he had set out north-west and reached the frontiers of Peru to find that it had already been conquered from the Pacific. His last enterprise was to send one of his captains, Nuflo de Chaves, to found a town on the upper waters of the Paraguay. In the independent manner of the conquistadores, Chaves struck north-west and founded Santa Cruz de la Sierra which, in its new site, was to become the base for Jesuit missionary work among the Chiquitos branch of the Guaraní race.

After Irala came a series of feckless governors, court favourites or officers who had served on the frontier: few were capable and none had an interest in the Indian. Factions became endemic. Yet Asunción grew. On Irala's death it had a Spanish population of 1,500, a textile mill, a cathedral and a rudimentary stock industry; it was also the undisputed

capital city of an ill-defined territory that included, in addition
to modern Paraguay, the great expanse of Argentina, the
whole of Uruguay, parts of Bolivia and much of the Brazilian
provinces of S. Catarina, Guairá, Rio Grande do Sul, Paraná
and Mato Grosso. From Asunción expeditions founded, apart
from Santa Cruz de la Sierra, Santa Fe and Corrientes, and
in 1580 refounded Buenos Aires some miles to the west of its
original site. Other cities, such as Santiago de Estero, Salta,
Tucumán and Córdoba were established by Spaniards coming
down the old Inca trail from the province of Charcas. It was
the whole of this area that later formed the territorial extension of the famous Jesuit province of Paraguay.

The fall of Cabeza de Vaca had held back the serious
evangelization of the Guaraní; the first friars were occupied
almost entirely with the Spaniards. Only with the coming of
Fra Luis de Bolaños in February 1575 did anything like the
systematic evangelization of the Guaraní beyond the environs
of Asunción begin : he was the first to bring them into towns,
the first to master their language. In the province of Guairá,
now part of Brazil, he is credited with the establishment of
eighteen Guaraní villages between 1580 and 1593. He also
travelled on foot through the greater part of the Paraná and
Plata basin, living on the Indian diet of mandioca, roots, fruit
and herbs. The Jesuits who followed him owed much to his
enterprise. Between 1582 and 1585, nearly half a century
after the establishment of Asunción, he produced the first
Guaraní grammar, the first vocabulary and first prayer book;
he also translated sections of the catechism into Guaraní :
none of these works is extant, but they correspond with three
books of Christian Instruction issued in 1583 by the Council
of Lima.[3]

In his linguistic task Bolaños was helped by two creole
priests : his achievement was the starting-point of all the work
done by the Jesuits on the Guaraní language. Bolaños realized
that it was not merely a question of learning a formal
language, but also partly of constructing a new one. The
words most needed in catechesis had embedded associations
with idolatry, superstition and sorcery: they had to be rejected
and replaced by others. Only when these problems were

settled could the Guaraní become truly Christian : a further difficulty came from the great diversity of dialects and regional usages.

While Bolaños had called ecclesiastical attention to the Guaraní, his fellow Franciscan, Fra Francisco Solano, known also as St Francis of the Indies, had done the same for the Chaco Indians. Linguistically, Solano's task was more difficult, for the languages of the Chaco were multiple : contemporaries credited him with the gift of tongues : certainly between 1588 and 1589 he achieved the astonishing feat of crossing the Chaco to Asunción. On his arrival Jesuits were already established there.

In 1550, seven years before the death of Irala, in the life-time of Ignacio de Loyola, Jesuits had landed in San Salvador de Bahia in Brazil. They had sailed under the leadership of José de Anchieta, a priest whose achievement in Brazil is comparable to Javier's in the Far East. Some years later Anchieta was joined by an Englishman, John Yates, and a young Irishman from Limerick, Thomas Fields, who had been surreptitiously educated in his native city in a Jesuit school that for some years had escaped Government attention. Tomás Fildio, as he came to be called in the new world, became Anchieta's travelling companion.

The vast territory covered by Bolaños and Solano was governed by two Bishops at Tucumán and Asunción : Francis de Victoria, Bishop of Tucumán, was the first to invite the Jesuits to his diocese. In 1585, apart from a letter to Claudio Acquaviva, the General of the Jesuits, he had written to the Provincials both of Peru and Brazil. In response two Jesuits set out from Peru, six from Bahia. In January 1587 the Brazilian party reached the Plata estuary, where their boat was boarded by an English pirate, plundered and towed out to sea with only five barrels of water on board : eventually it drifted into Buenos Aires, where the Bishop of Asunción was on a visit. Three of the priests, Ortega, a Portuguese, Fields, the Irishman, and Saloni, an Italian, made their way to Asunción, an international nucleus of the Jesuit Province of Paraguay : the Bishop selected these men because the Indian language, Tupí, with which they were already familiar, was a branch of the Guaraní spoken in Guairá. At Córdoba the two Spaniards from Peru, later joined by others from Europe, established what was to become its headquarters and training establishments.

The next twelve years, 1587 to 1599, were passed in pioneer, ill co-ordinated work that held out little promise of development. In their first journey Fields with Ortega reached Villarrica, a Spanish settlement in Guairá, five hundred miles from Asunción, while Saloni remained at home. But in 1590 the worst plague of smallpox in South American history interrupted their preaching. A year later, Fields and Ortega made their way west through the forest to a point near the present town of Concepción on the upper reaches of the Paraguay. In 1593 a fresh group of priests, including an Andalusian, Juan Romero, and Marciel Lorenzana, a Spaniard from León, arrived from Europe and a College was founded at Asunción.

In 1599 Saloni died. About the same time Fields and Ortega were recalled to Asunción. It was eleven years before their work among the Guaraní was resumed. However, these pioneers had established three things that were to influence later decisions: that the Guaraní were numerous, that they were receptive to Christianity, and that more was needed than itinerant preachers who baptized and passed on to the next village. It might be claimed also that Fields and Ortega contributed to the spirit that was to inform the Paraguay Province. Already, within less than fifty years of Loyola's death, these men were said to possess the 'primitive spirit' of the Society of Jesus: 'humble, poor, mortified, eating little and sleeping less, clothed very poorly, but very contented with their life, favoured in prayer, most closely united to God and with one another in the true bond of charity.'[4]

The future of the mission to the Guaraní was now in the balance. Claudio Acquaviva ordered retrenchment; a meeting of the Jesuit Province of Peru, to which the priests then in Paraguay and Tucumán belonged, was called at Salta in 1602. After seeing each priest in private, the Provincial, Padre Páez, sought a common system of evangelizing such a diversity of tribes. His own experience in Peru convinced him that rambling missionaries achieved little: he reckoned nothing of rapid conversions, especially if these occurred under emotional stress. Lessons were to be learnt from Fra Solano: 'He had visited every part of Tucumán and a large part of the Chaco and in both had converted a vast number of Indians but there scarcely remained any trace of his work because he had made no permanent settlements.'[5]

The conference decided in effect to abandon Paraguay: rather, the rivers Paraguay and Paraná were to be the dividing line between the provinces of Peru and Brazil. Since it was unlikely that the Portuguese would undertake work in Spanish territory or even that the Spanish king would allow them in, the plan was unrealistic.

In Asunción the reaction was violent. Romero reflected it in a letter to Acquaviva. He asked bluntly whether the Jesuits were to abandon the difficult interior and concentrate on Peru, the Eldorado of the new world. Did gold come before souls? To the people of Asunción the clergy of Lima appeared scandalously rich. Already by 1620 it was reckoned that religious houses, with their properties, occupied more ground than the rest of the city. Priests were paid by tithes levied on the income of whites and on Indian produce, such as wheat, silk and cattle, that had originally been introduced from Europe. Fields and others also protested. Páez, although he did not immediately yield to the remonstrances against this part of his plan, took no steps to carry it out. The debate continued. In the end the decision came from the Bishop and Synod of Asunción.

Meeting in 1603, the Synod debated the experience of the Friars and first Jesuits among the Guaraní: it laid down that all instruction of Indians was to be given in their own language, that all priests with a cure of souls must know at least Guaraní: Bolaños's catechism was to be used as a guarantee that the same words and expressions became universal; on Sundays and feast days all were to learn their doctrine by repetitive chanting in church, absentees were to be punished, children under fourteen given instruction for two hours daily, adults let off work for three days before making their first confession. The Synod also demanded that the

Indians should be gathered into settlements for their own protection and singled out certain crimes for special castigation —for instance, the forcible removal of Indian girls from their guardians, the compulsory marriage of Indians or their compulsory separation. It insisted that no Indian was to be separated from his partner on any trifling pretext.

Fields, left behind at Asunción in ill health, was the only Jesuit present at the Synod, but Roque González de Santa Cruz, a young beneficed priest of the cathedral, was there: later as a Jesuit he was to take a large part in making its decrees effective. But now the moving spirit was Fra Luis de Bolaños, who saw official approval given to his works of translation.

Nothing of this programme could be carried out without priests to reinforce the few already at work in the colony. The Bishop who had summoned the Synod was a Franciscan, but he also happened to be Martín Ignacio de Loyola, a nephew of the founder of the Jesuits. First, he protested to the absent Romero that he would never have accepted the bishopric had he known that the Jesuits would abandon him: the Jesuits must be summoned back immediately, otherwise he would write to Acquaviva and, if necessary, to Madrid, even to the Pope. In fact, before receiving Romero's reply, he had sent off a letter to Acquaviva. As much as any other man, Martín de Loyola could claim to be the founder of the Jesuit Republic of Paraguay.

Ultimately Acquaviva appointed Padre Diego de Torres, a native of Castile, to replace Romero, putting him in charge of a joint Chile-Paraguay Province: his Roman advisers can have had little concept of the area this ecclesiastical creation covered, and can have known still less of the lines of communication that followed the old Inca trails from north to south. Torres, already aged fifty-six, but vigorous and imaginative, arrived in Lima in 1606 with fifteen priests; another eight reached Buenos Aires about the same time; from there they went up river to Asunción: the only Jesuit still in the city was Fields, lying very sick, 'but never done thanking God for seeing his brethren again in that distant country'.[6]

Torres was determined not to resume work among the

Guaraní until he had firmly established the Province : he had first to make Paraguay at least partly independent of manpower from Europe. With this aim, during his first five years of office, he built a novitiate at Córdoba, founded in the same city a seminary that soon developed into a university, as well as a college there and in several other cities; Romero's foundation at Asunción was re-opened. He also made it clear that the Jesuits were protectors of the Indians : his men would go to work among them to give effect to the freedom to which they were entitled in the Laws of the Indies, a collection of colonial decrees, often *ad hoc* rescripts, issued at different times over several decades, unmodified and sometimes contradictory. Whatever interpretation they might be made to bear on other points, they embodied unequivocally the principles of the Bull of Paul III (1537), condemning as a grave crime the enslavement of South American Indians, whether Christian or pagan. To their credit the kings of Spain had consistently taken the side of the Indian, but in many places the legitimate practice of *servicio personal* was often inextricably bound up with abuse. In theory the *servicio* was the performance of day labour in lieu of tribute : it took the form of a grant made by the Governor to a colonist or corporation or even to an estancia : this grant was the *encomienda* and the person who held it an *encomendero*.

As early as 1593 Padre Romero, the Jesuit then in charge of the rudimentary mission of Paraguay, had given up a piece of land near Salta presented to the Jesuits of Tucumán for their subsistence : his reason was that it could be cultivated only by Indians in encomienda and he did not wish risking an association between the Jesuits and malpractices of the *servicio*. To the west of Tucumán were the Calchaquí Indians, to the east the Lules of the Chaco; among them the first priests coming down from Peru had worked : the Calchaquí, resenting the drudgery of *servicio personal*, had revolted in 1590; for the same reason the Lules, among whom Solano also preached, had reverted to their primitive life.

The Fathers who had stepped ashore at Buenos Aires to help form the Paraguay Province faced the same dilemma. The port was now beginning to do well; although in theory it was closed to foreigners, ships of all nations put in under pretext of sheltering from bad weather. But attacks from the fierce Indians of the hinterland checked its development. The Jesuits were asked to work among them but they argued that it was too late : *servicio personal* had rendered fruitless earlier attempts to convert them.[7]

But it was in the Chaco, in the foothills of the Andes and other areas remote from Asunción that *servicio personal* was most abused. In 1586 Padre Angulo, who came to Paraguay after working in Peru, compared its encomenderos to Turks : under them Indians 'from birth to death, fathers and sons, men and women labour personally for the profit and enrichment of their masters, without so much as receiving a garment in return or even a handful of maize : so they continue to die rapidly.'[8] By 1612 the situation was worse : the separation of marriage partners, against which the Synod of Asunción had legislated, was still common; almost everywhere, without regard for family ties, Indians were secretly bought, sold, gambled or given away; in remote places like Guairá they were sometimes driven off their lands and carried into slavery.[9]

In taking their stand the Jesuits realized that the abolition of the *servicio* would threaten the economy of Paraguay : they knew well that they had public opinion against them. On the other hand their experience in Tucumán, at least, had proved that nothing could be achieved unless the Laws of the Indies were honoured. After much discussion, both in Paraguay and Rome, fourteen years after Juan Romero had renounced the farm near Salta, Diego de Torres reverted to his policy. In 1608, starting in Santiago de Chile, he gave orders for all the Indians presented to the College in encomienda to be freed : this was done, and the Indians continued to serve the Jesuits as free men. He did the same at Santiago del Estero, Tucumán, and Asunción. At Córdoba, when the Indians had finished erecting the novitiate building, he paid them for their work. This was a revolutionary step, but it left Torres free to preach in the city against the injustice done to the Indians in the neighbouring countryside. In the same year a meeting of the Province fathers in a Congregation endorsed Torres's policy. Full legal formalities confirmed the Indians' release.

Torres's revolutionary action was received with derision by the settlers: the Jesuits were accused of ignorance; it was said that they wanted to show themselves more just than the Friars who worked in peace with the encomenderos. In reply Torres wrote a pamphlet which had the endorsement of the Bishop of Asunción. From across the Atlantic Acquaviva counselled prudence: he feared that Torres's action might in the long run injure the Indians' cause. Torres, on the scene itself, knew that no safeguards of Indian liberty written into colonial laws worked in practice. He had seen that no effective appeal was open to the Indians; he knew that frequently they were the victims of well-intentioned men who had entered the encomienda system and then left their estates to be administered by subordinates: these men, anxious to make as much money as possible from compulsory labour, saw to it that the laws were a dead letter.

In their protest against the *de facto* enslavement of encomienda Indians, the Jesuits included two other classes of Indians, the *yanaconas* and *mitayos*: the former, called also in Paraguay *originarios*, were descendants of Indians captured in war: as such they were destined to perpetual slavery: they lived in the house of the encomendero who was obliged only to feed and instruct them; they could be sold at his will. The *mitayos*, originally Indians who had submitted to the Spaniards without fighting, were grouped into townships under a cacique: this occurred mainly in Alto Peru; from among them men between eighteen and fifty could be called upon for service in the mines: in the beginning this *mita*, as it was called, was only for two months: for the other ten the mitayos were as free as any Spaniard. But mine-work usually proved fatal to the health of Indians: *mita*, in fact, greatly reduced their number in the province of Charcas.

As a result of Torres's action, the people of Córdoba withdrew from the thirty-five Jesuits there the alms on which they lived. After consuming their store of maize and their garden vegetables they were forced to beg. Later Torres was given four hundred cattle and a thousand sheep with a farm outside the city for the support of the Jesuit establishments in Córdoba. In Santiago del Estero there was a worse outcry:

practices of slavery there were deeper rooted; the priests were refused provisions by the citizens and forced to leave for a residence in the country. But more sinister were the first slanders against the Paraguay Jesuits. They arose from this incident. It was said that the Jesuits, in defending the Indians, aimed ultimately to oust the encomenderos as their masters and so amass great wealth. Torres was the principal target of the attack. He was denounced as a 'turbulent and restless spirit'.[10] From their house in the country the Jesuits of Santiago del Estero organized expeditions to the Lules and Chalchaquí. Nothing was achieved. Severel Indian catechumens were carried into slavery under the eyes of the priests.

Meanwhile in 1609 Hernando de Saavedra, Governor of Asunción, received from Philip III letters instructing him to see to the submission of the Indians : priests should be used, not the military; the Indians were to be as free as any of the king's subjects; in no circumstances were the new converts to be given in encomienda to any Spaniard : only in this way would it be possible to win over an estimated 150,000 Guaraní in Guairá.

Towards the end of the same year Torres reached Asunción. There he negotiated the terms on which the Jesuits would undertake the work : the Indians were to be brought into towns directly subject to the Crown, independent of any Spanish city, fortress or other settlement; attempts at the enslavement of the Indians were to be opposed in the king's name with the backing of the royal governors.

On this agreement Torres sent two priests, significantly both non-Spanish, Simón Maceta and José Cataldino, to Guairá. They left Asunción on 8 December 1609. Following the decisions of the Salta conference, Torres determined to abandon transitory preaching and to establish instead a permanent Indian republic far from any Spanish settlements : 'The Indians loved the law of God', one Paraguayan priest had written, 'but not the Spaniards'. The remoteness of the new towns would protect the Indians from enslavement as well as from Spanish diseases and morals.

Soon after the two Italians had set out for Guairá, Torres's position was reinforced. In 1610 a royal commission under

Francisco de Alfaro, a member of the Council of Charcas, the supreme court for the La Plata area, was set up to enquire into slavery in Spanish America. Alfaro overtly used Torres as his right-hand man. In 1612 the commission reported : every Indian, regardless of his former status, was in law a free man who gave his labour in return for a fair wage and humane treatment. The report also endorsed Torres's plan of subjecting the Indian settlements immediately to the Spanish Crown.

This was a far-reaching legal victory for Torres. Many encomenderos gave up rights they believed they possessed and took back their Indians on a new footing. 'If Torres had done nothing else in his life,' writes the Spanish historian, Antonio Astraín, 'he would have a just title to be regarded throughout the world as one of mankind's principal benefactors.'[11]

2

The Triple Adventure

In January 1610 the two Italians, Simón Maceta and José Cataldino, reached Ciudad Real in Guairá, a province defined on the west by the upper Paraná, on the south by the Iguazú, and on the east by the vague line drawn by the Treaty of Tordesillas between Spain and Portugal in 1494. From here they sailed north to the confluence of the Paraná and the Paranapanema. Following this tributary eastwards, they settled in March the same year on a site for an Indian township near the river bank. This was the first 'Reduction'* of the Jesuits in Guairá. First to come into the town were Indians among whom Fields and Ortega had begun to preach. Here, as Cunninghame Graham writes,[1] the Jesuits 'built up a system with which their name is linked forever—the system which for two hundred years was able to hold together wandering Indian tribes, restless as Arabs, suspicious above every other race of men—and which to-day has disappeared, leaving nothing of a like nature in all the world.'

The Guairá party formed one section of a three-pronged expedition planned by Torres in consultation with Fra Reginaldo de Lizárraga, who was now Bishop of Asunción, and the Governor, Hernando de Saavedra. The other parties, each consisting of two men, set out about the same time, one

---

* The word 'Reduction' (from the Spanish *reducir*, to reduce – into townships) is first found in an instruction of the Spanish Crown dated Saragossa 29 March 1503; it charges officials in Española to bring all Indians into Reductions, with church, priest and school, and there, after giving them clothing, introduce them into civilized life. Cf. R. Streit and J. Dindinger, *Bibliotheca Missionum* (Aachen, 1924), vol. ii, 14.

going south to the Paraná, the second west across the Paraguay into the Chaco.

But it was in Guairá that the pattern of Indian life under Jesuit direction first evolved in its essential features. For the first decade all went well. The Indians, glad to escape the Spaniards who exploited them and the Portuguese who enslaved them, flocked in large numbers to Loreto. A second Reduction, San Ignacio, was founded the next year four miles higher up the Paranapanema.

However, there were setbacks even in these years. In 1618 the first of a series of plagues struck Loreto and then San Ignacio. Believing they were safer from the contagion away from the townships, the Indians fled 'in shoals into their ancient woods and marshes'. There they rejoined their heathen tribesfolk, who tried to persuade them to abandon their new faith and 'have one merry bout of drinking out of a priest's skull'.[2]

When the plague was over, the priests, guided by Indians who had stayed behind, recovered many of the refugees. In their search between the rivers Paraná and Itubaio they came across a small unnamed tribe; these Indians 'fastened three or four little stones to their lips, which stuck out and made them look hideous. They lived in cottages not so high as themselves : their entire food was dates, the pith of palm trees, some little venison and roots. They supplied the absence of iron with sharp stones and bones fixed to long wooden handles. They had no name to express God but worshipped the thunder as their only deity.'[3] Seventy-three of these primitive Indians were brought into the two Reductions, but they were unable to survive outside their forests. All but four died within twelve months.

In the first period of the Guairá foundations there was intermittent reversion to paganism among the neophytes. For this reason the Jesuits did their utmost to expose the sorcerers who at intervals found their way into the townships. The story of the sorcerer who entered Loreto, was exposed by the Fathers and given a hundred lashes has been told in a recent book.[4] The incident occurred in 1618. The source is del Techo. The wizard, as he is called, entered Loreto accompanied by a man-servant and a woman: on his approach through the forests he had practised his frauds. Cataldino was ready for him. 'Gathering a multitude by the riverside, the man put on a garment of feathers used by sorcerers and shaking a sort of rattle made of a goat's skull, cried in a mad manner, proclaiming himself absolute lord of death, seed and harvest,' and announced that he was god. Everything was subject to his power. He could destroy all things with his breath and re-create them. 'There he stood three in persons but one God. For, said the blasphemous wretch, "I begot my companion (*that was his man*) with the splendour of my face, and this young woman proceeded from us both, whom we equally love, making use of her by turns." '

It seems that, while he was raving, Cataldino came up. The blasphemies and rattle-shaking were repeated in the priest's face. Then destruction was threatened on him and his neophytes.

The father, justly provoked, ordered those that were near to seize him, and being delivered to the officers, the sham god was well whipped; and though he cried out after a few stripes that he was no god nor anything different from any other vile fellow, that all his divinity was vanished and that he had no power in his breath, yet the lusty converts who took him in hand left not off until they had given him a hundred lashes by tale, the boys laughing and making sport at him.

Del Techo concludes: 'The two following days he was again publicly scourged that he might three times abjure his being God three in person.'[5]

The story reveals that even in the first years of the Jesuit Reductions judicial authority was already exercised by the Indians: the sorcerer was 'delivered to the officers', who determined and administered the punishment. Excessive as it was, the Indians reckoned it just. The wizard survived: he was banished from the district for a time, returned and became a Christian.

Without adding to the number of the Reductions, Maceta and Cataldino, in these first ten years, searched for a direction in which to expand. First they explored northward. Here they encountered a diversity of small tribes, all with painted bodies, abundance of wives, warlike disposition, dressed in skirts of feathers and shells, the prey of absurd superstitions : they believed that because an owl rarely flew and never built a nest, they had only to touch it to become lazy for life; if a girl saw a parrot during her first menstrual cycle, she would never stop chattering. 'The laws men have to observe when their wives are with child are these : not to kill any wild beast, not to make arrows, clubs, or handles to any other instruments; to abstain from eating flesh fifteen days after the wife is brought to bed, to unbend the bow, not to lay snares for birds; to lie at home idle and fasting till the infant's navel-string is cut.'[6]

The descriptions of tribes that recur in the accounts of the priest explorers are the earliest of their kind. For their time they are scientific, yet, in spite of detail, it is difficult to identify these Indians today. Many are extinct, others have migrated more deeply into the forests.

Already the Jesuits in Guairá would seem to have envisaged an Indian reservation stretching from the Paraná to the Amazon, embracing the vast unexplored central area of South America. But the fierceness of the Indians forced them to look south and south-east instead. First they explored the country from the Paranapanema three hundred miles south to the Iguazú, another eastern tributary of the Paraná, then with the appointment of Ruiz de Montoya as Superior in 1620 they pushed out more to the north towards São Paulo in Brazil. It was in this mountainous area at great intervals that Montoya, executing the plan of Torres, established between 1622 and 1628 eleven new towns containing some forty thousand Indians.* The farthest from Loreto, Concepción, in the territory of the Gualacos, was less than a hundred miles from the coast. Montoya's adventures in these years are recorded in a diary he kept and published under the title *Conquista Espiritual.*

* San Javier (1622), Encarnación and San José (1625), San Miguel and San Pablo (1625), San Antonio, Concepción and San Pedro (1627), Arcángeles, Santo Tomás and Jesús María (1628).

A Peruvian creole, at the age of fifteen he had joined the Spanish forces in a campaign against the Araucano Indians of Chile. He then entered the Jesuits. In phrases reminiscent of St Paul he summarized his life as a missionary : 'I have lived all through the period of thirty years in Paraguay as in a desert searching for savage animals, that is for primitive Indians, crossing wild country, passing over mountain ranges . . . going hungry, naked, in frequent dangers to my life which the imagination cannot capture.'[7] No one knew the country as well as he. His travels were almost continuous, his only baggage a hammock and some mandioca flour. Usually he journeyed on foot in sandals. For the space of eight or nine years he never tasted bread. About the time of the foundation of Arcángeles he and his Indian guides were offered a pot of maize and meat in the country of the Payes, a subdivision of the Guaraní. 'When they came to the bottom of the vessel a human head and hands were found and recognized for those of a man who used to attend [Montoya] at the altar and had fallen in the last battle.'[8]

Only in the first months after their arrival in Guairá did the Jesuits use Spanish guides. Imperfect in their knowledge of Guaraní, they accepted the offer of a Spaniard from Ciudad Real to act as interpreter.

The man affected to be totally disinterested : he never returned to the common hut except with one less article of baggage or clothing until he was left only with his underpants. Standing in this attire he admonished the two priests: 'You Fathers have the gift of eloquence but I make up for my lack of it with my good works. Everything I brought with me I have given to the Indians of the country.' The Fathers thanked him, then when he had gone, discovered he had bartered everything to buy women and children in exchange and was carrying them off as slaves. The Indians suspected the Fathers of complicity : only after much effort could they repair the damage done.[9]

Among the causes of the astonishing initial success of the Jesuits was the character of the Guaraní race : Ortega and Fields had been the first to discover that they were not only numerous, but appeared to be 'close to the Kingdom of God'. This assessment was now confirmed. Monotheists, believing in a Father God without offering him any worship, they had a natural aptitude for a Christian experiment.*

An early problem was caused by the plurality of wives allowed to Guaraní caciques by tribal custom. The cacique treated his wife as a servant : he would dismiss her if she felt sick and was unable to dress the meat or sew his garments or, most commonly, because she had grown old; often he would take to wife a woman with all her daughters, whom he would distribute among his followers, then later take them back for his own use; some caciques left behind their wives when they moved to another place. The more scrupulous missionaries urged that a cacique, before receiving baptism, should return to his first wife, but the majority argued that the concept of 'first' wife was meaningless : apart from the practical difficulty of remembering among so many wives the first to be taken, there was the further problem of finding her; when found it might be discovered that she had been previously married or so might her first husband. The tangle was inextricable. Moreover the Indians would lie, state before baptism that their present wife was their first or make pretence of returning to her and come forward again with another woman. In such a society, according to the more common view, all wives were concubines : there was no contractual bond, consequently a cacique after baptism was free to take a true wife and keep to her.

A judgement on the issue affected more than the personal concern of the cacique : the whole structure of Reduction life was based on his authority : it was he who brought his followers in from the forest and he retained his leadership over them under Jesuit supervision. A harsh decision based on European law, not on the realities of Guaraní tribal life, would

* This is also the judgement of Bartolomé Meliá, a Spanish Jesuit of Asunción who is on terms of friendship with primitive Guaraní Indians as well as other races in the forests of Paraguay between Coronel Oviedo and Iguazú. These Indians have never been touched by the historic Jesuit missions. Meliá has no difficulty in finding sufficient common religious ground to stay up three or four hours a night praying with them to their big Father.

have made substantial progress impossible. Fortunately the liberal view prevailed before the end of the second decade of the Guaraní Reductions, but not without an appeal to Urban VIII 'on behalf of Paraguay in the West Indies' by the Jesuit theologian, Cardinal de Lugo. The Pope, himself a pupil of the Jesuits, was asked to empower the Jesuit Provincial to dissolve all marriages of Guaraní caciques before baptism, leaving them free to marry again for the first time. Urban's reply registered irritation at being consulted : if there was a majority or even a probable opinion that the marriage of caciques was void, then there was no need for him to grant powers of dispensation. The priests should act on their own opinion.[10]

Two other parties of Jesuits had set out from Asunción in 1609, within months of the departure of Cataldino and Maceta for Guairá : the second, made up of an Italian, Vicente Griffi, and the creole, Roque González de Santa Cruz, crossed the Paraguay at Asunción and struck west to convert the Guaycurú, one of the largest groups of savage Indians in the Chaco. Confined before the coming of the Spaniards to the area between the west bank of the Paraguay and the Pilcomayo, now, with the acquisition of horses, they terrorized the country from Santa Fe to the marshes of Xarayes. Only by civilizing these Indians could a short route be opened up across the Chaco to Peru. Torres, the Provincial, believed that this party would have the easiest task, for it would never be more than a few days distant from the capital, at least in the first stages of its assigned mission.

After a few weeks Griffi fell sick : for nine months he was laid up with fever while González continued alone. On 10 May 1610 González reached a considerable group of Indians. His preaching appeared to prosper. At the end of the year Torres, after visiting the mission, reported enthusiastically to Rome that although only a few Guaycurú had been baptized, many hundreds had been pacified. 'Formerly they used to cross the river to pillage and do damage,' he continued, 'now they come in their scores, walk in the streets, enter houses and sleep safely in the town. . . . González and Griffi have been teaching them with great devotion to plough, sow, tend the land and harvest crops.' He described how he had been carried shoulder high to visit the principal cacique and choose with him the site for a settlement.

But the rains came, the land was flooded and the Guaycurú dispersed. For two years the priests lived among the Guaycurú without bringing them any closer to Christianity: 'They preached often, travelling through the country and penetrating to its remotest parts, teaching children and conveying by signs what they could not express in words.' In 1613 they were withdrawn and replaced by two fresh priests, who succeeded in forming a Reduction, St Mary of the Kings. But it did not develop. The Guaycurú could not settle. For months the new men lived miserably in reed huts, feeding on the same roots as the Indians, suffering from lack of fresh water and from the stench of rancid fish oil with which the Indians smeared their bodies. At night they listened to the drunken cries of the Guaycurú; in the day they were forced to watch them 'perform their hellish ceremonies and lascivious actions in the face of the sun'.

Reluctantly they acknowledged their failure. After a second visit from the Provincial, the priests were withdrawn: in the words of del Techo, 'The Guaycurú loved their nights to fight in, their strength lying in the suddenness of their onset; having done their damage by night, they withdrew to their lurking places infested by jaguars.' It was wild country: swamps, waving pampas grass, forests of thorny trees, thickets of cane; the climate was heavy and humid, a transitional area between the plains and the tropical forest, infested with vinchucas and mosquitoes; no landmarks but only an occasional clearing with a straggling settlement. It was the country that had defeated Cabeza de Vaca when he set out in 1542 to subdue it with four hundred Spaniards and a thousand friendly Indians. Within a few months he had returned to Asunción. Now the Guaycurú, 'keeping many spies abroad . . . not only opposed the Spaniards during almost a whole century, but often made slaughter of them, continuing in their ancient superstitions.'[11]

The third party left on 16 December 1609. It also was made up of two priests, Marciel de Lorenzana, formerly

Rector of the College of Asunción, and a novice, Francisco
de San Martín. In company with the cacique Arapizandu
they struck south towards the Paraná where today it forms
the frontier between Paraguay and Argentina. On their arrival
the next day at Yaguarón, a mission founded by the Franciscans in 1586, they were joined by a Paraguayan priest,
Hernando de la Cueva, with a small group of Christian
Indians. Continuing south they crossed the broad Tebicuary
river. At this point they crossed into unknown territory. On
Christmas Eve they reached Arapizandu's rancho, which they
attempted to convert into a permanent settlement. After a few
days Lorenzana reported that nine caciques had offered to
come in with their people and that some of them had begun
to build huts, 'the best sign we could have'. Early in January
the priest Cueva returned to Asunción.

The site chosen by Arapizandu did not please Lorenzana;
his search for a better place took him to the shores of the
Paraná, where he visited the veteran Franciscan missionary,
Luis de Bolaños, now working eastward from his base at
Corrientes. This encounter was important in the development
of the Jesuit mission. Lorenzana wrote that this 'great linguist
and great servant of God' gave him grammatical notes on
the Guaraní language, instructed him in the Guaraní verbs
and showed him his course of sermons and aids for hearing
confessions. Hitherto he and San Martín had only a rudimentary knowledge of the language.

The two Jesuits then moved some sixty miles east and
found there a suitable site for a town. Huts were built, one
larger than the rest serving for a church. Buildings, food
supply, everything that later was to be so exactly ordered, was
improvised: the main effort of the Fathers was directed to
winning the affection of the Indians. Drunkenness, lust and
cannibalism, the Fathers noted, were the principal shortcom-
ings of the Guaraní. Wisely the priests bided their time. In
a letter of 19 July 1610 Lorenzana told Torres that at two
or three every morning the Indians got up to drink and stayed
up drinking until dawn; that after their return from hunting
there was a community drinking bout lasting two or three
days. Possibly by dealing with the Indians individually they

might achieve something: the caciques commanded obedience only in time of war. 'Although we reproach them,' he wrote, 'they don't get angry with us.'

On reliable sources the eighteenth-century Jesuit Sánchez Labrador states that this Reduction, San Ignacio Guazú, was founded at a place called Itaguy in the corner formed by the confluence of the Paraguay and Paraná, opposite the later Franciscan foundation of Itatí; that eighteen years later, in 1628, it was transferred to a place where there was a chapel dedicated to San Angel, and finally, in 1668, about a mile to the east, where the pueblo of San Ignacio now stands on the southern highway from Asunción.

In its first location the founding Fathers hesitated whether or not to hand Ignacio Guazú over to the Franciscans who were working to the north and south: earlier in the field than the Jesuits, they had organized for their Indians protected townships, from which their neophytes went out daily to work for the settlers in return for a legal wage; the Jesuits, starting out after Alvaro's report, were able to claim total independence from the encomenderos. The Indians of the area had made freedom from encomienda a condition of their joining San Ignacio Guazú. Both sides agreed that it would be unwise to have townships of the two Orders too close to one another. A compromise was finally arranged. The Jesuits, while remaining at San Ignacio, would drive eastwards, following the waters of the Paraná upstream. It was in this almost fortuitous way that the territory between the Paraná and Uruguay rivers, and to the north and south of both, became the land of the Jesuit Republic.

Caciques continued to come into Ignacio Guazú. In August 1610 Lorenzana again wrote to Torres: no less than ten with their followers were expected in the next ten days, including Tabacambay who bore the high-sounding title of 'Captain-General of Paraná'. Lorenzana concluded: 'Within two or three months I hope with God's help to have in my Reduction another 1,000 married men which means 6,000 more souls.' Of the original number, he expected to have two hundred and thirty instructed before the first anniversary of the foundation.

But hostile Indians soon threatened the existence of San Ignacio. Fierce Guaraní tribes attacked a group of Christian Indians living close to the Reduction—some were killed, some were taken off as prisoners and fattened for a banquet. An attack on San Ignacio was then planned. Lorenzana posted his companion San Martín to Asunción for military aid, then made emergency disposition for defence. But fifty harquebusiers with two hundred friendly Indians arrived from the capital within a few weeks : these forces advanced with the Reduction Indians and routed the enemy.

This was the first of countless engagements which involved the Indians of the Jesuit townships. Without help from Asunción the early Paraná missions might have collapsed as shortly did those of Guairá. Sporadic attacks continued for the next century and a half; for the most part they were contained, and only occasionally was the regular life of the townships interrupted.

This action was fought a short time before the arrival of Roque González, who after his failure with the Guaycurú had been sent south to deal with the unexpected expansion. His coming marks the turning-point of this mission. Until then organization had been embryonic. Architect, mason and carpenter, he laid out the plaza, supervised the construction of blocks of houses, founded a school, built a church, working the wood and carrying it to the construction site. He also taught the Indians to plough, sow and protect their harvest from wild animals; in 1613 he wrote : 'Yes, we have some cattle, about forty head, and the same number of sheep. It is a beginning.'

So it was : within a hundred years many thousand head of cattle were found on the estancias attached to the Paraná towns : González understood clearly that a sound economic foundation was necessary for the Reductions to flourish. It was the beginning also of the peculiar way of life that was to characterize the Paraná Reductions. A creole, González spoke Guaraní and understood the Indian temperament : hymns, processions, music, catechisms in rhyming verses, fiestas and other features of Reduction life were introduced by him. He was a natural missionary. With strong feelings for the Indians, especially those made to work by the Spaniards for the exploitation of the Paraguayan *yerba*, he quickly won their confidence. His eloquence was effortless. From all contemporary accounts he would seem to have been an impressive man, tall, slender, with a high broad forehead, regular nose, fine lips, and a mobile, sympathetic expression and, further, he had the advantage of coming from an influential family. In the year he was sent to San Ignacio, his brother was *teniente* or acting Governor of Asunción. He possessed an optimistic temperament. His contribution to the shaping of Guaraní Republic was as great as that of any other single man. Among other achievements he conceived the plan of a school for the Guaraní language for future missionaries. He settled on San Ignacio Guazú for the purpose : the Reduction could support at least four priests, its economy was flourishing; also it was the natives of this part of Paraguay who spoke Guaraní in its purest form.[12] González appreciated that knowledge of their language would create ties with the Guaraní that nothing could replace : it would produce sympathy, even a sort of magical power, especially in the case of a people for whom the cacique was often a 'master of words'. As an earlier missionary had observed, 'There is no greater bond of friendship than a common language.'[13] In his instructions to his priests, Torres had insisted that, after the grace of God, the most effective means of winning the Indians was always to talk their tongue.

With permission to establish three more Reductions, Roque González, without an escort of soldiers or any Spanish assistance, continued south. On 25 March 1615 he raised a cross on a site that was soon to become the centre of a pueblo, and began building a church and houses for Indians. This was the beginning of the township of Itapúa or Nuestra Señora de la Encarnación on the Argentine bank of the Paraná at or near the present town of Posadas. The position was well chosen : the area was thickly populated with Indians and the lake running into the river formed a natural port. The first baptisms were held on 11 June that year, but the harvest of maize failed. After surviving on soup made of thistles, González and his companions were eventually succoured by

Franciscans from Corrientes. Two other Reductions founded soon afterwards failed. Itapúa, transferred to the north side of the river in 1621, survived to become, under the name of Encarnación, the third largest city of modern Paraguay.

In his journeys over the next thirteen years González traced the outline of the future Jesuit state, fixing its frontiers beyond their final limits. Towards the end of 1619 he was visited at Itapuá by Nicolás Neenguirú, a cacique from the eastern bank of the Uruguay, who wanted the Jesuits to found a town for his people. On 25 October González set out

> attended by a small number of converts, and after travelling through dismal places as far as the stream Aracuta which runs into the river Uruguay, found there a large number of Indians, who had notice of his coming by their spies. They were naked, armed with clubs and bows, and haughtily commanded him to proceed no further because it would certainly cost him his life. His companions, terrified by their threats, left him but he lay in a wood all night with only two boys who served his Mass the next morning. Then with a cacique of the district, who promised him protection,[14]

he made his way south and about a league from the river bank founded the town of Concepción on 8 December the same year. It was sited to be a base for exploration up and down the Uruguay and the centre of other Reductions to the east.

Within a few months Roque González, with the cacique Neenguirú, 'the captain', as he now called him, 'not merely of this pueblo but of all Uruguay and the whole country of Tape', crossed the Uruguay at its confluence with the Ibicuí and reached the village of the cacique Tabacan about a hundred and fifty miles from the river. In this land, now the Brazilian province of Rio Grande do Sul, which González was the first non-Indian to enter, he put up a cross and founded the Reduction of Nuestra Señora de la Candelaria. In its final location, across the Paraná from Encarnación, Candelaria was to become the headquarters of the Jesuit Republic.

At this time González was named Superior of the Reductions. Almost immediately he set out on a further exploration. In 1621 he crossed the cordillera by what is now the pass of Santiago into the country of Tape. The Indians here were hostile, but by showing the women and children they had nothing to fear from him, he gained their confidence and on 3 May 1622 founded the pueblo of San Nicolás Piratini. Shortly afterwards he got news that Candelaria had been destroyed by hostile Indians.

In spite of famine and smallpox San Nicolás prospered. In a few years it counted five hundred families.

Next, with Padre Pedro Romero, González went to the north of the Piratini, an area well suited to Reductions, won over a hostile cacique and on 2 February refounded Candelaria, leaving Romero to take care of it.

Earlier, González on his exploration of the Uruguay to the south had discussed with the Indians in the country near the confluence of the Ibicuí his plan for founding a Reduction there. The site was admirable; ninety miles below Concepción and three hundred above Buenos Aires, it guarded upper Uruguay pueblos against attack from the south; it was also not far from the territory to the east occupied by the Charrua, Yaró and other savage tribes and would serve as a base for their conversion. The difficulty was the sparseness of the population, 'only three Indian houses with a hundred Indians'. However, González made the decision to start. The local Guaraní were joined by non-Guaraní groups, Charrua and others, who adopted the Guaraní language and customs along with Christianity. Perhaps this mixture of blood accounted for the cultural lead later given by Yapeyú. Success came quickly. Before the end of the century, Yapeyú was famous throughout the Plata area as an academy of painting and music.

The last pueblo founded by González was in the forests to the north of Río Iyuí Grande: he called it Asunción del Iyuí. This was in 1628. It was a bold step, for he had chosen a place in the centre of a district dominated by the sorcerer cacique Nezu. Later in the same year and in the same area, only seventeen days after his return to the locality to chose a site for yet another town, as he was fastening the tongue to a bell designed for a yet unbuilt church, an Indian cracked open González's skull. Padre Alonso Rodríguez, his companion, died with him. The following day the third priest in the party was killed.

Montoya tells the story of González's horse : when the priest was murdered the horse refused all food and wept, two streams running continuously from its eyes. It never allowed an Indian to mount it after its master's death and finally lay down to die of grief close to its master's grave.

In 1628, the year of González's death, the Indians from the Reductions of Alto Paraná were already travelling to Santa Fe where they sold their products, using the Jesuits of the College in that city as their agents. It is likely that even then among their products was *yerba*, the Paraguayan tea, which Montoya in Guairá had forbidden the Reductions to market for fear of seeming to compete with the encomenderos.[15]

3

The Great Exodus

The vision and initiative of Roque González accounted largely for the remarkable expansion from the Paraná to within a hundred miles of the Atlantic. González had also visited Guairá and for eighteen months he had worked in the Chaco, the two other mission districts of the Paraguay Jesuits. In 1627 he had concluded an account of his most recent explorations with an estimate of the likely number of Indians that might eventually be brought into the townships in the vast area he had covered by canoe, on horseback and on foot.

> With truth I can say that no journey I have ever made has been so full of perils as that to the Ibicuy and Tape. . . . But now I am in a position to give you a reliable account of that territory: in the first place I can affirm that the whole land of Uruguay is no more than a single province, extensive though it is; its length at least 300 leagues, its breadth in parts more than 100 leagues. From the port of Buenos Aires to our first Reduction [Yapeyú] it is 100 leagues: from there to the cordillera that lies about ten leagues beyond the Reduction of San Nicolás, the furthest of all, it is 50 leagues: . . . then 50 leagues of dense forest until you come out on to the plains towards Guairá, and from there to the borders of Brazil another 100 leagues, which makes 300 in all.
> All these lands are peopled by Indians but very sparsely: in the entire province there might be 20,000 families, more

51

or less, That would come to 100,000 souls, all cultivating the land.*

In this year, 1627, it seemed likely that the Indian reservation would soon extend from Yapeyú to Loreto in Guairá in the north and in the east to within a hundred miles of the Atlantic.

González's vision was perhaps common to the Jesuits of Paraguay or at least to those who were in position to influence the development of the missions. In 1629 these prospects evoked some of the wildest dreams ever formed by Jesuit missionaries. There had been one major failure, the mission to the Guaycurú of the Chaco: Guairá, Tape and the Paraná more than compensated for the failure across the Paraguay west from Asunción.

In their first .years, the missions of Guairá and Paraná were dependent on the College at Asunción. In fact in all the South American cities where the Jesuits had either a residence or College, they were expected to undertake both the religious education of the Spanish population and work at the same time for the conversion of the Indians in their area. Success varied. The most striking was the missionary work undertaken by the College of Santa Fe: in May 1656 a Belgian Jesuit, Noel Berthot, was able to write: 'There is no infidel left in the whole of the Province.' By contrast the Jesuits of Tucumán could record only failure. As early as 1617 an attempt was made to Christianize the Indians of the Calchaquira valley, a narrow strip of fertile land hemmed in to east and west by the foothills of the Andes. This was the most southerly point of the Inca empire at its greatest. The Calchaquí remembered their proud past; they were suspicious of the Spaniards who let it be known that they believed that mines were once worked in this area; fierce as well as independent 'they defended themselves in battle with such resolution that women have been seen to force their husbands back to fight, driving them with firebrands when they saw them give way or fly'.

During an interval in the chronic warfare between the Spaniards of Tucumán and the Calchaquí two Jesuits from

* Modern estimates greatly exceed Roque González's figure.

the College made an expedition into the valley. Glad of a respite from fighting, the Calchaquí welcomed the priests; two towns, San Carlo Borromeo and Santa María, were built as a base for deeper penetration into the valley.

The reports sent back by the priests gave little ground for hope: the Calchaquí were sun-worshippers; thunder and lightning were their minor deities; they honoured heaps of stones, the monuments of Inca times; and they clung fiercely to their filthy funeral rites: 'As soon as a man is dead, they place all sorts of meat and wine about his body . . . clap meat into the carcass's mouth and then swallow it themselves; finally they cast into the grave the man's dogs, horses, arms and clothes and then burn his house.'[1] On the anniversary the ceremonies were repeated; as a sign of mourning they painted their bodies black.

An estimated 30,000 Calchaquí lived scattered in the valley. They threw over Christianity as quickly as they accepted it: after several years' preaching the priests reported despondently: "None who formerly had been baptized lived at this time like a Christian, but dwelt promiscuously among the heathens, following the customs of his forefathers."[2] Henceforth the priests baptized only Calchaquí near the point of death: until their subjection to sorcerers was uprooted, no advance could be expected. However, by 1630 they could claim to have brought thirteen years' peace to the valley. It was broken early the next year: the Calchaquí revolted, destroyed Spanish estates, invaded Tucumán and carried on an intermittent warfare for the next ten years. In 1640 the Fathers returned: the town of San Carlo was rebuilt, but the mission never prospered.

The Fathers from the College of Mendoza to the south did no better among the Indians of Cuyo, an Andean valley about 500 miles in length, holding the passes into Chile: here there was an abundance of corn, grapes and fruit of almost every kind; there was no need for the Indians to settle, there was food in abundance to support a nomadic life: attempts by the Fathers to gather the Cuyo Indians into towns failed: not even a rudimentary settlement was made; the Indians continued in their old ways. 'Carrying about their mats which were their only houses, they lived in small holes in the ground like rabbits in a warren.'[3]

Too well provided by nature and given to heavy drinking, they shrugged off attempts to make them Christians. The Guaraní, however, living mainly in dense forests, gave the Fathers boundless hopes. Success in Guairá and on the Paraná led to the detachment of these missions from the College of Asunción : by 1620 they had their own Superior, Montoya, dependent directly on the Provincial of Paraguay : later there were two mission Superiors, Montoya in Guairá, González on the Paraná : both were given complete freedom in the field by two remarkable Provincials, first Torres, then Durán. It was the latter's directives, drawn up in 1626,[4] that determined the internal structure of the townships, their system of government and relations with the Spanish settlers : they provided a labour charter and penal code suited to the Indian. Until the expulsion of the Jesuits a century and a half later, Durán's directives remained the law of the Jesuit republic : adaptations, revisions, additions were made, but the principles stayed unaltered.

But no amount of sheer administration could of itself account for the phenomenal expansion of the missions. At Rome Claudio Aquaviva backed his men in the field to the full : he and his immediate successor, Mutio Vitelleschi, did as much to secure their work as Ignatio Visconti and Lorenzo Ricci, the last two Jesuit Generals before the suppression of the Order, later did to destroy it. It was Aquaviva who directed to Paraguay the superfluous Jesuits from Flanders and thus provided the priests needed for the rapidly growing number of Reductions.

At this time all missions entrusted to the Jesuits were made the responsibility of Assistancies or groupings of Jesuit Provinces according to geographical or linguistic divisions : to the Portuguese were assigned Brazil, the east and west coasts of Africa, the east Indies, and extreme east, including Japan; to Spain, South America from Mexico to Chile and the Philippines; to the French and Italians, the coast and islands of the eastern Mediterranean, parts of the Middle East and their hinterland, North America and the Antilles. Left out of this division of the non-Christian world was the German Assistancy, which included the two Provinces formed in 1611 in the Spanish Netherlands : their 'mission' was to combat heresy in the homeland.

By the time the first Paraguay townships had been founded, there was an altered situation which Acquaviva was quick to appreciate : the fluid religious contours of sixteenth-century Europe had settled into fixed frontiers; this left Flanders and, later, parts of the Holy Roman Empire with a superfluity of vocations.*

Every six years an elected delegate from the Province of Paraguay visited Rome to attend the regular Congregations of the Jesuits.† This gave an opportunity for direct dealing with the Jesuit General : in addition, the delegate was often entrusted with negotiations with the court of Madrid; he was also expected to return with a sufficient number of recruits to replace losses and maintain growth. It was to the Catholic Netherlands that he naturally turned : the priests available there had the advantage of being subject to the Spanish Crown. But still the delegate had to negotiate with Madrid permits for them to embark for the Indies; he had also to raise the passage money or the balance of it—the king paid a third, which in the eighteenth century was cut to a quarter : lists were drawn up and passed through various officials in Madrid before the young recruits could sail from Cadiz.

A party sailed every six or seven years, the first to include Belgians in 1616; others about the same time left for Peru and Mexico; many never reached South America : some died at sea, others were taken into slavery by Barbary pirates. There is a laconic note to the 1681 list of Jesuits in Paraguay, *his accedunt qui in navigatione ad hanc Provinciam obierunt,* 'to these are to be added those who died on their way to this Province'. Their number was considerable. Even at the end

---

* For instance Josse van Suerck, an outstanding missionary in Guairá and later in Itatín (cf. inf. p. 69) was the third of seven sons of a merchant draper of Anvers, all of whom became Jesuits : one of them died at sea on the voyage to Buenos Aires.

† Although these Roman meetings were held every three years, overseas delegates attended only alternate meetings.

of the seventeenth century conditions were no better. Antonio Sepp, the Tyrolese priest who sailed from Cadiz with thirty-nine other Jesuits on 17 June 1690, did not reach Buenos Aires until 6 April the following year. In the second half of their voyage they were living on hard biscuits full of maggots and baked two years before, a daily ration of a pint of corrupted water, and some stinking beef. Their sleeping quarters were in the forecastle, where they used the ship's cables for pillows and were overrun by rats in their sleep.[5]

The first contingent of Flemish priests that left Europe in 1616 completed their training in Córdoba and were then drafted to the Reductions; a remarkable group followed in 1628; the 1640 party included du Toit, better known as del Techo, the first historian of Paraguay. Like his compatriots, he concealed his Flemish origin under a Spanish approximation to his surname.* However, the war between Spain and France (1640–90) closed this source of supply: in 1647 twenty-nine Belgian priests gathered in Cadiz for the Paraguay mission were compelled to return to their country. In the eighteenth century the main non-Spanish element was South German, Swiss, Austrian and Bohemian, all from the Hapsburg dominions. They came first in the last decade of the seventeenth century: the party of recruits setting out from Europe in 1717, contained a German contingent whose influence marked a turning-point in the cultural and economic life of the missions.

Thanks to the aid from Flanders, each of the thirteen Guairá Reductions had a staff of two priests by 1629. In all of them the regime followed the lines laid down in Durán's instructions. No desk-bound bureaucrat, two years previously he had been on a historic visitation of Guairá: his reception everywhere was almost vice-regal in its grandeur, for hitherto 'no Bishop, Governor, or Provincial had been in Guairá.'[6] At Ciudad Real the officials of the town asked him to found a College; at the township of Loreto 'the converts staged a fight

---

* This was a ruse to deceive the emigration officials as to the number of non-Spanish priests in the party. Often it is difficult to trace the true nationality of priests working in Paraguay: for instance, van Seurck appears as Vansurque and van Seurq in Flemish documents, as Mansilla and Justo in Spanish; but also as Bancuir, Bansure, Bansurch, etc.

among themselves on the river, which resounded with song
and music'; the churches were decorated in his honour; at
San Ignacio the Indians already numbered more than 1,500
families: 'Wherever he went, he bestowed shirts, hooks, pins,
needles and glass beads among the Indians; he is said to have
spent to the value of 2,000 pieces of eight among them.'[7] On
leaving, he ordered Montoya to build three new towns.

His visit was undertaken with the secondary purpose of
finding a safer and shorter route from Asunción to Guairá.
The first Fathers had sailed up the Paraguay, then eastward
along its tributary, the Jujuy, and finally overland to Ciudad
Real, a distance of 1,500 miles in all. This route was now
'infested with Paiaguans, the most inhuman of Indians and
famed for the slaughter of numerous travellers'.[8] In 1626
Durán, setting out from Santa María, not far from the Iguazú
falls, followed the Paraná to a Reduction near the river
Acaray, then continued another hundred miles up the Paraná
to the first cataracts below the falls of Guairá. From there he
took a track cut through the forest by Montoya's Indians to
reach the summit of the falls, where he was met and escorted
to Ciudad Real. A few years later, Montoya was to make this
route famous when he followed it from north to south.

While still in Guairá, Durán heard rumours that the
Mamelucos, as the rabble population of São Paulo was called,
were preparing a slave-raiding expedition against the Reductions. The first raid, in fact, occurred in 1629.

Known also as Paulistas, they had converted São Paulo
into a stronghold virtually independent of the Portuguese
colonial Government. It was perfectly placed for their purpose. On a high rock surrounded by wild mountains and the
thick forests of Pernabacaba like a palisade on all sides, it had
a temperate climate, produced wheat, spices, sugar and
sulphur and at the same time provided rich pastures. Ironically it was the site chosen in 1554 by two Jesuits, Manoel da
Nóbrega and José de Anchieta, for a church and school in
which to educate the Portuguese on the plateau. They had
reached the place some years earlier, and on a nearby hill
naturally protected from hostile Indians had founded a
Reduction. The first Mass at the College had been said on

25 January, the feast of the Conversion of St Paul, after whom the College and later the city that grew up around it were called.

But soon the Portuguese through scarcity of women intermarried with escaped African slaves and the savage Tupí Indians and bred a race which in turn was joined by the criminal refuse of England, Holland, France and Portugal and by all who, in the phrase of a Jesuit writer, 'desired to lead a licentious life with impunity'.[9] Excellent horsemen, skilful at paddling canoes, able navigators along the coast, crack marksmen and brave fighters, they subsisted by procuring Indians and leading them chained and corded to São Paulo, where they were herded into pens and sold like cattle to work on the mines and plantations of sugar, cotton, mandioca and tobacco. 'Suckling babes were torn from the bosom of their mothers and cruelly dashed upon the ground by the way. All whom disease or age had rendered imbecile were either cut down or shot as being unequal to the daily march. Others, in sound health, were often thrown at night into prepared pits so that they should not take advantage of the darkness and flee.'[10] Whole families were enrolled by the Paulistas in these raids—old, young, whites and half-breeds : with them went cattle for slaughter and pack mules. At times, shortage of provisions made them settle in a forest clearing, where they planted a crop of quick-growing mandioca and waited until it ripened. It was reckoned that in the course of a hundred and thirty years they made two million slaves. The colonial Governor 'abandoned not only the desire but all hope of subduing their stronghold'.[11]

About the time of Durán's departure from Guairá, the Mamelucos had combed the district around São Paulo and were driven to search further afield. The Jesuit towns gave them the chance of seizing large numbers of Indians in a single haul, and Indians already disciplined, attached to the soil and, at least in the first encounters, unarmed. Moreover, the rivers of the tableland on which São Paulo was built flowed, not to the near-by coast, but eastward into the interior. Following their course, the Mamelucos appeared in 1629 before San Antonio, destroyed it, set fire to the church and drove off the Indians. They did the same at San Miguel and Jesús María. In Concepción Padre Diego de Salazar was under continuous siege and with his Indians was reduced to a diet of dogs, cats, rats, mice and snakes : he was about to surrender when Cataldino came to his relief with a force of Indians armed with any and every kind of rough weapon.

Ordinarily the Reduction Indians, with their clubs and arrows, had no chance against the Mamelucos with their horses, guns, bloodhounds and enlisted bands of savage Tupí allies. Despair overcame them : many who escaped capture fled into the forest, others turned on the Jesuits, to whom they attributed their suffering, and on occasion threatened them with death.

It was perhaps with the purpose of convincing the Indians of their goodwill that Maceta from Jesús María and van Suerck from San Miguel followed their neophytes through the forest into Brazil. Fifteen thousand Indians had been herded together, mainly from these two Reductions : their caciques had been secured with fetters linked to a long chain, the rest made to march with bound hands. The story is told by del Techo :

> Maceta ran among these poor wretches embracing them and begging of their keepers for his children in Christ, but they scoffed at him, saying he was mad; and yet he did not stop until he had mollified one of three thieves and rescued some few of the Indians. Encouraged by his success, he went to another company where with much entreaty he obtained the release of eight, including their chief, the famous cacique Guiravera and his wife.*
>
> The priests then followed the thieves through a vast tract of land, feeding on berries and other wild fruit. The Mamelucos marched their prisoners slowly so that they should not faint by the way; yet very often some dropped, spent with sickness or hunger or failing through age or

---

* Guiravera, a recent convert, was a man of great authority among the Indians of Guairá: he confirmed caciques in their power, killed and ate his adversaries and threatened to titillate the palate of his concubines with a roast Jesuit. Maxime Haubert, *La Vie Quotidienne en Paraguay* (Hachette, 1967), p. 155.

weakness: the Fathers prepared these men for death but were obliged to leave them exposed in the wilderness in order to give the same help to others. It was common to see young men burdened with their mothers, mothers with their children, sons with their fathers, wives with their husbands, and husbands supporting their wives who had their infants in their arms. If anyone tried to make his escape he was cruelly whipped, and no one, even if his mother or father dropped by the way, was permitted to stay behind: wherever anyone fell, there he was left to die alone.[12]

At São Paulo the Mamelucos divided the prey among themselves; they confessed they had never made a more successful expedition.

At São Paulo also the two priests pleaded with the Mamelucos chiefs, but they were referred to the central criminal courts of Brazil at Rio de Janeiro six hundred miles away, and from there back to the governor of the colony at Santos. From him they obtained an order for the restoration of their Indians. This was specious satisfaction: no form of law, only force of arms, could be effective: the Indians had already been sold, and there was now hardly a planter in Brazil who had not a stake in the human loot.* Padre van Suerck considered accepting an offer of his passage money to Europe to pursue the cause there, but rumours reached him that the Mamelucos were planning another expedition. With only a handful of their Indians now released from slavery, the Fathers set out from São Paulo, sailed down the Aniembi river into the Paraná, and reached their ruined townships 'after a whole year's toil to little purpose'.[13]

Meawhile the Guairá Reductions were in confusion: the Indians rightly believed greater safety was to be found in the forests: there was one report that the Jesuits were in league with the Mamelucos and had received payment from them. It was just the situation which the pagan sorcerers required to recover their influence. In the area of the ruined Reductions,

* In the five years 1627–32 some 60,000 Indians were put up for sale in the public markets of Brazil. Cf. G. Furlong, *Misiones y sus Pueblos* (Buenos Aires, 1962), p. 384.

on a high mountain, two temples were built to which the Indians now resorted on Sundays and the Christian holidays. The description of the ceremonies there is more detailed than the accounts left by the Augustinian friars of the Inca temples of Peru. The buildings were spacious, decorated with curious hangings in plaited straw; one section, a kind of sanctuary, was protected by an ornamental wall: here the bones of a dead sorcerer were kept in a hammock slung between two pillars; its cords and the fine cotton fabrics which protected the mummy were decorated with multi-coloured plumes and with garlands of flowers renewed each day: lamps burned continuously before the holy relics. In the body of the church, benches were laid out for worshippers: panniers for offerings hung from the walls and pillars; balsam perfumed the sanctuary. The priests, who belonged to both sexes, were supported by first fruits and tithes; women with dishevelled hair fed a perpetual fire in honour of the devil, while men, like possessed persons, went into violent convulsions and in that state received an oracular message from the dead sorcerer, now risen from the dead, when he was questioned in the name of the people. In the sacrifice the officiating priest consumed part of the offering and distributed the rest among the faithful.

It was a highly organized cult with a number of features borrowed from the recently preached Christianity, yet Indian in spirit. In the hierarchy of the gods even the Jesuits had a place, petty divinities with feeble powers. The sorcerers, on the other hand, were at the apex, makers of heaven and earth, masters of the elements. Their death was apparent only.

It was through the oracles also that the man-god preached his messianic doctrine: the Jesuits were impostors who ingratiated themselves with the Indians under the cloak of piety; they spread epidemics by the touch of their hands; the salt they used in the baptismal exorcism contained poisonous gunpowder; all Indians must fly from the Jesuits' churches and take up the new religion, otherwise the Mamelucos would attack their towns and fire envelop them; the rivers would burst their banks and not a soul would be saved.

Even Indian officials from the Reductions and catechists

were caught up in the fervour of the new national religion;
whole towns were deserted on Sundays, the crosses erected at
the corners of the plazas were uprooted during the night. The
relapse into paganism seemed complete. For a period the
Indians became ungovernable.

It was at this moment of crisis that Montoya showed his
powers of leadership. He sought out the Indians, burned their
temples, and with the help of the cacique Guiravera drew
them back in sufficient numbers to start rebuilding Jesús
María. Within a few months the town was moved further to
the west: van Suerck had returned from São Paulo with the
news that the Mamelucos were preparing another raid. Weeks
later San Pablo was destroyed, then Encarnación, the neighbouring town, abandoned through fear: the Indians from
there fled to San Javier, which now became the Jesuit outpost
to the east. Montoya was faced with the problem of feeding
the refugees; he had also to contend with the Spaniards of
Villarrica who had seized homeless Christian Indians and sold
them to plantations in Paraguay.

The only hope of saving the missions and with them the
whole province of Guairá for Spain was military. The
Governor of Asunción, Luis de Céspedes, was a high-born
adventurer. On his way to Asunción to take up his appointment in 1628, he had travelled overland through Brazil from
Rio de Janeiro instead of sailing up the Río Plata as he had
been ordered. At São Paulo he had allied himself with the
Mamelucos; at Loreto he had been entertained by Montoya,
who asked him to provide military aid against the Mamelucos.
'All the return he made was abusive language.' His departure
from Guairá had been quickly followed by the first Mamelucos
raid.

Montoya now sent one of his priests, Díaz Taño, to
Asunción: the case for Spanish forces could no longer be
questioned, yet the governor asserted that the Jesuits were
exaggerating the danger. From Asunción, Taño went to
Charcas to plead with the supreme Court of the Indies.

Meanwhile Durán's successor, Vásquez Trujillo, visited
Guairá himself: he arrived too late to save San Javier, which
fell after a short siege: only one hundred out of fifteen

hundred families were saved. San José, half-way between San Javier and San Ignacio, was abandoned : rumours spread that there was a still larger force of Mamelucos on the way.

The Mamelucos were now perfecting their tactics. Normally they rushed a town when the Indians were gathered in church and blocked all the exits. But coming up as they did now against improvised defences, they infiltrated disguised as Jesuits, wearing rosaries, crosses and black gowns, attended, as the Jesuits usually were, by a number of Indians. On meeting isolated groups in the forest, they would mimic the gestures and speech of the Jesuits and persuade their victims to leave their forest dwellings and form themselves into larger units both for their safety and instruction. 'When they had brought together a large number, they amused them until their soldiers came up, put them in irons and drove them off to São Paulo.'[14]

At this point the Provincial gathered as many priests as he could in the township of Jesús María for a strategic consultation. After a hot debate between the men in favour of resistance and those who urged flight, Trujillo himself for purely military reasons came down on the side of the latter : he argued that the Reduction Indians, almost naked as they were and armed only with their arrows, 'could do little execution among the Mamelucos who had coats stuffed with cotton to resist them : although they outnumbered the enemy, they had no firearms'. By a majority vote, it was resolved to move the Reductions to the lower reaches of the upper Paraná to what was judged a safe distance from the marauders. On the side of resistance was Louis Ernot, the son of a Flemish officer : he was later to write to the Jesuit General, Vitelleschi, complaining that the evacuation plan had been hurriedly conceived and carried out with wretched organization.[15] But with his military instincts he obeyed the Provincial's orders loyally. For sixty days he marched with his Indians through the forest, and brought them to the assembly point for evacuation without losing one Indian. Other priests were less successful. Ernot himself was attacked later, on 25 January 1631, but his life was saved by the chance misfire of the arquebus shot at him by one of the raiders.

There were rumours now that another thrust was being prepared by the Mamelucos from the south against Loreto and San Ignacio, the first two and last remaining Guairá Reductions. Foreseeing that not even these two towns could be held, Montoya had ordered a fleet of rafts and canoes to be constructed: he knew that the Mamelucos had no craft to pursue by river. 'These two colonies built twenty years before this time were so improved by the industry of the Fathers that they could compare with the best Spanish towns in those parts,' writes del Techo.[16] 'Their churches were more stately and better adorned than any in Tucumán or Paraguay. Padre Vaisseau had trained choirs of musicians that differed but very little from those in Europe. . . . There was a good increase of kine and other cattle brought there with much trouble by the Society.' Another writer is more idyllic in his description:

Each house had its patio in the rear in which hens, geese, flocks of domestic birds were kept. The fields produced cereals and cotton, so that the Indians carried on a real trade in their cloth and at the same time provided clothing by way of an alms to all naked travellers, both Indian and European. Flocks of sheep and goats could be seen in the fields and herds of cattle and mules in the lowland pastures intersected by rivers that abounded in fish. With these and other blessings the Indians led a happy life.[17]

The Jesuits could justly claim that Guairá was the most flourishing province under the Governor of Paraguay. There had been thirteen towns under their direction.

Understandably, the Indians were reluctant to leave. The journey to safety was nearly four hundred miles; it was likely that no more than a handful of the old, sick or very young would survive it, yet they promised to follow Montoya.

On the river beneath Loreto, Montoya gathered his great flotilla; about 2,500 families or some 12,000 Indians were embarked, the remnants of eleven Reductions; a few statues were salvaged from the wreckage and loaded on to the craft with provisions sufficient for several weeks. The Spaniards of

Villarrica and Ciudad Real protested : if the Jesuits left, they would be exposed to the depredations of the Mamelucos. After passing the fleet in review, Montoya set sail. A few days later the Mamelucos, coming on Loreto and San Ignacio, set them on fire.

All went as Montoya had planned until the flotilla entered the broad lake above the Guairá falls. At this point the Paraná, about three miles wide at the crest of the falls, thunders over a ledge between a hundred and a hundred and thirty feet high in eighteen separate cataracts, then funnels its way through a canyon less than three hundred feet wide in a cauldron of foam stretching some thirty-five miles until it becomes navigable again.*

Montoya had hoped to send his boats empty down the falls and re-embark his Indians at the foot. Here the lack of planning of which Ernot complained was apparent. While events were still recent, del Techo wrote : 'The difficulty was finding boats for such a multitude after they were down the precipice, for there was no hope that any craft could escape wreck if they were let down from the top of the precipice to the pool at the bottom.' But as the craft could not be transported through a jungle that even the Indians found almost impenetrable, Montoya made the experiment : 'Taking out the loads, he turned loose almost all the boats which in a moment were shattered into fragments and vanished beaten against the rocks or swallowed by whirlpools.'[18]

When the Indian sent to the foot of the falls reported that all three hundred craft had been broken into pieces, Montoya began the descent by land : he would encamp at the pool until other boats had been made or until the Jesuits from Iguazú and Acaray sent up transports for the second part of the migration.

With depleted provisions, the descent began through country where game was so scarce that according to an Indian fable no living thing could survive near the cataracts. It was

---

* At extreme flood the falls of Guairá have eight-and-a-third times Niagara's volume. Most of the gorges between the islands at the lip of the falls are now bridged. There is a light railway operating on the eastern bank parallel with this unnavigable stretch of the Paraná.

a dense forest area of dank vegetation over which clouds of vapour descended like a continuous rain.[19] To add to Montoya's difficulties there was a report that Spaniards from Guairá, angered at the flight of the Indians, had planned to intercept them a few miles from the head of the falls : they had built a wooden fortress there and surrounded it with a stockade, into which they would herd the Indians and take them back as slaves. Montoya, disguised as an Indian, went ahead alone to reconnoitre. On his return he led his people through a forest track that skirted the ambush : by the time it was known that they had passed, they were beyond reach of the Spaniards.

Montoya tells how each Indian, even children, carried a load on his back, the priests taking the equipment for Mass and some statues saved from the wreckage of the Reduction churches. The advance party was made up of Indians armed with hatchets : they cut open a path through the forest. As the column advanced, hymns were sung and fugitive Indians came out of hiding and joined it.

Soon the going became more difficult. The hymns ceased, the instruments brought by the Indians were left, strings broken, wood unglued, on the rocks. There is a record of each day of the eight-day march to the foot of the cataract. The multitude divided into columns each with a priest at its head. 'Every now and then they met with streams and were forced to fell trees and make some sort of bridge. Sometimes the steepness of the rocks, sometimes the hot burning sands and sometimes impassable woods obstructed their passage.'[20] A great number died in the descent, a distance of thirty-five miles in a direct line, but many more with the circuits they were compelled to make.

At the foot, the river differed greatly from its placid upper reaches : steep banks on both sides held in narrow, deep, fast-flowing waters no more than three hundred yards at their broadest. Whirlpools and jagged outcrops of rock soon took toll of the boats sent upriver from the missions at Acaray and Iguazú. Of this relief flotilla loaded with provisions only a few craft survived. Instead of taking all his Indians downriver Montoya was now forced to divide them into four parties.

The first, under Padre Espinosa, followed the river bank, the second and third made their way as best they could across country, on the east side to Santa María la Mayor on the Iguazú and on the west to Natividad on the Acaray. The fourth went downstream with Montoya,

> but as he did not have sufficient craft to carry so great a number, Maceta was ordered to stay at the foot of the precipice with the rest of the people until the craft could return from Acaray. There Maceta and his company lived three months on wild fruits. . . . [But of the rest] whether they went by land or water, very many died, some fainting with hunger, some with weariness and other misfortunes. As the boats were small and the surges great those on the river were often overturned and many drowned. Many had made boats of cane, fifty feet long and thicker than a man's leg, bound together, in which many were lost.[21]

The survivors of the four parties were cared for by the Guaraní of Jesuit townships on the Iguazú and Acaray: they were then dispersed in smaller numbers among the Reductions on the Uruguay and Paraná: 'San Ignacio distributed two-thirds of the provisions they had among the strangers; Itapúa gave them three thousand oxen; the inhabitants of Corpus Christi slaughtered a great number of cattle to relieve them.'[22] But smallpox struck before the dispersal was completed: some again fled into the woods and died there from starvation; jaguars accounted for many others. 'To be brief,' concludes del Techo, 'of the remains of thirteen towns of Guairá scarce four thousand survived the first year after their migration, all the rest either died on the way, scattered, or perished by hunger or famine.'[23]

When the plague abated, Montoya gathered these remains and on the Jabebuir, a tributary of the Paraná, laid the foundations of two towns; he gave them their old names of Loreto and San Ignacio: to feed his Indians while the towns were under construction, he bought ten thousand oxen with the money the Spanish Crown allotted each priest. Slowly the two places began to prosper in comparative safety.*

For twenty-three years the Jesuits had been in Guairá. With the exception of a few heathen pockets the Province was now Christian. At their departure the two Spanish towns were in turn overthrown. The whole area fell to the Mamelucos, who continued to push westward. Traces of the Jesuit occupation —some piles of masonry, orange and banana groves—were found by roving Brazilian bandits as late as 1771 and then lost again.[24]

When he had seized the throne of Portugal in 1570, Philip II of Spain had confidently expected the vast Portuguese possessions in Africa, Asia and America to remain always under the Spanish Crown. Neither he nor his two immediate successors had taken steps to defend Spanish overseas territories against encroachment from their old rivals. Assuming that Brazil was theirs for ever, they were not concerned with the loss of Guairá and other lands to the west of the line of Tordesillas.†

When in 1640 Portugal regained her independence under John IV it was too late to recover them.

* Both towns were later transferred to the area between the Paraná and Uruguay. Loreto is now a ruin. San Ignacio, called Ignacio Miní (Little) to distinguish it from the other Ignacio called Guazú (Big) founded by Lorenzana in Paraguay, has been partially restored as a tourist attraction for visitors to Argentina.

† The Treaty of Tordesillas (1490) drew a line from pole to pole dividing the new world nine hundred miles to the west of the line drawn by Pope Alexander VI the previous year. This adjustment gave Portugal a small segment of the eastern bulge of South America.

4

Defeat of the Mamelucos

On the fourth day of the descent of the Guairá cataracts,
Montoya had detached four priests, including the seasoned
van Suerck, to Itatín, a province bounded by the river Jujuy
to the south, the Mbotetey to the north, and by Chiquitos and
Guairá to the west and east. As early as 1612, caciques from
Itatín had sent to Loreto for Jesuits, but only with the abandonment of the thirteen Guairá towns were any available. It
was a low-lying, partly marshy province later to become
notorious in the Brazilian rubber boom. The first Jesuits there
reported home on the marvel of the 'rebounding balls of
Itatín, made from the gum of trees, which thrown on the
ground start up again as if filled with air, and when toasted
are used for curing the flux'.[1]

Montoya had planned this development with the Provincial,
Vásquez de Trujillo, when they had conferred over the
evacuation of Guairá. But they did not foresee that the story
of Guairá would be repeated. Possibly it was hoped that the
new towns to the west would be allowed to provide their own
military forces to meet the Mamelucos. However, the work
was begun without the kind of debate that accompanied the
evacuation of Guairá. If Montoya entertained grandiose ideas
of 'spiritual conquest', the temptation was great. These were
Guaraní Indians: though they were not numerous in the
province, it was hoped that when it became Christian 'the
light of the gospel might be carried beyond Paraguay as far
as Peru one way, and the other way to the lands of the river
Marañon, all famous for multitudes of Indians'.[2] Overtures
had already been received from the Chiquitos west of Itatín.

The Jesuits perhaps looked too quickly for compensation for the loss of Guairá; on the other hand they may have regarded themselves tied by promises made many years earlier to send priests to the province as soon as they could.

The ground had already been reconnoitred : while Montoya was preparing the migration from Guairá, he had sent Ransonnier, a Fleming, to the Itatines. Passing south from the Spanish border town of Jerez he met unexpected opposition : a Portuguese priest, Acosta, after bringing many Itatines into a settlement, had tried to drive them off to Brazil as slaves, but was set upon and murdered by the Indians. Their fear was increased by sorcerers who gave out that Ransonnier had come to gather the people into churches and burn them there.[3]

The Indians, however, changed their attitude when famine reduced them to living off locusts and the pith of the palm. San José, the first primitive Reduction, to which the bells of Loreto had been taken, soon had two hundred families; Los Angeles, the second, about the same number. After this the Jesuits were welcomed by Nianduabusu, a cacique who boasted overlordship over the present Paraguayan Chaco as far south as Asunción. A third Reduction, Pedro y Pablo, was established for his people ten miles from the river Paraguay. San Benito and Natividad followed soon after. On the west bank of the Paraguay, contact was made with the savage Paiaguans, but they scattered again as soon as a town was built. The Fathers now dreamed of pushing north : 'Beyond this Province [Itatín] in the land towards the great river of the Amazon, there were pigmies and Amazons living in war all their lives : they were reported for a short time every year to call men from the neighbourhood to get them with child; and other natives as well, so numerous that Ransonnier in a letter to his Superior affirmed that many towns might be built up in their country if there were Fathers to serve them.'[4]

Itatín was largely the mission field of the Belgians, van Suerck, Hénard and Ernot, as well as Ransonnier, all of whom had some years of experience in Guairá to guide them. This in part accounts for their very rapid progress. But it was brief. In two years in which they founded six Reductions, Villarrica and Ciudad Real fell to the Mamelucos. In 1633 the first bands entered the province of Itatín. What remained of the six were gathered into two new foundations further south. In 1634 these two were reduced to one, Yatebo. After twelve years this split into two, Santa María de Fe and San Ignacio de Caaguazú. Each successive move was nearer Asunción, until finally in 1659 they occupied the sites between the Paraná and Paraguay, where they developed into the present towns of Santa María and Santiago.[5] Here the Belgians who had been critical of Montoya's move were able at least to fight a holding operation against the Mamelucos: they also won at the Court of Charcas their appeal against the Spaniards of Paraguay, who argued that, since the Indians of Itatín had never been granted the same privileges as those of Guairá, they could be dispersed in encomiendas.

The arrival of a large number of priests from Guairá in the Paraná Reductions to the south of Asunción gave the opportunity to the Superior to realize the dream of González's eastward expansion. There, between the cordillera and the sea, was a fertile land with excellent pastures, an abundance of streams and brooks, and a people similar to the Guaraní of Guairá but gentler and, according to some priests, even more apt for Christianity. This territory, between the Uruguay and the Yacuí rivers, now the Brazilian Province of Rio Grande do Sul, was known to the Jesuits as Tape, a name extant only in a branch of the mountain system called Sierra de los Tapes.

González had visited the country before his martyrdom. In 1631, three years afterwards, Montoya, following the rivers, and Romero, taking an overland route, converged in the centre of the province. In 1632 the first town, San Miguel, was started. The priests made good progress. Within a year seven hundred and fifty families had been collected. As the priests advanced into the province they found that the Indians were already building rudimentary churches and huts in places they judged suitable for Reductions. On their arrival the priests were welcomed with bonfires. The old, now familiar, names of towns recur—San José, Natividad, Santa Teresa. Among the most active of the priests was Cataldino, the pioneer of Guairá.

Another two hundred and fifty miles still lay between the most easterly Reduction and the sea. In 1634 Diego de Boroa was appointed Provincial, the third in a line of brilliant organizers, which must be uncommon in Jesuit annals: he quickly saw not just the opportunities, like Montoya, but also, unlike him, the dangers. 'He ordered excursions to be made into the country of the heathens towards the ocean to found new towns and to invite Indians to join existing ones, and also to make friends with those Indians and join with them to oppose the Mamelucos because it was clear that an invasion was only a matter of time.'[6]

Pedro Jiménez was detailed for this task: he sailed along the rivers to the east and finally reached the Tebiquary. 'He searched the rocks, woods and forests along these rivers, was conducted from village to village and found many Indians anxious to become Christians. Sometimes he was met by thirty canoes at a time all resounding with mirth and jollity.'[7] The Indians implored Jiménez to erect crosses and build churches on the spot: they were disinclined to leave their territory. Some however did and joined the Reductions of Santa Teresa and Visitación; more followed, driven into the Jesuit towns by famine and later by an outbreak of smallpox.

Even while the towns were building, the Mamelucos were preparing an invasion. Christobal Mendoza, acting mission Superior in the absence of Romero, provided as best he could for the defence of Jesús María, the Reduction nearest the Atlantic, not far from the modern city of Porto Alegre. For many years now, the Mamelucos had run down the coast from Santos in their schooners and then sailed up the rivers of Tape trading with the Indians, who exchanged their own prisoners of war with European trash. Already these Indian allies of the Mamelucos were raiding villages subject to the Reduction of Jesús María. There was danger that all the Indians living on the coast would join with the Mamelucos in the destruction of the new Reductions.

It seemed likely that the Mamelucos would attack also from the south through the land of the Caaguas: on occasion, mainly from curiosity, these savage Indians had visited Jesús María and other Reductions. Mendoza now accepted an invitation to make a return visit to their country, and he had no sooner crossed into it than a sorcerer whose name is given in Latin as Tabaius worked on a hostile tribe, the Ibiani,* to murder him on his return journey. On 24 April 1635 Mendoza, caught in an ambush, frightened off the savages by charging his horse at them in the manner of a conquistador, but going to baptize a child the next day, he stuck in a bog, was hemmed in, wounded and left for dead. He crept away, but was discovered twenty-four hours later and tortured to death. His two young Guaraní escorts were killed and eaten. 'At the same time three hundred lately baptized Indians were killed and devoured by the same savages in the town of Jesús María.'⁸

Far from securing an alliance with the Caaguas, Mendoza's death triggered off the first war in which the Reduction Indians were to be engaged. Fifteen hundred Indians from Jesús María attacked and defeated the Ibiani. This proved only a preliminary skirmish. The Ibiani, urged on by their numerous sorcerers, attempted to win back the Tape Indians to heathenism. Three caciques penetrated the area of the Reductions administering mock baptism. At a meeting of seven hundred savages one sorcerer proclaimed himself God and threatened his converts with destruction; another announced he would assume the shape of a jaguar and consume the Christians: only those who accepted his new baptism would escape massacre. In a subsequent battle five hundred mission Indians routed the invaders, killed seven of their sorcerers and captured another three. Only two escaped.

However, these savages had unwittingly created a diversion for the Mamelucos. Romero, on completing his period as Superior of the Missions, was appointed to Jesús María. The Mamelucos were reported to be approaching. Romero hastily threw up some earthworks, but the Mamelucos, with 1,500 Tupí Indians, were on him before he could complete the circuit. Only four hundred Reduction Indians could be mustered, the rest were out hunting or in search of provisions against a siege; the church was fired, the town razed to the

* Probably a small subdivision of the Guaraní who have disappeared without trace.

ground. In three years in this Reduction of Jesús María 5,057 Indians had received baptism; more were being prepared for it; those that survived were moved to the west.

During the engagement Romero and his assistant had been held prisoner to prevent the neighbouring Reduction, San Christóbal, receiving warning: the town, however, was evacuated, but in a rearguard action the Christian Indians were again defeated by the well-armed Mamelucos and many taken into slavery.

The remnants of the two Reductions, along with Santa Ana, were moved across the Yacuí river to Natividad: the plan was to use the river for defence and behind it to coordinate forces with other Reductions in the neighbourhood. Initially the plan succeeded: a fortress-like wood structure was erected on the Jesuit bank of the river, guards were posted where the river could be forded and ambushes laid: by this means many Mamelucos and Tupí were slain.

But the Jesuits could organize no more than a delaying action. The governor at Asunción once more refused help: he argued that he could not disperse his small military contingent which was already engaged against the northern prong of the Mamelucos invasion in Itatín. Left to their own devices, the Jesuits counter-attacked to gain time: Montoya with a party of Indians crossed the Yacuí but the Mamelucos had withdrawn with 25,000 captive Indians.

During this time Montoya appears to have maintained his prestige among his fellow-missionaries. He was a determined fighter, and it was perhaps this quality that led to his election as delegate of the Paraguay Province to do its business in Europe. Apart from gathering recruits, his tasks were to negotiate with the King, Philip IV, complete exemption from encomienda for all Indians in Jesuit Reductions (the Spaniards argued that the privilege had been granted only to Guairá for a limited period of years); he was also to negotiate for the Reduction Indians to be free from taxation of every kind for the first twenty years after coming in from the forest, so that the towns could recover from the devastation of the Mamelucos; and he was commissioned finally to have printed in Madrid a Guaraní dictionary, catechism and grammar.

All these tasks he carried out successfully. At Lisbon on his return journey he got news that the Mamelucos had again broken into Tape: he returned to Madrid to seek permission for the Reduction Indians to carry firearms. Royal letters dated May 1640 authorized the Viceroy in Lima to allow this if he judged it necessary.

Diego de Alfaro, who had taken charge of the Guaraní mission during Montoya's absence, had been forced to abandon San Joaquín in Tape. As usual the Indians objected to being transplanted: many fled into the forest: the rest left only when their houses had been fired and it became impossible to rebuild them.

The assault on Santa Teresa was a greater tragedy: it had 4,000 inhabitants, was growing daily and seemed likely to become the parent town of many more along the river Tebiquary. At the end of 1637 the Mamelucos broke in. The town was destroyed, most Indians were captured, the survivors transferred to Itapúa. The area to the east of Serra Geral was abandoned. Visitación, only recently founded, was dissolved, Santa Ana scattered for the second time: 'It was frequent to rail at the Society saying that the Fathers gathered the people into towns the better to betray them to the Mamelucos.'[9] On their side, the Mamelucos gave out that they had an arrangement with the Fathers for this end. It was understandable in this atmosphere that many Reduction Indians tried to murder the Fathers.

In January the following year, 1638, reports reached the Fathers that the Mamelucos had renewed their advance and were approaching also through the territory of the Caagua: the two-pronged attack was designed to penetrate across the Uruguay to the Paraná. It had been anticipated.

Diego de Alfaro exhorted the Indians to self-defence: he arranged a rendezvous for the Reduction forces at San Pedro y Pablo: this seemed the most defensible position and lay on the direct line of the Mamelucos' advance. But panic seized the colony: the Indians of San Pedro y Pablo fled: the troops of the other Reductions retired in disorder. The Guaraní had no military leaders: Pedro y Pablo and San Carolo were destroyed. In the space of seven years the Jesuits had baptized

4,337 Indians in San Carolo and 5,845 in San Pedro y Pablo: hardly one-third of this number was saved.

The advance continued towards the Uruguay. Another large force, some 1,500, was gathered, still badly led and without field communications, no match for the experience and cunning of the enemy. There was another series of defeats and withdrawals: whenever the Mamelucos were locally worsted, they retreated behind their palisades; the Indians, when pressed, scattered. San Nicolás, already 'famous for its stately church',[10] was lost. The Uruguay became the last line of the Jesuit defences. 'It was now that the caciques of the Paraná and Uruguay, joining their forces, assembled the greatest army that had ever been seen there in the field to oppose the enemy if they ventured to cross the Uruguay.'[11] But instead of continuing their advance, the Mamelucos drew back with their booty of Indian slaves. The Reduction Indians crossed the river in pursuit and won several encounters.

But the change of fortune came with the arrival of a mere eleven Spanish soldiers sent up from Buenos Aires to officer the Indians. When the Mamelucos suddenly found themselves confronted by 4,500 Christian Indians drawn up for battle, they knew they could neither defeat them nor escape. They sued for an armistice.

At a parley Alfaro, in his simplicity, made the Mamelucos swear they would never return, then he let them go unpunished: the folly was immeasurable: other Mamelucos were still active and four of the six Tape towns were still intact.

With the threat remaining, the Provincial decided to withdraw the surviving Tape towns to the territory between the Uruguay and Paraná: the average distance between these rivers was no more than forty miles. The towns on the Iguazú and Acaray were also pulled in. Here, in what is today the Argentine province of Misiones, the great crowd of Christian Indians would make their stand. To the north-east the falls of Iguazú, twelve miles above the point where the river joins the Paraná, formed a natural barrier—a great cataract twice the height of Niagara and as fearful as the falls of Guairá a hundred and twenty miles to the north. To the south another cataract below Yapeyú blocked any approach up the Uruguay from Colonia, intermittently in the hands of the Portuguese. The Spaniards in their search for silver and the Mamelucos on their slave raids had to stop there. 'Our missionaries', wrote Padre Sepp, 'are all of the opinion that God made these rapids for the benefit of the poor Indians. The Spaniards have come thus far in their great ships but no further.' To the north, across the Paraná, between Ignacio Guazú and Asunción, lay the ranches of the Spanish encomenderos. Only to the west was there no natural protection : the towns lay open there to attack from the wild tribes of the Chaco. Within these limits the land was fertile and able amply to support all who had been pulled back into it.

First Cosme y Damián was brought across the sierra of Tape and over the Uruguay. Santa Ana was twice transferred. With little loss 12,000 Indians were led through a barren wilderness for nearly two hundred miles. On reaching their destination 'the forest was cut down to make space for this multitude to sow its crops; at great expense seed and cattle were bought, houses and churches built and all other necessaries provided'.[12] When the settlements were established, the priests, 'going up and down the rivers, gathered in many thousands of fugitive Christians and Indians'.[13]

This withdrawal was strategic, intended only as a temporary measure until the Jesuits had armed and trained sufficient Indians to repel the Mamelucos : when the withdrawal was completed the caciques from the Paraná and Uruguay asked the Provincial for their own firearms : 'How can we defend ourselves with arrows of reed, which do hardly any execution, when our enemies attack with guns that fling bullets a vast distance?'[14]

This was the moment of crisis : either the Indians were adequately armed or the Jesuit enterprise was abandoned; it might also well be the end of the Spanish possessions in South America : if the line of the Uruguay was lost, only the Paraná remained between the Mamelucos and Asunción. With the fall of Asunción, the way lay open to the mines in the province of Charcas.

On Montoya's return, the Provincial argued with the

Viceroy and, on a lower level, with the provincial governors and civil magistrates, the case for arming the Indians. Many officials opposed it for fear of an Indian rebellion. However, the Viceroy finally consented.

Muskets were obtained. Some towns started rudimentary arms factories. A Jesuit lay brother, Domingo de Torres, who had served in the Spanish forces, was put in charge of training. Even before the defence line was stabilized, the Reduction forces, although still without firearms, gained field experience. In 1638 and again in 1639 the Governor of Buenos Aires, Mendo de la Cueva, requisitioned the newly-formed Indian contingents, first 230, then 600, to repel attacks of the Chaco tribes on Santa Fe and Corrientes.[15]

Early in 1641 spies reported that in the reaches of the Uruguay above the cataract, two Mamelucos leaders, Pedroso de Barros and Manuel Pires, were building a fleet of barges to surprise the Reduction by an assault from the river, outflanking its land defences. More detailed information followed: in all there were four hundred Mamelucos, three hundred boats and 2,700 fierce Tupí allies. Against this force the Jesuits could now muster 4,000 Indians, but only three hundred of them carried firearms. Now they in turn set to making rafts and canoes of every kind; then they took up a position on the right bank of the Uruguay a little to the north of San Javier, at the confluence of a small river, Mbororé, today called Acaragua.

In the first days of March 1641 the Reduction army was in position behind their fortifications: their canoes and other craft were manned and armed.

On Friday 8 March a hundred Mameluco craft advanced upriver. The Jesuits threw into the first stage of the battle only thirty boats manned by two hundred and fifty Indians.

This encounter lasted eight hours. The Mamelucos, surprised, turned back. Several of their boats were sunk. Three days later, 11 March, the Mamelucos returned to the attack. Romero, the soul of the resistance, was ready for them: seventy Reduction craft were waiting behind the stockade, fifty manned by harquebusiers. Their commandant was the cacique Abiarú: his flagship was surmounted by a bridge armed with a cannon. The land forces were under Brother Domingo de Torres.

Proudly Abiarú opened battle by discharging his cannon. Firing was heavy. Pedroso de Barros attempted to encircle the Guaraní squadron. The manoeuvre was defeated. The Reduction fleet then put into action a plan drawn up by Claude Ruyer, a Fleming: they drove the Mamelucos flotilla towards the stockade from which they came under heavy arrow and firearm attack from the land forces.

Although the Mamelucos had committed nearly twice the number of vessels as their opponents, a hundred and thirty to seventy, the fire from the Reduction stockade forced them to retire with the loss of fourteen boats and many dead.

Further down on the east bank the Mamelucos, learning from their victors, began to build their own stockade, but immediately they were attacked. Ruyer knew better than Alfaro to show mercy. He knew that the Mamelucos would certainly attack again, for their supply of slaves from Angola was drying up. He seems to have taken personal command of the pursuit.* On 13 March, two days after the river battle, the land forces advanced: the Mamelucos suffered heavily. During the night the pursuit was maintained; to gain time the Mamelucos tried to parley but were merely mocked. Encircled by the Indians, they broke up into small groups to make away as best they could. Under cover of a sudden storm many got through. But the pursuit continued the next day. Varied fortunes overtook them; one party was savagely handled by the Gualaches: del Techo, normally uncommitted, betrays relish in narrating their fate: 'The Gualaches tore off their beards and hair and the flesh from their arms and thighs before eating them; they then mangled their bodies and fixed their heads to poles on the roof of their huts to frighten off others.'[16] Probably a hundred and twenty Mamelucos died and nearly all their Tupí allies.

The success of Abiarú with his improvised armament sug-

* Padre Diego Alfaro had been shot dead by the Mamelucos in January 1639. Ruyer succeeded him as Superior. Ruyer's account of the engagement (*Relación de la guerra*), dated 6 April 1641, is printed in Pastells, vol. ii, pp. 58–66. It is a despatch of high literary quality, describing an extended battle in country that is wild and difficult to reach even today.

gested a development that surprised visitors to the Reductions
in the seventeenth century: a canoe adapted to serve as a
man-of-war. These craft operated mainly from the southern
Reductions of the Uruguay—Yapeyú, San Borja and Santo
Tomé. A priest newly appointed to Yapeyú in 1691 was entertained on his arrival with a regatta: 'They sent to meet us
two boats well equipped like galleys, mounting firelocks on
both sides: these two vessels started a mock engagement, discharged their guns at each other to the noise of drums,
trumpets and hautboys till at last, wheeling about, they fired
a triple salvo and joined our craft.'[17] Development of this
canoe continued to the end of the Jesuit period: a French
visitor in the eighteenth century spoke of 'this formidable arm,
a small craft armed like an updated chariot with crenels for
her guns'; and then he added: 'The Indians are very clever
navigators and are as courageous in their canoes as they are
on horseback.'[18]

The victory of Mbororé encouraged the Indians who had
scattered to return to the Reductions. It also secured the
Spanish settlements in the district south of Asunción. No
difficulties were made when the Jesuits applied for a renewal
of the licence for their Indians to carry firearms. As the
Reductions gradually established themselves in permanent
sites, a regular well-drilled defence force was formed.

Constant watch was still kept against the Mamelucos. The
entire summer following the victory of Mbororé, Reduction
Indians scoured the country: they would go out 150 to 180
miles to look for signs of their approach. At last the Indians
had won the initiative. They had their strategy worked out:
they would engage the enemy in the open country where their
superior horsemanship gave them the edge.

The last attack came in 1642. It was easily repelled. Fresh
supplies of arms had been constantly arriving. Each Reduction
soon had its own armoury; some manufactured their own
gunpowder and small arms.

The towns now fell into two groups: those north of the
Paraná within the jurisdiction of the Governor of Asunción,
the other between the Paraná and Uruguay under the
Governor of the Río de la Plata in Buenos Aires. From the

start to the end of the period the Jesuits were on happy terms with Buenos Aires: it was the handful of soldiers sent up from there that had first checked the Mamelucos. There had been no history of strained relations as with Asunción. Moreover, Buenos Aires was three times the distance of Asunción from the Reductions. In the intervening country there were no jealous encomenderos but mainly forests, swamps and the savage Charrua.

Between 1641 and 1687 ten Reductions were firmly settled in present Paraguayan territory and another twelve including the capital, Candelaria, south of the Paraná and north of the Uruguay. In 1685 Jesús, the first of another eleven Reductions, was founded on the river Monday, then moved finally to its present site about the beginning of the next century. Ten years later Santa Rosa, an offshoot of Santa Maria, was established. Trinidad followed in 1706, north of the Paraná. And at the same time the Jesuits advanced again south over the Uruguay. Seven further towns were founded in a compact area centred round Santo Angel in the Brazilian province of Rio Grande do Sul.

Most of the country between the upper Paraná and Uruguay consisted of *campos quebrantados*, or undulating plains with dense forest on the bank of the main and tributary rivers, more uninhabited and wild today than in the later seventeenth century. These plains, covered with fine short grass and yatais or stunted palms, provided admirable pasture. The red soil in most places was between four and twenty feet deep: a French traveller referred to this country as *la terre rouge des missions*: this soil, sandy in texture and soon turning to mud after heavy rain, gave its tint to the fine churches that soon rose in the Reductions. The forest provided hardwood in abundance, and there were many lakes and backwaters. Between Yapeyú in the far south and the seven towns later built to the north-east lay large tracts of marshes called *esteros*, an impassable defence in winter but fine grazing in spring and summer. These Jesuit lands lying well south of the tropics were as pleasant as any in South America.

5

Jesuit Mines

Before the frontiers of the Paraná Reductions were established against the Mamelucos, the infant state was threatened from Asunción.

Don Bernardino de Cárdenas, a creole born at Sucre, then called La Plata, the capital of the province of Charcas, took over the administration of the diocese as bishop in 1642. The disruption he failed to achieve in his lifetime was completed more than a century later when the campaign he initiated was taken up with fresh vigour. The most favourable judgement that can be passed on him was that he possessed 'an unusually ambitious, energetic and ruthless personality'.[1]

When he was an immature priest, his dream had been to emulate the great apostle of his Order, Francisco Solano. As the historian Charlevoix points out,[2] 'he engaged in preaching in which, with his memory, assurance and facility, he found it easy to succeed in a country where brilliant gifts are more esteemed than solid learning'. More dangerous were the visions and revelations which he was careful to publicize. The Jesuits considered him the most gifted and pernicious spiritual clown they had encountered in South America.

When he was named Guardian of the Franciscan convent at Sucre he embarrassed his Provincial by carrying a wooden cross through the streets : he was followed by his community disciplining themselves in the manner of fourteenth-century flagellants. He was ordered to stay at home, but managed to get himself appointed Apostolic Visitor to the Indians : his mission was to reform their morals by means of preaching. It was at this point that he became interested in the work of the Jesuits.

All through the province of Charcas, Cárdenas made his apostolic progress. Dressed as a pilgrim bearing his wooden cross, he was followed by a multitude of Indians. Everywhere he had been preceded by his fame as a wonder-worker and recipient of visions.

There were reports that his Indian entourage had told him of the existence of rich silver and gold mines, comparable to the mountain behind Potosí, on condition that he did not divulge the secret to the Spaniards. This was the epoch of the mad gold rush in the Altiplano. The story grew in the telling and Cárdenas was summoned to Lima. There was a rumour that he was to be given a mitre. Friends, believing that the mines were real, came forward with presents and loans, trusting that he would repay with interest all he had borrowed; the more cynical said repayment could be expected only in 'that better country where no usury exists and no gold corrupts'.

When a government enquiry showed that the mines were fictitious, Cárdenas was again confined to his house by the Franciscans at Lima. But he was able to stir up further trouble. Drawing on his brief experience in the Altiplano, he made out a memorandum for the Council of the Indies on methods of evangelizing the still unconverted tribes. His opponents saw in this a move to gain favour with the government, for every Christian Indian meant an increase of revenue for the Crown. Already there had been complaints that the number of Christian Indians in the Jesuit Reductions remained the same in the annual returns. Cárdenas urged that it was unwise to place Indians in the care of Jesuits, with their exemption from the jurisdiction of bishops who alone could check whether their information was not falsified.

Thanks to this memorandum Cárdenas, while still in house confinement, found himself nominated Bishop of Asunción. Within this diocese lay the Reductions north of the Paraná as well as those of Itatín. However, the Bishop still lacked the papal bull authorizing his consecration and entitling him to take possession of his see.

From Lima Cárdenas went to Potosí where he resumed his spiritual histrionics while awaiting the bull. This was the richest city in the Spanish colonial empire. Moving up and down its steep streets Cárdenas, in the habit of the Franciscans improved by a small wooden cross on his breast and a green hat to replace the hood, preached sermon after sermon. After each performance the green hat was passed round his hearers. To enhance his reputation for sanctity he took on the duties of parish priest of the cathedral, an impressive gesture of humility from a bishop-elect. He finally left the city with a mule train carrying his silver, furniture and plate. He had entered the city penniless.

Instead of going to Asunción to obtain the consent of the chapter to govern his diocese provisionally, he went to Salta. Anxious to get consecrated quickly, he showed the Jesuits of the College there a letter from Cardinal Antonio Barberini, dated 1638, and another, undated, from the king: could he be consecrated on the strength of these papers? The Jesuits, anxious not to give offence, stalled: they referred south to the theological faculty of their university at Córdoba. The Fathers there had no hesitations. They declared against Cárdenas who was at Santiago del Estero when he received the judgement. He instantly fell into a rage and tore up the paper without showing it to anyone.

Then he moved north to Tucumán. Here he carried on as he had done in the dioceses of Sucre and Potosí. However, he scored a success. The Bishop, Melchior Maldonado, anxious to be rid of him, agreed under pressure to consecrate Cárdenas.* The consecration was valid (Cárdenas was a Bishop) but irregular (he could not lawfully exercise his functions). Taking the customary route to Asunción, Cárdenas stopped at Santa Fe, which formed part of the vacant diocese of Buenos Aires four hundred miles away. At the request of the chapter he stayed on to make a visitation of that part of the diocese, then proceeded to Corrientes, at the junction of the Paraná and Paraguay rivers, very close to the Jesüit

---

* Owing to the small number of bishops in South America, a single bishop was privileged to consecrate without assistants.

Reductions. Here he embarked for Asunción, flanked by two ships sent down the Paraguay to form an escort of honour.

As he progressed upriver, Indian canoes and Spanish launches put out to catch a glimpse of the saint and to accompany him on the next stage of his journey. Each evening at dusk he called on the flotilla to retire a little from his ship; then towards midnight his followers were awakened by the sound of scourging: it was the bishop preparing himself for his apostolate. This happened every night. During the day he celebrated Mass pontifically on deck. Rumour had already reached Asunción that a second Saint Thomas was on his way: the first Saint Thomas, the apostle, was supposed to have preached in central South America and at the end of his life to have retired to a cave south of Asunción.*

About twelve miles from the capital Cárdenas disembarked at an estancia belonging to the Jesuit College. A description of it by a priest who on a later occasion stayed there for convalescence explains why Cárdenas was soon to covet it. Stretching out 'on one side into a pleasant plain affording pasture to a vast quantity of cattle, on the other, where it looks to the south, it is surrounded by hills and rocks, on one of which a cross piled up of three large stones is visited and held in great reverence for the sake of St Thomas, for they firmly believe that St Thomas, seated on these stones as a chair, formerly preached to the assembled Indians.'³

On reaching Asunción Cárdenas offered Mass, preached to the people with his mitre on his head and then dismissed them, saying that he himself had no need to eat for he was nourished by an invisible food. With the adroitness so often found in maladjusted ecclesiastics he sought public support to boost his status which was not yet regularized. Gradually he built up his position. He addressed himself to the self-interest of the Spaniards, reviving their old quarrels with the Jesuits, whom he held responsible for the reduced number of Indians available to the encomenderos. At the same time, he won the

---

* Possibly the legend dates from the journey from Santa Catarina to Asunción made by the two Franciscan Fathers with Cabeza de Vaca in 1542 and has its origin in a corruption of *Zumé*, the Guaraní word for Padre.

adulation of the creoles by his theatrical piety: two Masses on weekdays when one was the rule, barefoot processions along the roads lined with bitter orange trees, blessings scattered in profusion to left, right and centre.

First Cárdenas fell out with his chapter, half of whom declined to recognize his authority, then with the rest of his clergy when he took to ordaining young men who knew no Latin: among them were some criminals, but the Bishop held that ordination, like a second baptism, effected a spiritual regeneration: finally he revived the endemic struggle between Bishop and Governor, the latter now a Chilean, Gregorio de Hinestrosa.

A natural stage for the next drama was provided by the geographical setting of Asunción, with its mile-broad stretch of water surrounding it on three sides. On the further bank roved the Guaycurú, untamed even by Roque González, an irresistible challenge to the self-acclaimed second Apostle of the Indians.

Already before Cárdenas's arrival, the Guaycurú had agreed to a meeting with the Governor; but the bishop-elect declared that all dealings with Indians came under his jurisdiction. With an operatic gesture Cárdenas crossed the Paraguay in full pontificals and with a Governor's escort. He met some Guaycurú caciques, preached to them through an interpreter, baptized them without instruction, and on his triumphant return to Asunción wrote to Philip IV claiming that through his apostolic exertions he had converted the most savage Indians; at the same time he had removed a perennial threat to the safety of Asunción. Less than a week later, a party of Guaycurú crossed the river above the city and burned a Spanish settlement.

When finally the papal bull arrived, it was found to contain a clause to the effect that if any irregularity had occurred (as indeed it had) in the Bishop's consecration he was liable to suspension. The Jesuit translation of this document for public reading retained this clause but Cárdenas threw it out as hairsplitting. What was more sinister, Cárdenas interpolated into the bull the grant of unlimited power to him by the Pope in temporal matters.

The bull had been brought to Asunción by the Bishop's nephew, a Franciscan, Pedro de Cárdenas. At Corrientes, on his way upriver, Pedro had taken on board a lady whom Charlevoix describes as *'une jeune femme, bien faite'*. On his arrival at Asunción, his uncle overlooked this, gave him a vacant prebendary, denounced the gossip as calumny and installed Pedro in his palace. Meanwhile a fresh series of quarrels had broken out between Governor and Bishop. In the end the frantic Governor threw the conduct of Pedro in the Bishop's teeth.

Hell was let loose; Cárdenas excommunicated the Governor and declared him incapable of carrying the royal standard at a religious festival shortly to take place. A second excommunication followed within seven days when the Governor came with a troop of soldiers to arrest Pedro, who had insulted him in the streets. Cárdenas was now in charge of civic affairs, for no excommunicate could command the obedience of Christians. But even Cárdenas had to face up to realities. When only the Governor could provide troops to save Asunción from another threatened attack from the Guaycurú, Cárdenas lifted the double excommunication.

Cárdenas had now to look for broader support. Afraid that the Jesuits and the upper statum of Asunción society educated at their College would declare against him, he began to woo them with unwonted favours. He praised them from his pulpit. In complete reversal of the statements made in his Lima memorandum, he wrote to the king declaring they were the only persons fitted to have charge of the Indians.

There was a purpose in his volte-face. Excessive praise from Cárdenas at this juncture was the one thing calculated to make a person or body unpopular. Cárdenas further embarrassed the Jesuits by giving them tasks which he declared the diocesan clergy were unfit to perform. A still more delicate situation occurred when he ordered two Jesuits from the College to take over a mission at Villarrica east of Asunción. Here the Indians were under the encomienda system. Rather than countenance what they had fought against from the beginning, the two Jesuits lived out in the forest with the Indians. At Asunción, as Cárdenas had correctly judged, the

Jesuits were accused of intruding into the spiritual domain of other priests.

Cárdenas's flirtation with the Jesuits was short-lived. When the Governor arrested Pedro and sent him downriver in a canoe, the air again became thick with excommunications. The confusion was made worse when Pedro escaped back to Asunción. To do reparation for his nephew's misdeeds, Cárdenas stripped himself to the waist and scourged himself in the streets. This won him supporters among the women of Asunción.

The Governor now appealed to the Court of Charcas. The Bishop did the same, then left the city for Yaguarón, a Franciscan mission about twenty miles to the south. For two years, 1642 to 1644, Yaguarón was Cárdenas's entrenched camp. Meanwhile Asunción lay under an interdict, the poor starved in the street, three hundred Guaycurú appeared before the river defences. Since most of the civic and military officers lay under excommunication no resistance could be organized. Cárdenas was forced temporarily to lift his excommunications. The evening of the day the Indians were beaten off the excommunications were re-imposed.

Finally Cárdenas made a full-fronted assault on the Jesuit Reductions. He promised the priests of his Order and the cluster of clergy who still clung to him that they would take over from the Jesuit 'heretics' : his jealousy had been aroused by the contrast between the poor pueblos of the Franciscans with their encomienda Indians and the apparent prosperity of the Reductions. He forbade all Jesuits to preach or hear confessions in his diocese, which included the Reductions north of the Paraná, and in a sermon at Yaguarón he formulated his celebrated charges against the Jesuits which were revived a century and a quarter later to justify their expulsion from Paraguay. The accusations were 'so ingeniously contrived that royal, national and domestic indignation were all aroused by them'.[4]

None of the charges was original but each was presented with authority and conviction : the Jesuits prevented the Indians paying their annual taxes to the Crown; they also withheld from the bishops the tithes that were their due;

moreover they had rich mines in their territory which were worked by Indian labour for the benefit of their headquarters in Europe; they were not careful in maintaining the secrecy of the confessional; the information they acquired by this means was used for their own advancement; Montoya had deliberately deceived the king, who under misapprehension had granted the territory covered by the Reductions to the Jesuits and thus had deprived the Spaniards of their rightful conquest; the Jesuits had entered Paraguay with nothing but the clothes that covered them, now they were sovereigns of a great land; he, Cárdenas, and the Bishop of Tucumán and other bishops had secret orders to expel the Jesuits from their diocese, but he alone had shown the courage to carry out the decree.

The historic sermon ended with a fitting peroration. Only when the Jesuits were out of the country would the king enjoy his rights. Then there would be a plentiful supply of Indians for the encomenderos; every section of the community would have its share of the Jesuit riches; the country would be saved. Just as the Venetians had expelled the Jesuits from their territory and the Portuguese from São Paulo, he would drive them from Paraguay.

Certainly Cárdenas was unaware of the impact his eloquence would have. As the Jesuits recognized, his brilliance as a speaker was unmatched in the country, only his facts and forecast were questionable. In their last years in Paraguay the Jesuits were still striving to undo the harm this sermon had done them.

There were stories of Jesuit riches before Cárdenas arrived in Asunción. To many settlers it had seemed incredible that the Jesuits should bury themselves in the jungle merely to preach to savages. Cárdenas's sermon reinforced the legend of their wealth and added circumstantial detail, for instance, that the Jesuits worked their mines without paying the royal fifth to the treasury. But in spite of continuing efforts to expose their falsehood, the stories were never taken by the populace as disproved.

There were fragments of truth and half-truths in Cárdenas's sermon : Montoya had obtained the royal decree at Madrid after a thorough exposition of the facts; the decree had been renewed on several occasions; ecclesiastical tithes were not made regular until 1649, five years after Cárdenas's sermon; the Venetians had not expelled the Jesuits, who, in fact, had left Venetia of their own accord; no decree, royal or papal, had, of course, been issued for the expulsion of the Jesuits. Cárdenas's statement contained more threats than facts.

In his diatribe against the Jesuits, the Bishop had risked losing his support among the non-Reduction Indians, who were now the mainstay of his position, for he came down firmly on the side of the encomenderos. His logic was smothered by his eloquence. It was true that the Jesuits of São Paulo had been expelled from their College but Cárdenas had omitted the reason, namely, a royal decree and a bull of Urban VIII, brought back by Montoya from Rome, forbidding the enslavement of the Indians: both documents had been fastened to the door of the Jesuit church, and in the subsequent uproar the Jesuits had been forced to leave the city.

Cárdenas's next step was to show that he was a man of his word. This he did with results that were disastrous in the short term for himself and in the long term for the Jesuits. He would set an example to his fellow-bishops by confiscating the Jesuit estancia at San Isidro on the Paraguay, where he had first set foot on diocesan soil. This was equivalent to closing the Jesuit College at Asunción, since the revenue from the estancia provided free tuition for the pupils. The Governor intervened on behalf of the Jesuits. In retaliation Cárdenas armed his partisans and threatened to expel the Jesuits from their College by force. In spite of his sermon Cárdenas still had the populace on his side. The Governor was uncertain of the loyalty of his simple troops. To his defence he summoned six hundred armed Indians from the Jesuit Reductions. 'Thus the supremacy of the royal government', writes Cunninghame Graham,[5] 'fell to be supported by men just emerging from a semi-nomad life, who owed the tincture of civilization they possessed to the calumniated Jesuits.'

It was not long since the Governor of Río de la Plata had asked for and received military help from the Reductions against hostile Indians; but to use these troops against refractory Spaniards was an innovation.

Cárdenas opened his campaign with the expected fanfare of excommunications. His supporters from all over the diocese mustered at Yaguarón. The Governor waited the arrival of the Reduction Indians by river, then marched south. Confronting Cárdenas in the church at Yaguarón, he told the Bishop that he had come on orders of the Viceroy to banish him from Paraguay: he had six days in which to leave. Returning to Asunción on the pretext of preparing his departure, Cárdenas shut himself up in the Franciscan monastery, which he proceeded to convert into a fortress: he constructed embrasures for his guns and pierced the walls for his musketry. This done, he wrote off to the Council of Charcas: he alleged that the Jesuits had offered the Governor 30,000 crowns and a thousand soldiers if he would get rid of him because he knew the secret of the Jesuit mines.

Cárdenas refused to leave Asunción. The Governor surrounded the Franciscan house with a troop of fifty soldiers, declared the Bishop deposed, appointed in his place an administrator who, judging his life unsafe in the cathedral, took up his residence in the College of the Jesuits.

At this point the Bishop had to acknowledge defeat. All he could do now was to make a dramatic departure by river, sitting in the poop of his ship surrounded by his faithful clergy. But the immediate effect of the two years' struggle had been disastrous for the missions: particularly harmful for the simple converts was the sight of their own troops marching out to fight their bishop: it was more than the Jesuits could explain. During these years many Indians left the Reductions and returned to the forests.

At Corrientes, in the neighbouring diocese of Buenos Aires, Cárdenas continued his campaign against the Jesuits. He ignored two citations to appear before the court of Charcas: he argued he must first return to Asunción to install an administrator of his own appointment. His attempt to do this was frustrated by the Governor, who turned back his boat before it reached Asunción.

Cárdenas was not to be defeated. His opportunity came in

1647 when Gregorio Hinestrosa was superseded as Governor by Don Diego Escobar y Osorio. He set out immediately for Asunción and was quick to see that he had another vacillating Governor to confront. The fiction concerning mines was only part of Cárdenas's campaign against the Jesuits. Simultaneously he got up a petition signed largely by women and children for the expulsion of the Jesuits from Paraguay : blank forms were passed round on which the people wrote out their complaints. The forms were then despatched to Madrid. One bundle sent to Cárdenas's agent in Spain fell into the hands of an English pirate, who expressed disgust at the underhand devices and bad faith of Cárdenas.

In the following year, 1648, the Bishop moved once more against the Reductions. He selected as his target Santiago and Nuestra Señora de Fe, the last of the Itatín townships, recently in the wild district of Caaguazú close to the mountains of Mbaracayú, and serving as outposts against incursions from Chaco Indians and the Mamelucos. Under pressure from Cárdenas the new Governor, Don Diego, and the cabildo of Asunción decided as an alleged measure of safety to move the settlement nearer to Asunción : the real motive was to hand over the Indians to the encomenderos. The Jesuits were duly replaced, then the Indians, rather than be taken over by the Spaniards, fled to the forest. The two towns were left deserted.

In moving against these two Reductions, Cárdenas had charged the Jesuits before the cabildo with the design of building up a rival kingdom to Spain. His main witness was a soldier from the garrison at Asunción who in 1639, ten years earlier, had formed part of the troops sent to save the Uruguay Reductions from the Mamelucos. This man testified that 'the chief of the Reduction Indians', Nicolás, who had worn a crown on his head over his hat, had welcomed the soldiers to his territory in the name of the Pope.*

The Council of Charcas, anxious about the northern frontier of Paraguay, gave orders that the Jesuits were to return. For twelve months the Fathers went out in search of the Indians. Only half the original population was recovered.

* This is probably the origin of the legend of King Nicolás in the Guaraní war. Cf. inf. p. 256.

Van Suerck, the pioneer of the Itatín missions, died in the effort. Until the nineteenth century the district remained a desert. In 1830 it was used as a penal settlement.

Cárdenas now sought to re-establish himself by repeating the rumours of Jesuit mines in the Uruguay Reductions. It was his line of attack when no other was open to him. But this time there seemed to be substance in the reports.

They had originated with an Indian called Bienaventura, who had made his way from Buenos Aires to the Jesuit mission of Yapeyú; there he had been whipped for running away with another man's wife. Back in Buenos Aires he invented a plausible story about gold found by the Jesuits near the river Uruguay: 'He confidently affirmed that he himself had worked a long time in Uruguay at digging gold; and it was there in such plenty that in three days a man might fill a half-bushel with pure gold dust. He said further that when he resolved to run off he was tempted to hide away a great parcel of gold for his own use, but he was betrayed by an Indian, whipped by the Fathers and banished.'[6]

Bienaventura was a plausible story-teller : the detail he gave was so convincing that many speculators in Buenos Aires believed him. On their side the Jesuits demanded and got an official enquiry which issued in a public declaration by the Governor, Isteban de Avila, that the report of mines was a fabrication by enemies of the Jesuits. After a time the rumour died, only to be resurrected by Bienaventura among a group of newly-arrived Europeans. A new Governor, Jacinto de Laríz, was uncertain about what to do when he received a letter from Cárdenas, then at Asunción, affirming that there were certainly gold mines near the Uruguay. Bienaventura was delighted. A search party was formed made up of forty soldiers from the garrison of Buenos Aires and led by the Governor himself and a mining magnate from Peru, Martín de Vera. It made its way upriver. When Bienaventura suddenly disappeared the Governor was disturbed but he continued his search. He was well received by Díaz Taño, the mission Superior, in the Jesuit towns. He promised promotion and rich rewards to the first man to find a mine : the soldiers became keen : 'Some of them travelled several days with an

Indian who promised to discover the mines, but were only laughed at when they returned after finding nothing but some bright shining snails.'[7]

De Laríz's search was observed with mixed feelings by both the Governor of Paraguay, who feared the violation of Paraguayan territory by Laríz, and Cárdenas, who wanted to deny to all but himself the satisfaction of discovering the mines. Cárdenas was less specific than Bienaventura on their exact situation, but he pointed out to the Viceroy that even greater wealth would accrue to the Crown from the expulsion of the Jesuits than from the discovery of the mines.

At last Laríz was forced to acknowledge that he had been misled. Bienaventura was caught near Yapeyú and handed over by the Jesuits to the Governor, who ordered him to be given two hundred *azotes*: he was then condemned to death. On the ground that he was a madman the Jesuits secured his release. But it required two further governmental enquiries in the twenty years that followed before the matter of the mines was allowed to rest.

Meanwhile, the case of Cárdenas's consecration was still before the authorities in Rome. More than four plenary meetings of the Congregation of Propaganda were called between May and October 1645 to discuss it. But it dragged on.*

Nevertheless the anti-Jesuit virus now affected all classes. Cárdenas made much of the use of Reduction troops by the Governor. The popular hatred fell chiefly on Díaz Taño, the mission Superior, who was insulted in the streets of Asunción. Another Jesuit, a quiet learned Italian, Ferrufino, the Provincial, was nearly murdered by a fanatic who wanted to 'eat his heart'.

With the auguries in his favour, Cárdenas struck again. He declared the Jesuits excommunicated. Since the Bishop had been absent for more than a year, people took this measure seriously. In February 1649 the position of the Jesuits became even more critical when the new Governor, Don Diego, died, so suddenly that poisoning was suspected. Cárdenas declared

---

* A decision was not reached until 1658, by which time Cárdenas had been appointed to another see.

himself Diego's interim successor and nominated an interim government. His action was totally illegal : the nomination belonged to the Viceroy in Lima. Cárdenas had based his action on a non-existent edict of the Emperor Charles V.

At once Cárdenas began to govern. In his cathedral he proclaimed that he had an order from the King to expel the Jesuits. To win over the Paraguayan encomenderos, he proposed to divide among them 20,000 Reduction Indians.

In March 1649 the Jesuits were ordered to leave Asunción and at the same time hand over their Reductions within the jurisdiction of Paraguay. With hands tied, they were taken from the College a few hundred yards across the plaza to the port, where they were put into canoes and sent downriver. At Corrientes, in the diocese of Buenos Aires, the exiled community was asked to start a school. Meanwhile in Asunción they had been declared heretics and their church a temple unclean. The College was sacked but no treasure was found. Cárdenas, however, lost no time in laying his hands on the cattle in San Isidro, the estancia belonging to the College.

There was commotion beyond the boundaries of Paraguay. It was feared that if the Jesuits left the Reductions, the present frontiers would be lost to Spain; there was thought to be danger also that the Indians might revolt. Cárdenas was summoned to the court of Charcas to show the edict of Charles V entitling him to govern Paraguay. In the interim, the Viceroy, Conde de Salvatierra, appointed another Governor, Don Sebastián de León y Zárate, and then, at the instance of the untiring Montoya, he issued on 21 June 1649 an important *provisión real* which was virtually a charter of independence for the Reductions. It defined exactly the duties of the Jesuits to the Crown and reaffirmed the exemption of the Reduction Indians in Itatín and on the Paraná and Uruguay from *servicio personal.* Every male Indian in the Reductions between the ages of eighteen and fifty had to pay one peso at eight *reales* annually to the king. In return for the low tribute, the Indians were given the task of protecting the frontier against the Portuguese. Three years later Montoya died.

Cárdenas ignored the summons to the court of Charcas.

The new Governor was compelled to advance on Asunción. The main part of his army was made up of seven hundred Reduction Indians. Cárdenas led out his forces in person. The two met on the sandy plain of Campo Grande, not far from the village of Luque. Cárdenas was routed. When the Governor entered the cathedral to give thanks he found Cárdenas seated on his throne. However, his supporters had fallen away and in the following year, 1650, he left Asunción for Charcas.

Tracts, books and pamphlets were written for and against Cárdenas. Certainly the Indians revered him. In Charcas, where he lived for years on a pension while his case dragged on in Rome, Madrid and Lima, he was always greeted with flowers when he appeared in public. There may have been a streak of the saint in the schemer. Without question he was a talented preacher. He was also a personality. Anyone who differed from him was accursed of God, headstrong and obstinate. Finally in 1665 Philip IV made him bishop of Santa Cruz in the province of Charcas.

While the quarrel between Cárdenas and the Jesuits lasted, the financial resources of the Jesuits were strained: it was reckoned that in 1650 and 1651 alone some 38,000 pesos were sent from the Jesuit Province of Paraguay to European lawyers, who were the only persons to derive unquestioned benefit from the disturbance. At the time the Government in Madrid had been distracted by war with Portugal. Moreover, in 1650 the Araucano Indians in Chile rose against the Spaniards. At the same time Corrientes and Santa Fe were threatened by Chaco Indians who now had acquired horses and were using them with great skill in lightning raids on the Spaniards. In 1657 occurred the second Calchaquí revolt, which smothered the Jesuit missions and threatened the safety of Tucumán. Worse was ahead. The Guaraní Indians who already formed part of the Paraguay community rose in revolt against the growing demands on their diminishing numbers by the encomenderos; then in the next year the Mbayá Indians from the Chaco crossed the Paraguay and destroyed what remained of the Itatín missions. Cárdenas's agents in Spain made the most of the unrest. Reports of great quantities of firearms stored in the Jesuit Reductions had reached the Council of the Indies, which issued an instruction in 1664 that all the firearms from the Reductions were to be deposited in Asunción. The agent of the Paraguay Jesuits in Spain, in a memorandum dated 1665, made the point that if all the eight hundred muskets of the Indians were stored at Asunción there would be no firearms available to meet a sudden attack. Also, no training in their use could be given to the Indians; finally, many of the Reductions belonged to the La Plata jurisdiction, which depended on their arms for the defence of Buenos Aires. The instruction was revoked.

In spite of the effort of the Jesuits both in Spain and South America to refute Cárdenas's charges, the government at Madrid, from the middle of the seventeenth century, became increasingly suspicious of the Jesuits in Paraguay. Cárdenas's agents and, in particular, his nephew, kept the Bishop's calumnies alive. For their own ends the governors of Asunción continued to favour the Reductions, but the very efficiency and discipline of their troops brought on them unwanted attention. From 1650 the Reductions were exposed to the almost perennial threat that their privileges on which they depended for survival would be taken from them.

The first enduring damage done by Cárdenas's campaign was the ban on the entry of Jesuits from outside Spain into Paraguay. In Cárdenas's second period at Asunción, an Italian, Ferrufino, had been Provincial, van Suerck, the Belgian, Superior in Itatín; under van Suerck had been Berthot, a Frenchman and a Portuguese, Benavides. These foreign Jesuits had been openly charged by Cárdenas with sending back to their own countries vast quantities of gold. Cárdenas was plausible enough to secure in 1647 letters from Madrid to the Viceroy, Salvatierra, instructing him to send back immediately to Spain all foreign Jesuits working in Paraguay. Goswin Nickel, the Jesuit General, wrote in alarm to the Paraguay Provincial to get the decree rescinded at all costs. On his own initiative the Viceroy suspended it until the Jesuit agent in Madrid could present the Jesuit case to the King. The foreigners at work in Paraguay were not, in fact, expelled but seventy non-Spanish Jesuits awaiting embarkation for South America, twenty-five of them destined for Paraguay, were sent back to their own countries.

For the next forty years the Jesuits in Paraguay were forced back on a holding policy: there were Spaniards enough to maintain two priests in each township, three or more at Candelaria, the headquarters of the Paraná missions. None was available for pioneering work.

Further expansion came rapidly at the end of the seventeenth century with reinforcements from the German-speaking dominions of the Hapsburg Emperors. Many of these men were among the most talented missionaries the Society of Jesus had sent to any continent.

In Cárdenas's defence it must be said that from the early seventeenth century Paraguay had suffered an economic crisis. It is debatable whether or not it was aggravated by the loss of a large body of Guaraní labour to the Jesuit Reductions: it was only in Itatín that the Indians under Jesuit protection lived in proximity to the settlers. The Paraguayans, anxious to replace the diminishing number of encomienda Indians, could hardly be sympathetic to the Jesuit enterprise.

It was from this section of the people that Cárdenas had drawn his most consistent support, and among them his name was never forgotten. A series of enquiries and reports favourable to the Jesuits never wholly obliterated suspicion of the Paraguay Jesuits in Madrid, and in the last decade of the Jesuit missions, when German, Czech, Swiss and Austrian priests gave promise of subduing the Chaco and Pampas Indians and had already won over the Chiquitos on the borders of the Mato Grosso, the revival of Cárdenas's charges was in considerable part responsible for the ruin of their work.

6

Defence and Independence

The armies of the Jesuit missions consisted mainly of cavalry.
Although the Incas and their allies were so frightened of the
first Spanish horses that they climbed trees to escape them as
they would jaguars or the South American puma, the Indians,
soon learnt to sit a horse as well as any conquistador. In a
short time the Reduction cavalry became the crack force at
the service of the Spanish Crown. Mounted and carrying firearms they were almost invincible. Their tactics were to engage
the enemy in open country where their horsemanship would
turn the scales in a hard-contested battle.

The Guaraní marched in the manner of a South American
army in the last decades of the nineteenth century. The
caballada or spare horses led, followed by the vanguard made
up of the best cavalry under the caciques, then the baggage
train with the herdsmen driving the cattle for the men's
commons.

To avoid surprise attacks and to make it easier to guard the
animals, camp was usually pitched in the plain. The troops
were accompanied by a Jesuit chaplain.

For success in the field, the Guaraní depended on their
Spanish officers. Left to themselves, they were unable even to
draw themselves up in battle order, still less to maintain it.
Their native tactics were simple : to rush the enemy in a mass,
howling ferociously. This served sometimes against other
Indians but not against the Mamelucos. Their main armament was composed of traditional weapons, lances, slings,

99

chuzos or broad-pointed spears, *lazos* and *bolas*; sometimes they used another kind of sling, the *hande*. There was also the *macana*, a huge club of hardwood with a double edge, thick in the middle and tapering to a sharp point; it was a deadly weapon in close fighting. Then, apart from their muskets, they ordinarily carried some not particularly heavy but far-ranging English guns fired from rests.

With the experience of Mbororé behind them, each Reduction was kept on a war footing: in emergencies their men would go armed to church, for it was the Mamelucos' favoured time for a surprise assault. Instruction for the most part was given by the Spanish officers who succeeded Torres and Ruyer. Every Sunday evening after Vespers military and perhaps also naval exercises were held. A regular course of training was established; after target practice prizes were awarded—usually a quid of tobacco, a fish hook or harpoon; then a mock battle would be held. At the same time the Spaniards trained select troops in the use of the arquebus or cannon.

At drill and ceremonial reviews the troops carried sabres and shoulder bands. Their uniforms—jerkins and drawers—were cut in French military style, their dragoons' caps decorated with an ostrich feather, the name Jesus inscribed in front, a skull behind. Each Reduction contributed a regiment consisting ordinarily of six companies each made up of sixty men, a colonel, six captains, six lieutenants and a general officer. Each company carried a different arm. All weapons were kept in the armoury and given out only on the day of the exercise or review. Boys had their own military exercises on alternate Sundays.

The Guaraní soldier was equipped and campaigned at the expense of the Reduction in return for certain remissions of taxes. To mount a horse and possess a title of rank was sufficient recompense for the Indian. After two or three winters in the field he was happy if he returned with a captain's staff. 'At all times,' writes Dobrizhoffer,[1] 'even when employed in building or in agriculture they ostentatiously hold their captain's staff in their hands . . . On the point of death and about to receive Extreme Unction, a Guaraní captain puts on his military boots and spurs, takes hold of his staff, and awaits the priest. "This", they say, "is the way for a captain to die." '

The allotment of firearms to the Indians had alarmed the Spanish settlers: they feared that the Indians, recently savages, might turn against the Jesuits and perhaps attempt a reconquest of their country. Protests were made regularly to Madrid. But in the critical years of Cárdenas's power the Jesuits were supported by the governors of Paraguay, and at the same time their case was being pressed by Montoya in Lima. Permission for the Reduction Indians to use firearms was renewed several times. Montoya's case was based on the declared policy of the Crown to protect the Indians : he estimated, probably with exaggeration, that between the establishment of the first Guairá mission in 1610 and the first grant of firearms 300,000 Indians from Spanish territories had been enslaved, and that between the first raid on a Guairá Reduction in 1627 and the last in 1632, at least 60,000 had been sold in the public market : firearms had accounted for the enemy's success, as earlier they had accounted for the Spanish conquest of Peru.

Objections, however, persisted especially from Asunción, where the governors continued to call upon Indian troops for service against fractious settlers : exaggerated reports were quickly spread : 14,000 firearms were piled up in the Jesuit armouries to protect, not the Indian, but the secret Jesuit treasure. The total number of firearms, in fact, was nearer 1,000.[2]

Because both Asunción and Buenos Aires depended on the Reduction forces the Jesuits in Lima, the Viceroy's seat, as well as in Madrid, were able in most disputes to obtain a settlement in their favour. This, together with the economic strength of the Reductions, put them at still worse enmity with the Spaniards. It was easy to represent the Jesuits as a disloyal or foreign element in the State. Moreover the rivalry at Asunción between the Bishop and Governor was continuous. For moral as well as military support the governors were anxious to keep on good terms with the Jesuits. On their side the bishops resented the exemptions claimed by the Reductions.

It was with relief that the Jesuits received Jacinto de Laríz, Governor of Río de la Plata, on a military inspection of the Reductions in 1647. Laríz reported to the Viceroy his satisfaction with the Jesuits' military dispositions: none of the supposed abuses had any foundation. In that year the total Indian population of the fifteen Guaraní towns was only 21,116. Together they furnished 6,968 armed and trained men. Santa María, for instance, on the north bank of the Uruguay, with its 2,000 Indians, produced a quota of 500 men.[3] Even at the time of the Jesuits' expulsion, a hundred and thirty years later, Santa Rosa in Paraguay possessed only four stone mortars, one small cannon on its estancia, to be used presumably against savage Indians, a fifth mortar in the armoury, a sixth on a boat that had been sequestered at Corrientes, two blunderbuses, seventy-one muskets and fourteen pistols. The number of firearms varied with the size of each Reduction, its geographical position and the openness of its estancias to attack.

The present frontiers of Paraguay, Argentina, Equador and Colombia are explained by the position of the missions run by Jesuits who were subjects of the Spanish Crown. Each colonizing Power had its own institution to protect or extend its American frontier: in the French colonies the pioneers were the fur traders, principally the beaver hunters, and missionaries; in the English colonies the backwoodsmen hewed down the forest and drove the Indian further west; the Portuguese worked through the Mamelucos; the Spaniards used their missionaries.

If the king had been forced to defend the frontiers with his own troops, the expense could not have been met by his exchequer. And it was out of the question to found Spanish settlements along the frontier at a time when Buenos Aires, Córdoba and Santa Fe had not the resources for their own defence. Even at the beginning of the eighteenth century, Buenos Aires had only 4,000 inhabitants; at the end of the century in the area that came under its governor, stretching south to the Straits of Magellan and west to the Andes, the Spanish population was estimated at 25,000, roughly the number of Indians in three Jesuit towns.

It fell to the Guaraní troops, therefore, to hold the frontier in Paraguay against the Chaco Indians, and on the Uruguay and later beyond the river against other savages as well as the Mamelucos. The chain of Chiquitos missions did the same on the fringe of the Mato Grosso, and the Mojos Reductions, belonging to the Peruvian Jesuits, further west on the line of the river Beni. It was said with truth that the Spanish Jesuits effectively barred the Portuguese from the silver mountain of Potosí.

From the middle of the seventeenth century there were few years in which the Reduction forces were not called out against the Guaycurú, who came in from the Paraguay river up the Tebicuary north of Ignacio Guazú; and there was a fairly continuous warfare against the Abipones of the Chaco, who despised the Guaraní as Christians and still more as soldiers of the King of Spain. The towns closest to the corner formed by the confluence of the Paraguay river and the Paraná were most frequently attacked. Innumerable Guaraní were killed, their cattle driven off, their young men taken prisoner.

Over a period of some sixty years Ignacio Guazú, in its exposed position both to the north and west, suffered most. The forest made it easy for the Abipones to conceal their approach. In spite of day and night watches, murders were frequent. Quick to learn from the Mamelucos in points of warfare, the Abipones surprised Ignacio Guazú on a holy day, burst into the plaza and slew more than three hundred Guaraní. 'This', says Dobrizhoffer, 'happened when Padre Francisco Maria Rasponi was *Cura.*'*

This success encouraged the savages. Some days later they carried off four hundred oxen and droves of horses. Ditches and palisades were ineffective. Additional guards were posted, armed with muskets; scouts were sent out daily. The attacks continued. At Santiago, immediately to the south of Ignacio Guazú, and at Nuestra Señora de Fe, the defensive ditches can still be traced. Several wagons conveying *yerba maté* from Santa Rosa, another town in the district, were attacked on

---

* Dobrizhoffer, vol. iii, p. 22. Rasponi was *Cura* of Ignacio Guazú 1742-9.

their way to the Paraná for shipment to Buenos Aires : fifty Guaraní were left dead.

Occasionally the Guaraní got the better of the raiders but defeat was more common and affected their morale : 'Whenever they fought an engagement with the Abipones they thought more of suffering death than inflicting it.'[4] The Spanish troops sent down from Asunción at the expense of the towns were of little use. Their purpose was to patrol the forest tracks. Usually they were outwitted.

Dobrizhoffer, the Czech missionary, asks why the Guaraní were 'such timid hares at home, when they are said by historians to have fought like lions in the royal camps against the Portuguese and even against savages'. He gives two answers : the Guaraní were slack in keeping watch, and at home they were not captained by Spaniards but left to their own devices. Freedom from these attacks came only with the pacification of the Abipones.

Seven times between 1657 and 1697 the Guaraní troops came down the Paraná to defend Buenos Aires : on the last occasion 2,000 drove back the French from the city. Across Río de la Plata from Buenos Aires Colonia was constantly saved by the Guaraní for the Spaniards. In 1704 perhaps one of the largest expeditions was mounted : 4,000 men with a train of 6,000 horses, 2,000 mules, 30,000 cattle and a fleet of barges to carry their equipment, provisions and yerba. In an eight-month campaign a hundred and thirty Guaraní were killed and two hundred wounded. There was a campaign on a similar scale in 1718. Three years later they were called on to defend Corrientes against an attack by the Payaguas in their canoes; in 1724 they chased the Portuguese out of Montevideo and stayed on to build fortifications for the city. Altogether, between 1637 and 1745, the Reduction Indians entered the field at least fifty times on behalf of the king, at considerable sacrifice of lives, working time, and money. The gratitude of the Spanish cities was never evident.

It was a heavy price to pay for their safety. On the other hand, the expense and drain of manpower did not noticeably affect the economy of the Reductions : in return for services the Jesuits secured tax exemptions.

About 1748 the Provincial, Manuel Querini, codified the regulations concerning military matters. There was conscription for all able-bodied men; youths were to have their own military exercises; watches were to be mounted both inside and outside every town; priests should not 'laud' warfare, but accept it as the lesser of two evils.

War manoeuvres, however, did at times disturb the life of the Reductions. The Indians themselves were known to object. In 1733, some 580 Indians sent to the King a memorial drawn up at Guaibiti, where they were encamped: they set out the hardships endured by their families at home and the disorder caused there by their long period in the field.

The Jesuits did their best to reduce the time given to military affairs. In 1746, when the Spaniards were anxious to establish a fort at a strategic point among the Reductions, the Provincial, Bernardo Nusdorffer, opposed the plan: only in an emergency would he allow troops to be employed in the construction of defences, and then they were to return when work was complete.[5]

Nusdorffer's protest was prompted by the increasing number of Jesuits occupied in military affairs when he could have used them to open new Reductions in the Chaco. From 1714 if not earlier, certain Jesuits were set in charge of the equipment of the Guaraní forces: there were two in 1724, one for the Paraná, the other for the Uruguay; in 1725 the number was increased to five, by 1745 it reached eight when the estancias were included in the defence system. These supervisors were often Jesuit Brothers, like Anton Bernal, who had distinguished himself in Chile: he was known to the Marqués de Macera, Viceroy of Peru, who wrote in 1646 that he was confident that the Jesuits could defend the frontier against the Portuguese so long as Bernal was with them; at the same time Brother Herricht, a fine military technician, was working in the Reductions. Every week during the 1740s there was increasing Portuguese infiltration. At a consultation held by the Provincial, Antonio Machoni, at Ignacio Miní on 14 November 1741 it was decided that each town was to have at least fifty Indians trained in the use of the musket, a total force of more than 1,500 musketeers: any difficulties, such as lack of arms or powder, were to be referred to Brother Herricht.

Although the Jesuits played a pivotal role in frontier defence, still first and last they regarded themselves as preachers of the gospel: 'To doubt this is to confess complete and disqualifying ignorance of the great mass of existing missionary correspondence, printed and unprinted, so fraught with unmistakable proofs of the religious zeal and devotion of the vast majority of the missionaries.'[6] Rather, the priests held or extended the frontiers for the sake of Indians to be made Christians, and in doing this they served the purposes of the Crown: the system explains how Spain took possession of the new world with a handful of men, while most of her military strength was engaged in Europe: in this way she was able to spread her religion, culture and language over half the American continent as well as across the Philippines.

The military organization of the Reductions was only one aspect of their sheer efficiency, discipline and method. Certainly the Spanish South American Jesuits in their privileged position considered themselves in fact a self-sufficient state. One of their writers, José Peramás, speaks of the 'Jesuit Republic of Paraguay' and devotes a book to comparing it feature by feature with Plato's Republic.*

Politically and administratively the Reductions belonged to the Viceroyalty of Peru, but as a territorial unit they were in practice autonomous. In the vast area they ultimately covered from San Ignacio Guazú in Paraguay almost down to the Atlantic coast of Rio Grande do Sul, there was not a single resident Spanish official. But there was no question of the Reductions forming an independent state. Theoretically as well as in practice they were a peculiar administrative unit under the Spanish Crown.

On 15 March 1624, for instance, the Governor of Asunción, Don Manuel Frías, certified to Madrid that all the Jesuit towns under his jurisdiction had been founded with the authority and approbation of either himself or his predeces-

---

* José M. Peramás, S.J., *La República de Platón y los Guaraníes.* Original edition, Faenza, 1793. Modern edition, Buenos Aires, 1946.

sors.[7] Two years later, Francisco de Céspedes, Governor of Buenos Aires, acting in the name of the Crown, granted the Jesuits the province of Uruguay 'to reduce and convert the natives there': he gave them 'full faculties and power to establish and found all the Reductions they can, and to appoint caciques and justices as they think right, giving them all the power and authority they judge convenient' for the service of the Crown.[8]

On their side, the minutes of the Provincials' meetings illustrate the same dependence of the Reductions on the Spanish authorities. For instance, at Santa Fe on 1 September 1741 Padre Jerónimo Herrán, the Provincial, in conference with his advisers, 'ordered a letter to be read from the Deputy Governor of Santa Fe and also the decree of the Governor of Buenos Aires concerning the hoped-for conversion of the Mocobíes: his Reverence enquired whether the papers came in the form that would permit the Society to undertake the "reduction" of that nation. All replied, no. And it was agreed that letters should be sought in the correct form which the Society uses and insists on for its own safety':[9] if this were not done there would be risk of trouble with the Spanish settlers. Other instances of this procedure can be found in the same book of minutes. In 1774, the Marqués de Cevallos, Governor of Buenos Aires, wrote in defence of the Jesuits after their expulsion, that all they had done in Paraguay had been done either on an express command of the Viceroy or with his sanction.

Unless explicit exception was made, all royal decrees were promulgated in the Reductions; both priests and the Indian civic officers were confirmed in office by the district governors, who made official visits; taxes and tithes were paid; any differences with the governors were adjusted through the royal court in Charcas: either adjudicators were appointed or an investigating committee that reported to the king.

Loyalty of the Indians to the king was expressed on the occasion of their solemn processions. Then the royal standard was borne to the church with great ceremony: the *alférez real*, who carried it, was received there with regal honours; it was then planted in the centre of the plaza, with a picture of the King: then, standing on the spot, the Indian officers renewed their oath of homage before it.[10]

Economically the Reductions were self-sufficient, while socially they were more advanced than any Indian community since the passing of the Inca Empire. For the welfare of their citizens, they developed a system that European countries took another two centuries to attain. Consequently it was not surprising that they attracted the attention of social theorists long before the French Revolution. Many eighteenth-century writers saw in their organization a planned attempt to put into practice the ideas of Thomas More and Tommaso Campanella.

According to some writers[11] the Jesuits deliberately modelled their government on Campanella's *City of the Sun*: Maceta and Cataldino, the Italian founders of the Guairá mission, were Campanella's compatriots and contemporaries; they had set out to found a Christian communist community in Paraguay; before leaving Europe they had put their plan to Philip IV: he approved of it in theory, but did not give it practical support.

But there is nothing in the massive correspondence concerning the missions to support this theory, and there is no evidence that the two priests had dealings with Madrid. All negotiations with the court were carried on by the Jesuit procurator there, and it is absurd to imagine that two young foreign priests would have made contact with the King before sailing for South America: the Guaraní were then known in Europe as a warlike race, seemingly the last people to be chosen for such an experiment.* Moreover when the two Italians wrote to the Jesuit General asking to be sent to the missions, they made no mention of any idealistic programme nor did they ask specifically to be sent to America. Cataldino

---

* It is sometimes argued that Campanella's *City of the Sun* was not published until 1620, ten years after the foundation of Loreto in Guairá, but this is not decisive. Campanella, a Dominican, had been lecturing as early as 1587 in Naples, where Maceta was born in 1573. He was well known as a revolutionary thinker anxious to establish a new form of government in Naples on a theocratic communistic basis. For twenty-seven years he was in prison. His book had been circulating in manuscript for many years before it was published.

asked for 'some part of India, Muscovy or Turkey or wherever you may judge the greater glory of God might lie'.

Only in a restricted sense were Cataldino and Maceta founder-fathers of the Guaraní Republic. Earlier, soon after the perambulatory missions of Fields and his companions, a general resolution had been taken to 'reduce' the Indians. Moreover, in 1609, the year of the foundation of Loreto, Lorenzana established Ignacio Guazú. But there is no need to deny altogether the influence of social theorists. Certainly the ideas of Thomas More were very much in the air* and it is probable that they were known to the Paraguayan priests and compared with the more practical utopias of men like the Dominican, Bartolomé de las Casas : his treatise, published in 1518, three years after More's, prefigures the spirit and methods that characterized the Reductions. Seventy-five years before the foundation of Loreto, Las Casas created and directed at Vera Paz in Guatemala an Indian settlement directly dependent on the Spanish Crown; and he excluded from it all Spaniards, both military and civil. Other less publicized but similar experiments were made in the same region. It was a time when many thinkers in the old religious orders were giving thought to missionary methods and to the psychology of the American Indian. In this atmosphere the notion of a Christian republic continued to be mooted.

Ironically, if an idealist must be found, the role is best filled by the Portuguese Jesuit, Antonio de Vieira. At the age of forty-five, after a brilliant diplomatic career, he was charged by John IV with the task of organizing the Reductions in the Brazilian province of Pará : there he struggled to rescue the Indians from slavery and the forced labour imposed by his fellow-countrymen. His success was staggering, but on the death of John IV in 1556 he lost his protector : the colonists, inspired by the Mamelucos, cried for his arrest. In 1661 he

* There is evidence that several bishops in the Spanish possessions, long before the coming of the Jesuits, had studied *Utopia*: for instance, Vasco de Quiroga, Bishop of Michoacan, Mexico, in the 1530s, wanted a society in the new world based on More's principles. Quiroga left behind him a copy of *Utopia* annotated in his own hand: it is now in the seminary library of Michoacan. Cf. *Missionalia Hispanica*, no. 67 (1966).

was transported back to Lisbon as a criminal. In house confinement, first at Oporto then Coimbra, he wrote his *Quinto Imperio do Mundo*, a harmless but extravagant vision of a millennium in which the world would be ruled jointly by Portugal and the Church. The manuscript, now in the *Bibliothèque Nationale*, was examined at Coimbra, condemned by the Inquisition but not by the Jesuits.

After two years (1665–7) in prison, Vieira was absolved by the Pope, Alexander VII. When in 1669 he visited Rome, the Jesuits in a body went out to meet him. The Jesuit General gave him a triumphal welcome. A papal reception followed. With this backing, Vieira returned to Brazil and died at Bahia at the time his Paraguayan brethren were consolidating their work on the Paraná.

But in the final analysis, the Reductions owed their character more to the practical needs of the missionary situation than to any preconceived utopia. The ordinances of the Provincials also played their part, particularly Nicolás Durán's regulations, and other later directives codified in 1637 by a commission of priests and approved by the Jesuit General Vitelleschi. Further instructions were added almost every decade. A notable contribution also was made by the more capable priests who met in conference every three years.

These ordinances peculiar to Paraguay must be taken with the broader experience of the Jesuits in other places. For example, there was the new model mission at Juli where Torres had worked before his appointment to Asunción.* Further afield in the Philippines the Jesuits had been at work longer than in South America : the methods found successful

---

* The mission of Juli on an eminence encircled by high mountains near Lake Titicaca on the highway between Peru and Paraguay became a model Indian township of 10,000 to 12,000 inhabitants. Here Torres worked for some years before he was appointed its Superior. In organization it has been taken as one of the models of the Guaraní towns, the principal difference being that the Indians journeyed some four hundred and fifty miles from Juli to Potosí to serve their *mita* or fixed term in the mines. Torres's success in organizing schools, workshops, etc., and laying out satellite towns was acknowledged by the civic authorities, who appointed him Protector of the Indians, a title which hitherto had been held only by senior bishops.

there had been gathered into an instruction dated 1 May 1609 which Aquaviva gave to Padre Juan Romero, the first elected representative of the Paraguay Jesuits to be sent to Rome. The substance of this instruction was drawn from earlier documents sent in 1604 to the Philippines and in 1608 to New Granada : all contain many features clearly recognizable in the Paraguay Reductions.[12]

For instance it was laid down that the settlements were to be geographically remote from the Spanish towns; a school of languages was to be founded; two priests were to be stationed in every Reduction; the Indians were not to be imposed on; they were to be relieved of all tax burdens exacted by previous missionaries in contravention of the laws of the Indies; the more capable Indian children were to be taught reading, writing and singing; a fitting church and a hospital were to be built.

Other features, such as the military establishment, the peculiar system of land ownership, the position of the *cura*, stemmed from circumstances peculiar to Paraguay.

Seemingly rigid in several ways, the missionary principles of Acquaviva left much freedom to the priest working in the field : means and methods were his to choose or adapt, particularly in matters not directly apostolic, such for instance as administration, means of livelihood and the mechanical arts. In Paraguay the Guaraní were more unprepared for a stabilized life than the natives of the Philippines or New Granada : the Jesuits there naturally took on the duties of civic as well as religious chiefs, and the remoteness of the missions was never threatened.

It must be remembered also that the first Jesuit towns were founded a hundred years after the discovery of America. There was already a mass of legislation in existence concerning the treatment of Indians as well as an established bureaucracy—the Council of the Indies, the Viceroys, the regional governors.

Thanks to the dependence of the governors on the Guaraní troops, the Jesuits had the power to see that the laws guarding Indian liberties were strictly enforced, for instance, that no Spaniard should take off an Indian to a white settlement, introduce alcohol into an Indian village or even so much as set foot in it.

This legislation was based on the assumption of sixteenth-century Europe that the Indian was a minor and, as such, had to be protected by the law. The Jesuits did not subscribe to the theory; on the other hand it served their practical purpose.

The view that the Indian was a human being endowed with a soul and will was adopted universally only after a long debate. An extreme doctrine constituted him a species on his own half-way between man and beast: some writers worked out a number of Indian characteristics in common with quadrupeds, others maintained that the Indian was incapable of understanding spiritual things and therefore incapable of baptism.

These theories were explicitly rejected by Pope Paul III in his brief *Veritas Ipsa* of 12 June 1537: he declared emphatically that the Indian was a true human being called to salvation and entitled, even as a heathen, to complete freedom: he could not lawfully and ought not in fact be made a slave.* In 1567, thirty years later, in a letter to the Viceroy of Mexico Pius V went further: he asserted that the Indians had a right to civic honours and offices.

Nevertheless in practice the Indian continued to be treated at best as half human, a species with a limited intellectual capacity, sufficient for baptism and perhaps penance but not for the Eucharist. As late as 1638 the synod of La Paz discussed this opinion and re-asserted the teaching of *Veritas Ipsa* a hundred years after its first promulgation.

This strict isolation of the Indians from the Spanish community struck all European visitors to the Reductions. To some writers this policy of apartheid appeared a crime against human rights or, still worse, a sinister Jesuit method of building up an empire in the unknown wilds of South America; to Jesuit sympathizers it was a wise measure to shelter the Indian

---

* The phrase *licet extra fidem existant* (even if they are not Christians) was inserted against those who held that it was lawful to make slaves of heathens. There had been papal declarations against slavery before *Veritas Ipsa* which was issued at the request of Dominican Friars to reinforce previous condemnations. Cf. Article 'Esclavage' in *Dictionnaire de Théologie*.

from ruinous contact with the Spaniard. But friend and critic alike saw in this isolation the central flaw in the Jesuit system : according to both, it led to the failure of the priests to educate the Indian to take his place in society. The isolation was universally laid at the door of the Jesuits who were anxious to keep their charges *in statu pupillari.*

From the late sixteenth century the Spanish Crown, mainly for humanitarian reasons, had established a policy of segregation in the new world. By turn negroes, encomenderos, vagrants, mulattos, mestizos and finally Spaniards were excluded from living in Indian towns; in Spanish towns the Indians resided in quarters of their own; segregation was also observed in the estancias : at Jesús María and Santa Catalina, estancias belonging to the Jesuits of Córdoba, the separate Indian quarters can be seen today.

Vagrants were a particular trouble : they lived off the Indians, moving from one community to another, and through their evil habits became an obstacle to missionary work. Also the Crown realized that Spanish colonization had not gone ahead faster because vagrants and mestizos had preferred to settle in Indian villages. An exception was made in favour of mestizos who had grown up with an Indian mother in Indian villages. The Indians themselves, probably encouraged by the Friars, favoured the policy of segregation; the devastating epidemics of 1576–9 helped to establish this policy.[13]

The Jesuits in the Reductions followed a strict interpretation of these laws. The first instructions on segregation were given by Diego de Torres to Maceta and Cataldino when they set out for Guairá in 1609. Spaniards and mestizos from Villarrica and Ciudad Real were to be excluded altogether from the Indian towns. This policy was reaffirmed in 1618 in the ordinances of Alfaro which were largely inspired by Torres himself. Later, after the settlement of the Indians on the Paraná and Uruguay rivers, relaxations were introduced : Spaniards needed for a job in a Guaraní town were allowed to reside there; Spanish settlers from neighbouring towns were often invited to festivities or asked to be godparents in baptism; then, at the request of the Crown, the northern group of Reductions in the area of Ignacio Guazú were opened to merchants on certain days of each month; frequently the Indians themselves travelled to Buenos Aires and Santa Fe for trade or entertainment.

Only towards the end of the seventeenth century were the rules again tightened. In 1697, by order of the Jesuit General Tirso González, Spanish travellers were permitted only three days' stay in the Reductions: at the end of that time the corregidor had to fetch their mules and oxen so that they could continue their journey. Twelve years later, in 1709, a general prohibition was issued against Spaniards entering the missions except with permission of the mission Superior: Ignacio Guazú and Nuestra Señora de Fe were exempted because of their position on the trading route from Asunción to Corrientes. By 1742 the other Reductions in this group, Santa Rosa, Santiago, San Cosme y Damián and the capital, Candelaria, were included. Each of these six privileged missions had a *tambo* or spacious inn for travellers. According to one late Jesuit writer there was no week in the year when merchants from Asunción did not arrive in these pueblos: 'Many traders', he says, 'not only from Corrientes, Santa Fe and Buenos Aires, but also from Chile and Peru, five hundred or more leagues away, came and still come to trade with these pueblos.'[14] But there is no evidence of tambos in other missions; when Itapuá became a big commercial centre the tambo in the town was replaced by another near the *Capilla de los Mártires* where all business had to be done. In the other towns the Spaniards, while they did their business, were always escorted by an alcalde.

In other Reductions the Superior made exceptions in special cases: for instance, a Spaniard taken ill at Loreto was allowed to stay until he had recovered; another at Itapúa was given an extension until he had completed his business; a negro artisan could stay with his wife in another Reduction until the work he was doing on the church was finished; royal messengers, agents of the Spanish authorities, army and defence officials were all exempted.

Spaniards were feared mainly as bearers of diseases to which the Indians had no resistance; also their example of loose living was contagious and there was always danger that they would get among the Indian women. In May 1724 Bishop Fajardo of Buenos Aires, after a visitation, reported to the King that the morals of the six 'privileged' Reductions were less commendable than the rest and he concluded that if the Jesuits tried to keep the Indians away from the Spaniards, they did so with good reason.

The policy of segregation which was given such sinister interpretations—the military defence works at Santiago, for instance, were taken by some writers as a ditch to keep out foreigners—was peculiar neither to the Jesuits nor to Spanish South America. After the administration of the Reductions had been handed over to Spanish officials on the expulsion of the Jesuits, the Viceroy at Buenos Aires, Francisco de Bucareli, insisted on the maintenance of the system in the best interests of the Indians. 'You will not allow any strangers', he wrote in his code of instructions to his officials, 'of whatever estate, quality or condition they may be, to reside in the towns, even if they be artisans, and much less that they have dealings or take contracts in them . . . and you will take special care that the Laws of the Indies be executed and especially article 27 of book ix' which prohibited Spaniards from settling in an Indian town.[15]

7

Economy

It was common for nineteenth-century authors to see in the
Jesuit experiment in Paraguay the ideal of a Christian communist community in which everything was held in joint
ownership for the equal benefit of all.

In a sense the contrary is nearer the truth. Certainly in his
primitive state the Guaraní had nothing he could call his own;
nor was there any need for it : the forest and rivers provided
ample sustenance for all. The Guaraní knew everything that
the land spontaneously produced, when it ripened, where it
was to be found, where the animals lurked, how each species
could be most easily caught. There was no need to claim anything as private. What Dobrizhoffer wrote of the Abipones
applied equally to the Guaraní : 'All things are in common
among them. . . . Whatever flies in the air, swims in the water
and grows wild in the woods becomes the property of the first
person who chooses to take it.'[1]

Among the Guaraní of the forest, agriculture was sub-
ordinate to fishing and hunting. Land was cultivated in a
nomadic and intermittent manner, property and custom relat-
ing to it were unknown; only poultry were domesticated. But
the economy of a settled life demanded individual possession
of land at least in a rudimentary form. There is evidence that
the first Jesuits in Paraguay attempted to impress on the
Guaraní some sense of private ownership. Pedro Oñate, the
second Provincial, wrote in 1618 that 'in their barbaric state
the Indians possessed neither house nor field' and instructed
the Fathers on the Paraná to see that the Indians acquired

116

both. The division of fields according to the families under a cacique belongs to the first days of the Reductions: the word *abambaé*, private possession, was used to describe them.

In his account of the foundation of San Juan in 1696, Antonio Sepp describes how on reaching the site of the Reduction he allotted a portion of land to each cacique, who in turn divided it among his vassals. When this had been done Sepp then preached a sermon on the right of the Indians to their own land and their duty to respect the same right in others.[2] The allotment was sufficient for a married man to support his family on a crop of mandioca, a sturdy plant easily propagated by dividing the stock: the root could be eaten six months after planting though it required a year to ripen properly. It was an ideal crop for the Indian: it needed no attention, the root flourished even when the leaves were destroyed—locusts, ants and drought did it no harm.

Apart from mandioca the Guaraní also cultivated on his *hacienda* Indian wheat, vegetables, sweet potatoes, fruit and cotton. Oxen and agricultural instruments were lent in turn to each. 'In the town of Candelaria, where the farms lay across the great river Paraná, the Indians were taken over every morning in public transports without charge and in the evening brought back in the same way.'[3] The yield of his private field was the absolute property of the Indian: he disposed of it as he wished: he could consume it in a few days or over a long period, sell it or give it away. The production of cotton meant some labour which the Indian ordinarily shunned: he did not care whether he went half-naked or well-clothed. If he wished he could make a hammock or net or weave cloth. When he sold the cloth, the commune credited the proceeds of the sale to him individually; in exchange for his products the Indian received the goods he wanted. The only restriction on his ownership was that he could not sell either his field or house. Peramás sums up the position: 'With this system all the families were equal and had the same possessions. Some, however, cultivated their land with more diligence than others and so reaped a larger harvest. But this introduced only an insignificant inequality among them: in fact, it provided a stimulus to work, for any Indian who saw his neighbour's field produce more than his was incited not to be idle or indolent.'[4] If a man could work he was made to work, if not he was supported from public funds. Visitors were astonished to find that there were no beggars in the Guaraní towns.

Alongside the private hacienda there was the communal land called *túpambaé* or God's property. Left to himself the Indian could not be relied on to cultivate his own land. It was only for this reason that every town had these fields worked by all, including the young men who did not go to school : for them this was an agricultural apprenticeship. Girls helped mainly by clapping their hands to keep off the parrots from the crops; they were also used to collect cotton : their gentler touch ensured that the shrub did not suffer. All male adults, not excepting the mayor and civic officials, had to assist two days a week. Experts were also employed and paid piece wages. Of these common fields one was usually set aside for wheat and vegetables, a second for cotton. Rice was seldom planted : although it grew naturally on the western shore of the Paraguay, fear of the savage Payaguas prevented the Guaraní from gathering it. In the eighteenth century some Brazilian Jesuits in the Reductions grew it in quantity, but it was too much trouble for the Indian to take the grains from the ear for it to become a popular crop. The Paraguayan wheat, with a short stalk and a large ear, was more widely grown by the Guaraní than the Spaniards : the grain was pressed out by the feet of anything up to a hundred horses on the threshing floor. Though the climate was suitable for vines, they were invariably destroyed by ants, wasps and wood-pigeons : the little wine that was produced tasted like a drug to the European palate. Altar wine was brought at great expense from Chile. The *tupambaé* always yielded more than the private lots. This was partly because the Indians there were helped by music, partly also because communal ownership in primitive societies always took priority over private possession and was more in harmony with the conscience of the people, but most of all because the work was well organized and done under surveillance.

The produce of the *tupambaé* was placed in the Reduction

storehouse and held in trust for the community. It supported the sick, widows and orphans; it provided seed for next year's sowing, a reserve against famine and a medium of exchange for European goods. It was from this source also that the annual tribute was paid to the Crown, a *peso fuerte* for each male Indian Christian : women, minors under eighteen, men over fifty, caciques and their families, and sacristans were exempt. In other words the Jesuits of Paraguay hit on a co-operative system for the support of a welfare state long before either phrase was coined in Europe. Certain methods were similar to those used in parts of France for the threshing of wheat or the production of wine or cheese: they encouraged private enterprise and at the same time met the immediate need for a good return from the land. Independently the Jesuits discovered that only a well controlled co-operative system could overcome the problem of agricultural production in a people emerging from barbarism. Peramás, always in search of a comparison, writes : 'With this system of public and private land the Guaraní could be compared to bees who all have their own honey, their own livelihood and food, and only afterwards come together for collective work in the fields and hive and work for the common honeycomb.'[5]

The ownership of these communal lands was vested in the Reduction; the title of the Reduction was occupation. It is more difficult to determine the exact title the Indian had to his private lot : no author contemporary with the Reductions writes on this point with precision. It is perhaps best described as a life-interest.

Among the primitive Guaraní, hereditary succession was unknown. When the head of a family died, his relatives abandoned or destroyed his dwelling (if in fact it existed) and with it all his possessions, his hammock, canoe and everything else. In such conditions it is absurd to believe that the Jesuits introduced the notion of private property in the sense of Roman law : such a notion would have conflicted with the Guaraní tribal custom which made the means of subsistence common to all.[6] The Jesuits were pragmatists. When they divided the land among the caciques, they did in fact introduce a new notion into Indian civilization; they were not concerned with the nature of the Indian's right but only with the proper cultivation of the land. By the act of allotment the fields were not *ipso facto* transformed into classic private property. The Indians attached no value to soil as such. What occupation of the soil gave them was a strong sense of belonging to a place. Peramás sums up the system when he writes: 'Some things were held in private, others in common.' But the private ownership had so many limitations both in practice and theory that it carried a peculiar sense in the Guaraní towns.

In the first place, the Laws of the Indies, which treated the natives as minors, forbade them to dispose of real estate without the authorization of the local Spanish governor or of their guardians. This was written into the Laws as early as 1505. The Jesuits never considered it necessary to seek an alteration, nor is there any record of their ever granting the permissions they were empowered to give.

For this there were two reasons: the whites were forbidden access to the Reductions and could acquire no land in them: transactions in real estate among the Indians were superfluous. There was no reason why an Indian should buy, sell or inherit land: if he wanted a new field he did not treat with his fellow-citizens but was assigned one by the municipality. In any case, without money the sale of land was impossible, just as it was unnecessary to 'bequeath land when every Guaraní in the Jesuit towns at his marriage received from the community what he needed for the support of his dependants. On his death, his widow and children were cared for by the community. More land which he could always acquire meant more work.

Such a system of land tenure could work only if the number of Indians in a Reduction was fairly stable. For this reason among others, the Jesuits did not allow the population of any community to grow beyond a manageable number. For instance, when San Miguel became overpopulated some three thousand Indians under Antonio Sepp hived off and made the foundation of San Juan a few miles away.

Apart from the produce of the common lands, the herds of cattle, horses, mules, sheep, oxen, the distant yerbales, estancias and woods were all held in trust for the community. An Indian, if he wished, could have his own mule, but normally after keeping it for a week, he would lose interest in it, forget to remove its pack saddle or leave it tethered in a remote place without food. If he acquired a pair of oxen, as often as not he would slaughter them when he had ploughed his field, burn the plough and roast them on the fire. Many Indians in the early period of the Reductions owned their own horses, but they were later forbidden them: it was found that they rode all day and did no work, or that they stole or mutilated cattle being driven up from the estancias, or simply went off leaving the family behind. 'The Fathers are to seek gradually to take away their private horses by purchase or make them common property,' wrote one Provincial. Then another added: 'This is to be rigorously enforced and those who disobey punished.'[7]

The livestock belonging to the Reductions at the time of the expulsion of the Jesuits was far less numerous than at the beginning of the eighteenth century. An exact inventory was made on the orders of the Viceroy Bucareli:* it shows that the increasing demand in Europe for hides had greatly reduced the number of cattle as well as increasing their market value. The trade that was already well-established at the end of the seventeenth century was now at its peak. When Sepp landed in 1691 at Buenos Aires, he was amazed to see the three ships that had crossed from Cadiz in convoy take on a cargo of no less than 30,000 ox-hides which cost nothing more than the cost of killing, 'each piece of which they sell again in Spain for six crowns; and among all these there was not one cow's hide'.[8] The hides had been stretched with pegs in the place where the animals had been slaughtered, the tongue, suet and fat taken out and the rest of the flesh, 'enough to feed a numerous army in Europe, left on the plain to be devoured by jaguars, wild dogs and ravens'.[9] Then, as he wrote in the same letter, oxen, cows and horses

---

* The Guaraní towns then owned together 698,353 cows, 44,183 oxen, 11,408 calves, 240,027 sheep, 28,204 horses, 45,646 mares, 3,036 fillies, 771 young mares, 700 young fillies, 15,235 mules, 8,063 asses, 150 stallions, 343 pigs. Cf. Brabo, *Inventarios*, pp. 668–9.

roved the plains in such prodigious numbers that 'in some places the fields are covered with them as far as your eyes will reach'. At that time a good horse could be exchanged for a knife, three for a bridle, six for a European horseshoe. At Yapeyú, in the 1690s, in less than two months, the Indians rounded up 50,000 cows and might have brought in 100,000 if there had been need for them.[10] The same, Sepp wrote, held of the other Reductions. Even thirty years later the plains were still covered with such droves of wild oxen that travellers were obliged to send horsemen ahead of them to clear the way.[11] Books of valuation put a *real de plata* (5 groschen) on a full-grown ox: every Spaniard who wanted to increase his herd hired a troop of horse who brought him in thousands of bulls and cows in a week. Yapeyú then had a herd of 50,000, San Miguel more.

Every December there was a great round-up of cattle, what the Guaraní called *vagiares*. It lasted till February. A troop of anything up to thirty Indians rode out from each Reduction: every man had to return from the estancia driving before him not less than 1,000 head of cattle, sometimes for 600 miles across mountains, plains and rivers. At the end of the trail the animals were put into large parks, *mataderos*, twelve to fifteen miles in circumference; the surplus and those required for immediate slaughter were taken to an enclosure nearer the town. A French visitor described the meat as 'very succulent and extremely tasty'.[12]

With the increasing demand for hides, the price of an ox rose from one to four German florins in the last thirty years before the departure of the Jesuits. At home, hides came to be used for ropes, hedges, bedding, trunks, saddles, bags for tobacco, sugar, wheat, cotton and yerba. At the same time, what Dobrizhoffer calls the lower orders in Paraguay now lived mainly on beef.

Horses were as numerous and cheap as cattle and as many as a thousand of them also could be caught in a few days. They would be driven into an enclosure and there starved until they became tractable. In sales they fetched ten to thirteen cruitzers. The colts were given away gratis. In size, shape and good points the Paraguayan horse was no different from the European, but it lacked stamina for it was never stabled or fed on oats. Any difference in price depended on its method of going. 'An ambling nag covers two leagues in the space of an hour; a common horse only kept up if spurred by the rider.'[13]

In this evaluation the livestock of the Reductions amounted to very little real wealth. In 1768 San Javier on the Uruguay had in its pueblo 486 oxen driven up from its estancia for immediate consumption, perhaps a fortnight's supply, and only 12,136, less than sufficient for a year, in reserve. The number of its sheep, on the other hand, was growing. This did not denote any success of the Jesuits' attempt to get the Guaraní to vary their diet : the sheep were reared merely for wool. A sheep fetched usually three times the price of a cow.

None of this property belonged to the Jesuits. Like the church, the houses, the estancia buildings, it was *tupambaé*. The priests claimed only the 250 pesos which was the royal grant to all serving in the Reductions.* The Jesuit Generals in Rome kept an eye on abuses in the administration of the Indians' possessions. Any fish, eggs, vegetables or meat taken by the priests from the common fund had to be paid for, usually with salt, knives, shears, fish hooks, medals, pins and other objects sent from headquarters in Candelaria. There is a letter of Tirso González dated Rome 31 January 1696 reiterating firmly that everything, pensions apart, belonged in one way or another to the Indians. Any Jesuit students coming from the Colleges at Asunción, Santa Fe or Córdoba for a holiday or convalescence were to pay for their food and lodging; every Indian was to receive a fair return for any work he might do for the Fathers; if he sent timber belonging to the commune down river for use in the Jesuit houses of Santa Fe or Buenos Aires he was to be recompensed for both the timber and for the labour of felling it.[14] After a visitation of the Reductions in 1721, Don Pedro Fajardo, Bishop of Buenos Aires, wrote to Philip IV : 'I can assure your Majesty that I have found nowhere . . . more perfect unselfishness than among these religious who take nothing that belongs to

---

* This was less than half the salary paid to other priests, both religious and secular, in the Spanish overseas possessions.

their converts, whether it be for their attire or sustenance."[15]

By forming a commonwealth remote from Spanish settlements in the interior of the country, the Jesuits presented
themselves with the problem of making it viable. There would
be no chance of holding the Indians unless the towns were
self-supporting: they would be compelled again to search for
food in the forest and plains; before long they would again
become semi-nomads. If the Indians were to acquire árticles
that they could not themselves produce, they needed to trade.

The main marketable product of the Reductions was its
yerba, which served also as their main currency: but they
also exported a quantity of cotton, bundles of dried tobacco,
choice woods, furs, honey bees, sugar and aromatic resins:
they did not sell hides, for there was always a glut of them
from the Spanish towns: only a few carefully worked and
ornamented skins, perhaps 3,000 a year, were sent to Buenos
Aires, Santa Fe and Asunción. Articles produced in the
carpenters' shops, sculptures and other objects from the workshops were not exported at all: sometimes small statues and
rosaries were gratuitously distributed among the poorer
country folk.

In both Buenos Aires and Santa Fe there were agents for
the Jesuit towns: they noted in their books what each sent
down and from the sale of these goods paid the tribute due
to the Crown and purchased what each Reduction needed—
axes, saws, hatchets, chisels, scissors, anvils, paint, vinegar,
salt; also linen and silk goods for the church and estancia
chapels. The agent recorded the cost of each item and kept
an expense account. Sometimes at the end of a transaction a
Reduction was in debt, particularly if a large portion of its
produce was unsold when the Indians were due to re-embark.

The journey lasted several months. While the Indians were
away, their fields were cared for by the community, and on
their return they received a gift of food or furniture from the
common store.

According to a report of a royal commission, this trade by
barter netted an annual income of some 100,000 pesos or
seven reals per capita of the Indian population.[16] A royal
charter authorized the thirty Guaraní towns to put on the

market 12,000 arrobas* of yerba, roughly 300,000 lb a year. When the sacks reached Santa Fe or Buenos Aires a declaration was obtained from the fiscal inspectors that there was no excess of weight: only then were they sold by the agents. The Spaniards of Asunción were always fearful they might be put out of business by the Reductions.†

If alcoholism had not been the plague of all South American Indians it is unlikely that the Jesuits would ever have developed their yerba trade. The Guaraní were no exception, though they were not addicted to *chicha*, a fermented drink based on mandioca, to the same extent as the Chaco tribes. The Mocobíes, according to an early missionary, Padre Canelas, spent the greater part of the year drinking: Christian instruction was reserved to their sober intervals. Another writing of the Calchaquí in 1639 claimed that it was easier to kill a bull with a thorn than rid them of debauchery.

Reduction life was incompatible with chicha. At their war conferences the caciques would begin their discussions only after they were drunk; then they would declare for war, promising themselves spoils, prisoners and glory; at other times battles would break out between opposing factions: riots, assassination and lechery were the common thing.

At first the Jesuits did not ban chicha altogether but tried to restrict its use: the habit of drinking it was so engrained even in the young Indians and so universal that it was out of the question to punish delinquents. In the end the Jesuits substituted yerba.

For many years yerba, known to the Indians from time immemorial, had been ruled out as harmful. In 1610 Padre Torres described it as a 'pernicious drink'. Ten years later Lorenzana, the founder of Ignacio Guazú, wrote that it was the 'ruin of the land. It makes those who take it slothful, vile, brazen and dishonourable.'[17] Among Spaniards it was thought odious and was prohibited by excommunication unless taken

* The arroba is about twenty-five pounds weight.
† De Pauw, the eighteenth-century German writer, grossly exaggerated when he stated that the Jesuits sold 4 million lb of yerba per annum; and that the Indians employed in its production numbered 300,000, or twice the total of men, women and children at any one time in the Reductions.

as a medicine. But the habit soon became widespread and the bishop lifted the ban. Del Techo describes the effect of yerba as well as any modern writer : 'They say if you cannot sleep, it will compose you to it; that if you are lethargic, it drives away sleep; if hungry, it satisfies; if your meat does not digest, it causes an appetite; it refreshes after weariness and drives away melancholy and several diseases. Those who once become used to it, cannot easily leave it, for they affirm their strength fails them when they want it and cannot live long.'[18] But del Techo also saw the dangers : addicts would 'almost sell themselves rather than want the wherewithal to purchase it'; in excess it induced drunkenness and bred 'distempers like overmuch wine'. By the middle of the seventeenth century maté was popular also in Tucumán, Chile and Peru and had already reached Europe.

Grudgingly the Jesuits endorsed the raising of the bishop's ban. They had been against yerba also for another reason, the loss of Indian life involved in collecting it.

Mbaracuyurú, the region of the yerba forest, was nearly four hundred miles from Asunción. Expeditions would set out without sufficient food and with no medicines; sometimes as many as sixty Indians in a party of two hundred would die from snake-bites, undernourishment or attacks of jaguars. Francisco de Alfaro, the Governor, perhaps at the prompting of the Jesuits, forbade Spaniards to force the Indians to work the yerbales, but he was ignored.*

Without an alternative to chicha the Jesuits also gathered their yerba from Mbaracuyurú. The care they took of their Indians can be traced in the ordinances of the Provincials : stores had to be carefully checked before the caravans left the

---

* The Spaniards treated their Indians as all but slaves. Bands went out for six months at a time either with trains of ox-wagons and mules or on flat-bottomed rafts propelled by six to ten men in the manner of a punt. From their final camp they went in search of the yerbales or forests of *caa* trees, in shape and formation like an orange tree but larger. While some of the party cut the boughs, those at the base camp built a *barbacoa*, a large grid-iron of beams on which the boughs brought in from the forest were toasted for twenty-four hours. After this the leaves were placed on the ground and beaten to powder with sticks. This produced the *yerba de palos*, so called because it was partly made up of leaf stems.

Reductions: 500 to 1,000 head of cattle were taken, and an additional herd of 250 oxen to draw the loaded carts on the return journey, six pairs for each cart because of the difficulties of the forest track.

Eventually, to ease the burden of the Indians, the Jesuits tried to grow yerba trees near the Reductions. The plant was acclimatized only with the greatest difficulty. Cardiel writes of the tedious efforts to make the transferred seed take root: 'Finally after much experimenting it was found that only a dried-up gumless tree was produced. Then by transferring the tender shoots from a forcing bed to a second shelter and leaving them there until they became stronger, they were prepared for the final planting. Two or three years of careful watering and they began to grow; the yerba became full grown only at the end of eight or ten years.'[19]

The process, in fact, was even more complex: the seed, which was glutinous, had first to be washed thoroughly, and the ground in which it was sown drenched and rendered almost muddy; the seed had to be sown deep; when transplanted, a ditch two feet deep and two broad had to be dug to retain water and the plants placed singly in the middle; then a fence was erected to protect them from the frost and from the south wind.[20]

By 1670 yerba grew in some towns. It was of very poor quality and could be marketed only when the yerba of Mbaracuyurú was exhausted. But from the beginning of the eighteenth century it began at last to improve. Between 1740 and 1747 nearly all the Reductions had their own yerbales. By the middle of the century no yerba in Paraguay could compare with that of the Reductions. Their cultivated yerba, known as *caaminí*, was preferred to the uncultivated *yerba de palos*, especially in Peru, the largest market. It was also sold at twice the price of *yerba de palos*. It was prepared with infinite care. The Indians first removed the leaf stems and larger fibres, using only the tender parts of the leaves. They did not reduce the leaves to complete dust as the Spaniards did. They therefore retained a fragrance lost in the *yerba de palos*. As a refinement the Jesuits sprinkled their yerba with the rind or leaves of a fruit, the *quabiri mirí*, which doubled its flavour. In parching the yerba the Jesuits took care that it retained something of its glutinous character. The result was a 'nectar relished by every rank, age and sex, and is to the people of Peru what chocolate, Chinese tea and spirits are to other nations'.[21] Jealousies were inevitable. The Spaniards could hope to sell their crop to Peru only after the Jesuit quota was exhausted. To avoid tension the Reductions nearest Asunción produced only *yerba de palos*, the rest *caaminí*; some, like Santo Tomé and San Carlos, had their yerbales at a great distance away in the province of Corrientes.

By the mid-eighteenth century, the value of the Jesuit yerbales was considerable. Over 200,000 trees had been planted in the thirty Guaraní towns, each valued at five pesos.[22] But owing to the restriction on the sale of their yerba this wealth could not be realized.

It was not surprising that the Spaniards with their slave labour failed in their attempts to cultivate the yerba. The testimony of Cardiel is amusing: he writes: 'The Spaniards, seeing our yerbales, tried to imitate them on their own estates. . . . I gave them seed and directions; but they never had any success in spite of the fact that their lands in Paraguay are much better adapted to its cultivation than the other territory which we till.'[23]

Neither the Spaniards nor the Jesuits exported yerba to Europe: shipping space was needed for hides; moreover the yerba spoilt after a few years, losing its flavour: in this condition the Paraguayans used it to dye their clothes black.

Later it was said in Europe that the Jesuits had gained a monopoly of yerba. In fact, only the Spaniards traded in it without restriction. But they were short-sighted. The fortunes of the country could have been built on yerba and on the export of mules to Peru and Chile. Rightly, Dobrizhoffer observed that 'the few opulent men' in the country in his time were yerba merchants, other products were 'attended with infinite labour and little or uncertain profit'.[24] But the Spaniards were improvident. Instead of pruning the branches, as the Jesuits did, they felled the entire tree, consequently the yerba became more scarce every year. On the other hand in the Reductions whole forests grew up: the old trees continued, while fresh saplings were planted. In the year of the Jesuits' expulsion, in the three nurseries on the estancia of San Javier alone, the inventories listed 55,868 saplings waiting transplantation.[25] It is easy to see how in the circumstances yerba might be considered a Jesuit monopoly. Moreover, apart from its superior quality, the Reduction yerba was far more accessible and therefore more cheaply produced. After payment of their tribute to the Crown, the Indians had wealth over to extend and decorate their churches and improve their houses. Consequently the last decades of Jesuit rule saw an ambitious programme of public and domestic building which was incomplete when they left.

The economic future of Paraguay might have been different if the Jesuit forests had been maintained: they were the wealth, such as it was, of the Reductions, and the basis of their economic viability. A true picture can perhaps be drawn if a comparison is made with the cost of maintaining the Indian reservations in the United States: in 1874, just a century after the expulsion of the Jesuits from Paraguay, it amounted to 92 million dollars. Far from receiving a subsidy from the State, the Reductions, besides paying their per capita tribute, maintained all their buildings, equipped, trained and kept in the field a large force of auxiliary troops, and paid for all their imports from the restricted amount of yerba they were allowed to sell.

Certainly the Spaniards who passed through the Reductions gathered an impression of great wealth. The churches, the stone houses of the Indians, the paved streets, were splendid by comparison with Asunción; there were tanneries and workshops of different kinds; the storehouses were full of grain, the estancias were well stocked. Moreover, in a country where industry scarcely existed, the Reductions had small but thriving factories. There were ten to twenty looms at least in each town, as many as thirty-eight in Yapeyú: visitors could see at work highly trained and skilful carpenters, goldsmiths, masons, sculptors, stone-cutters, bell-founders, calligraphers, instrument makers, engravers, copyists, even armourers. Each man had been apprenticed and in turn transmitted his skill to others. The development was mainly in the eighteenth century, thanks to the influx of German, Czech and Swiss priests.

This was prosperity rather than wealth. The expenses of most Reductions accounted for almost the entire income. When the Reductions were taken over, no money was found, for there was no currency, apart from the yerba; no mines, no treasures except in the churches and estancia chapels. Cunninghame Graham writes: 'The Jesuits did not conduct the missions after the fashion of a business concern, but rather as the rulers of some Utopia—those foolish beings who think happiness preferable to wealth.'[26] Even in the principal Jesuit establishment, the College at Córdoba, the revenue from the estancias of Santa Catalina and Alta Gracia were insufficient to meet expenses.[27] In the Guaraní towns, when the account books were seized, it was found that several Reductions were in debt. Santa María was an exception: 'This town', runs the inventory,[28] 'owes nothing to any other town . . . nor to any person. Other towns owe this one 341 pesos, five reals and one cuartillo.''

8

Reduction Life, Medicine, Sickness and Danger

The lay-out of the Jesuit towns followed the instructions set down for all colonial towns by the Council of the Indies. It was the gridiron plan of the Graeco-Roman cities, straight streets intersecting one another at right angles to form rectangular blocks. In medieval times the plan had been abandoned. The first new world settlement to revive the Roman pattern was Mexico City founded in 1524: it happened also to be similar to the pattern of Aztec cities.

The laws governing the building of towns were eventually codified in 1573. The large rectangular square, the town centre, was to be sited on elevated ground in a healthy, fertile place near ample sources of fuel, timber and fresh water. This plaza with its longer sides at least one and a half times its width, was never to be less than 300 by 200 feet or more than 800 by 300; the four sides were to face the four points of the compass, so that the streets leaving it should not be exposed to the four principal winds: these streets and the streets round the plaza were to have arcades where business could be done. In order to emphasize their importance, the parish church and civic buildings were to occupy an entire side of the square as the temples had done in the pre-Conquest towns.

The houses of the settlers were in the rectangular blocks behind the plaza; and behind these blocks there was an open space of at least three hundred yards for the purposes of defence. Its perimeter was stockaded or walled off and sometimes also trenched. Beyond the stockade were the pasture and farm lands.

After a town had been marked out, the settlers were to plant their crops and construct their houses, which had to be 'of one form for the adornment of the town' : each had its patio and its corral backed against its neighbour's for mutual protection. In the first settlements walls were of adobe and roofs of straw or palm : later, stone replaced adobe and decoration was added—cornices, paved floors, iron grilles reminiscent of the mother country. This pattern was followed in Buenos Aires as well as in the Jesuit towns.[1]

Because of their remoteness, the Jesuit towns developed minor characteristics that distinguished them from Spanish settlements : the central plaza was commonly a regular square, not a rectangle. This can be seen in the surviving missionary towns of Paraguay like Santa Rosa and Santiago and as clearly in the engraving of Candelaria reproduced by Peramás : in the centre of the great square, each side of which measured 400 feet, is a statue of Our Lady, the patron of the township. The blocks of houses are ninety feet in length; on the right of the church the cemetery and a house for widows and orphaned girls, on the left the residence of the two priests in charge of the Reduction : it was built round a patio, and beside it, occupying an identical space, was another patio with warehouses and workshops. The Candelaria plan can be seen with some small differences in the reconstructed missions of Ignacio Miní (Argentina) and Cosme y Damián (Paraguay). San José in Chiquitos preserves an intact façade of the collegial side of the square : in the centre is a cross hewn from a single piece of stone.

The first Jesuits gained their expertise in the ill-fated Guairá mission : there are extant descriptions, among the earliest of South American provincial towns, of San Ignacio and Loreto in Guairá.[2] The streets were straight, all the same in length, the houses utilitarian and graceful, each with its corral where the Indians kept their hens, geese and domesticated birds. At their triennial meetings priests from all the missions pooled their experience; newcomers, especially the Swiss and Bohemians at the end of the seventeenth century, wrote home in astonishment at what they saw. Later still Dobrizhoffer found Asunción in spite of its imposing situation a dingy place compared with Candelaria, the Guaraní capital: no fine buildings, no houses above one storey high, untidy streets obstructed by ditches, a single grass-covered market, no proper seat either for the bishop or governor; and the people spoke neither correct Spanish nor correct Guaraní, but a kind of third dialect.[3]

For reasons of health the Jesuits always adhered to the recommendation that towns should be built on elevated ground: 'This also had the convenience', as one Jesuit pointed out,[4] 'that the rains and other waters were carried into the river.' The later missions of the Paraguay Jesuits in the province of Chiquitos ran along a ridge of high ground; in the Chaco they were spaced on convenient eminences above the river Salado.

In the Jesuit towns, crosses, still to be seen in the Chiquitos, were planted in the four corners of the Plaza; in the centre there was either a fountain, a statue of the patron saint or a fifth larger cross. At San Ignacio Miní, where the whole township can be traced, the plaza was 127 yards by 108; the houses in equal groups of six or seven are separated by uniform streets two and a half yards in width; the verandah stretching the length of the houses enabled the Indians to cross the town to the church or the priests' house sheltered from the rain or sun.

In all the Reductions the priests' house and the church occupied an entire side of the plaza: adjoining the house were the store houses for grain, yerba mate, cotton and other provisions, as well as the workshops for the different trades. The whole compound was surrounded by a wall about twenty feet high.

Only the priests' house had two floors, each with a verandah. The projecting roof was supported on columns to form an open and spacious hall below. The gardens in the rear extended the entire length of the enclosure and in some places also behind the church and cemetery. The cemetery was usually on the far side of the church from the priests' house. This pattern, set out clearly in Padre Torres's instructions to the Fathers appointed to Guairá in 1609, can be seen today in the ruins of Ignacio Miní: the walled-in burial ground, planted with oranges, cypresses and palms, was an innovation in South America, where hitherto all Christians had been interred within the walls of the church. In the same area also were the arsenal, the guest house, and in some Reductions the gaol, the hospital and the widows' home.

Antonio Sepp describes how his garden at Yapeyú was divided into sections for flowers, herbs, vegetables and fruit:

> In the kitchen garden grow all the year round diverse sorts of salep, herbs, endive, curled and not curled, chicory, roots, parsnips, turnips, spinach, radishes, cabbages, carrots, beetroots, parsley, aniseed, fennel, coriander, melons, cucumbers and diverse sorts of Indian roots; in my physic garden I have mint, rue, rosemary, pimpernel, sweet marjoram, etc.; my flower garden produces lilies, Indian lilies, yellow and blue violets, poppies and many sorts of Indian flowers. In my orchard I have apple and pear and hazel nut trees, but these last two will bear no fruit here though they grow very lofty; peaches, pomegranates, sweet and sour lemons, citrons, vanilla and diverse other Indian fruit.[5]

In this garden Sepp spent his leisure, or he would cross to an island, a stone's throw from the bank, to enjoy the cooler air with a group of his musicians or to paint. Sepp loved the Uruguay, the size of the Danube at Yapeyú, 'its waters so wholesome that you may drink as much as you please even after eating melons, peaches and figs, without receiving the least harm'.

By comparison with the Indians' dwellings, the priests' house was palatial; its furnishings, on the other hand, were more simple than a peasant's cottage in Europe. On the expulsion of the Jesuits a complete inventory of the contents of all the presbyteries was taken. In Ignacio Miní, for instance, the list includes these items only—eight mattresses, nine bedsteads and pillows, twelve candlesticks, six snuffers, seven tables, the same number of bookshelves, twenty chairs, three clocks and four bed-pans.[6] In Nuestra Señora de Fe the

inventory was made according to apartments: in the room
of each of the two priests there was one table, one bookshelf,
one mattress, one washbasin, 'curtained off for decency', and
three chairs.[7] An interesting regulation of the Provincial forbade paintings in private rooms, the refectory or passages—
they could be hung only in the church or sacristy. However,
devotional prints were permitted to priests, but not of princes
and princesses.*

Compared with the libraries in the Colleges of the Paraguay Province, the Reduction libraries were poor: between
250 and 700 books was the average content of their shelves.
Mártires had 382 of which thirty-two were different Guaraní
dictionaries; Candelaria, the capital, a kind of book deposit
from which the Paraná Fathers could draw 3,719 books, without taking into account another 503 in the rooms of the Cura,
his assistant and the Provincial. San Juan Bautista among the
Isistine Indians in the Chaco had a curious mélange: *Nuevo
Régimen de la Navegación*, the *Geografía de Schelton*, the
Guerras de Flandes and eleven volumes of Mariana's *Historia
de España*.[8]

It would seem that soon after 1715 all the missions had
their widows' home. At San Juan across the Uruguay, the
Provincial the previous year had ordered the construction of
a 'good, strong and commodious house where widows and
orphans can be taken in and also the wives of those who have
fled the pueblo'.[9]

In 1691 the only difference Sepp found in the Jesuit
Paraná towns from those of Europe was the simplicity of the
Indians' houses: at San Miguel they were constructed like
huts on bare ground with adobe walls and straw roofs (a few
only had been recently tiled) without chimneys or windows.
The door, made of oxhide about six spans high and three
broad, let in the only light. In the interior space father,
mother and children lived together along with three or four
dogs and as many cats—all in the same five or six square

---

* Finely coloured and engraved maps showing the position of the
missions were printed at intervals of about thirty years in the Reduction
presses. The Custom Book forbade prints of royalty in order not to
emphasize national differences among priests drawn from so many parts
of Europe.

metres. The smoke and stench nauseated priests fresh from Europe on occasions when they visited the sick. Most Indians slept on an oxhide or jaguar skin spread on the floor, a few only in a hammock fastened to posts above the hearth used in daytime for cooking. Interior furnishings were sparse: 'Their kitchen consists of two or three pots or pans; the hand serves instead of a spoon, the teeth in lieu of knives, the five fingers serve for forks';[10] sometimes there were a chest or two for clothes, some scooped-out pumpkins used for mugs, occasionally a rough chair, perhaps two: for the most part they squatted cross-legged round the fire that burned day and night. There were no locks or bolts on their houses. Thieving, except from the presbytery orchard, was unknown.

San Miguel was one of the poor townships. In 1714 the Provincial left instructions for the improvement of living conditions there: all other constructional work was to be suspended while decent dwellings were put up for the Indians: this was to be done 'with care so that it should not be necessary to tear down and rebuild or repair every year: stone was to be used. And because the need for housing is extreme, in order to carry out the work speedily, we will allow the Indians to work on holy days, a third part of the people working in shifts of a week or fifteen days.' The Provincial, familiar with the natural indolence of the Indians, urged the Fathers to keep them at work.

From the Provincial's notes it is clear that conditions at San Miguel were exceptional. Already before the end of the seventeenth century tiles, which were rare in the Spanish towns, were becoming common in the Reductions. 'Formerly,' wrote Sepp, 'they used also to bring tiles from Potosí, but since then we have begun to make our own. I have no less than six long streets in my canton, the huts whereof are covered with tiles.'[11] After the Provincial's visitation in 1714, which marked a rebuilding programme in nearly twenty Reductions, tiles became universal—and stone replaced adobe. The ruins of San Ignacio show three rows of houses on three sides of the plaza, all constructed from blocks of red stone perfectly cut and fitted. French travellers in the mid-eighteenth century commented on the fine masonry of the houses in other Reductions also.[12] In 1826 Dr Rugger, a Swiss visitor to Trinidad in Paraguay, commented that 'the houses from the Jesuit period were in cut stone and roofed with tiles, while the later buildings were of clay and straw'. All the streets were paved and arcaded though at the time there were still only dirt streets in Asunción.[13]

Even in the less developed Chiquitos towns and the neighbouring Mojos missions that belonged to the Jesuits of Peru, the Indian houses stood up well. A traveller visiting the Mojos town of Exaltación in 1868 had to admit that the Jesuits made the most of the poor materials available and put up houses which 'have resisted the storms of a century and a half and have been well adapted to their needs and the climate'. What impressed him was the residual vitality of these remote buildings : 'We expected every moment to see one of the padres appear from out of the dark background of the grey weather-beaten colonnade.'[14] Here he drew a sketch of the pueblo more than a century after the Jesuits had been expelled : in his own words the impression was a 'rather dreary one; large grass-grown streets bordered by mouldering house-posts, showing the former importance of the place and leading to a lonely plaza'. The low white-washed cottages, as in all the established Jesuit townships, had projecting roofs supported by wooden (or stone) columns and forming a continuous verandah. Only a few of them had the luxury of a small window, shut with a wooden grate; the rest, even at this time, had still no opening but the door.[15]

Dilapidation was often hastened by plagues of ants that burrowed beneath houses and even the church : the burrows they left after migration filled with water, causing the beams supporting the roof and walls to give way. 'This was a common spectacle in Paraguay,' writes Dobrizhoffer,[16] 'The whole of the hill on which San Joachín was built was covered with ant-hills and full of subterranean cavities . . . The high altar was rendered useless for many days for, it being rainy weather, the lurking ants flew in swarms from their caves, and not being able to support a long flight, fell upon the priest, the altar and the sacred utensils, defiling everything.' The floor of the church began to gape, the walls to crack and incline. Dobrizhoffer, rushing into the church, sank to his shoulders in a pit where the high altar had stood : 'the cavern had the appearance of a wine cellar' and as quickly as earth was thrown in by the Indians it was dug out by the ants. Eventually the church was saved by props set against its walls.

Toads were a minor pest and inflicted all towns alike. At Concepción on the Salado 'the streets became as slippery as ice' with swarms of them : they filled the chapel and house, falling from the roof on to the priests' beds and tables. 'In the colony of Rosario which I founded on the banks of a lake,' continues Dobrizhoffer,[17] 'there was the same abundance of toads. Whilst I performed divine service, the chapel swarmed with them, and though many were slain every hour of the day, for two years their number seemed to increase rather than diminish.'

There was a species of toad, larger than anything found in Europe, called by the Spanish *escuerzo*, that was dangerous as well as troublesome : when provoked it would squirt its urine; if the least drop of this liquid entered the eye, it immediately caused blindness : also its saliva, blood and gall were poisonous. An indefatigable researcher into natural history, Dobrizhoffer noted : 'We learn from creditable authors that the Brazilian savages roast toads and then reduce them to powder, which they infuse into the meat or drink of their enemies to cause them death; for it occasions a dryness or inflammation of the throat, together with vomiting, hiccups, sudden fainting, delirium, severe pains in the joints and stomach, and sometimes dysentery.'

Often there was no more than one priest in residence. The custom was for two to work each Reduction : one remained at home while the other made excursions into the countryside, visiting the sick, bringing into the township Indians still in the forest, saying Mass in the outlying chapels, visiting the estancias. It was laid down that the cura should visit neighbouring estancias twice a year; if the estancias were remote the assistant could be delegated on the second occasion.[18] 'Whenever any pressing occasion called, the neighbouring missionaries gave each other mutual help.'[19] The assistant was ordinarily the priest more recently appointed to the Reduction: his first task was to learn the language. At the end of three months he was permitted to hear confessions after an examination in Guaraní by a board of four priests appointed by the Provincial.[20]

When long distances could be covered by water, the Fathers used the Indian canoes which they adapted to their needs: two tree-trunks, about seventy or eighty feet long, were fastened a few feet apart, and the interstices filled to a depth of two feet with canes cut in twelve-foot lengths. On this a hut of straw, covered with an ox-hide, was erected: there was a small window on one side, a door on another. 'In these huts the missionaries divert themselves during the voyage, with as much satisfaction as if they were in a palace, and perform the same religious exercises as if they were in one of their colleges . . . the Indians rowing very orderly without the least noise.'[21]

River communications with Buenos Aires were open all the year round. One Jesuit, writing in 1715, reckoned that there were at least two thousand canoes from the Reductions in use on the Paraná and almost as many on the Uruguay. But there was also an excellent road system, based on Candelaria, the capital, and far superior to the tracks which were the only thoroughfares in the rest of the country until the end of the nineteenth century; the old Fathers travelled in coaches drawn by oxen, taking with them scores of caged hens to eat on the way; the younger Fathers preferred to ride, catch partridges and vary their diet with ostrich eggs. Roads ran to Corrientes and Asunción, others from Yapeyú to the Salto Grande, the main fall of the Guairá Falls on the upper Paraná. On the upper Uruguay were about eighty posts, all guarded and with horses ready to equip messengers. 'But', as Cunninghame Graham writes,[22] 'there were also roads in the district of the upper Paraná, which I myself remember as a wilderness, uncrossed, uncrossable, where tigers roamed about and Indians shot at the rare traveller with poisoned arrows out of a blow pipe whilst they remained unseen in the recesses of the woods.'

The maintenance of the roads was shared among the

Reductions. At San Borja on 21 June 1731 the Provincial called the attention of the Fathers to the need to repair bridges and roadside chapels; then, some months later when he was visiting Candelaria, 'there was a discussion on building a bridge over the river Igurupa, about a league from the town. Because frequent crossings must be made there is need of a stone bridge.'[23] A design of Primoli, the Milanese Jesuit, was accepted and the expense divided among the pueblos.*

The greatest distance between any two Reductions, 346 miles, separated San Ignacio Guazú and Yapeyú, but to the south and east of the seven towns established across the Uruguay were vast estancias extending almost to the Atlantic. The country produced every kind of South American fruit; it had ample pastures for innumerable cattle. After life in the forest in daily search of fresh venison, the Indians could experience plenty. The territory was well peopled; everywhere there rose houses for shepherds and farm workers; on the estancias and at resting-places on the road between them small chapels were built.† Here the Indians gathered for prayer on holy days when they were unable to attend their own churches. One Flemish priest wrote that the painters of his native land, with all their inventiveness, could produce nothing to compare with the natural beauty of this country.

Antonio Sepp, the Cura of Yapeyú early in the late seventeenth century, wrote to his family that his tasks would engage seven or eight priests in Europe.[24] Apart from overseeing the temporal administration, he and an assistant were responsible for the spiritual welfare of seven or eight thousand persons, little able to help themselves. He writes: 'Every morning, an hour before break of day, one of my boys awakens me, and sets up a candle, for we have no oil for lamps: the sanctuary lamp in the church is fed with tallow.'

* None of these bridges survive. Primoli, one of the builders of Buenos Aires cathedral, was perhaps the most distinguished architect of the La Plata region. Cf. inf. p. 230.
† None of these chapels survive in the area of the Guaraní Reductions; but there are a number in the province of Córdoba, gems of South American architecture, built by the Jesuits who worked also among the Guaraní. Cf. Illustration, p. 141.

After his private devotions in church, he attended the confessional. Mass followed and more confessions:

> then I instruct the children in the catechism, visit the sick, and if necessary, hear their confessions and give them holy communion and extreme unction, and, if it is not too late, prescribe medicines; and since hardly a day passes without somebody dying, I have daily burials. After the sick I visit the offices; first the school, where the boys are instructed in reading and writing and the girls in spinning and needlework; I also visit my musicians, singers, trumpets, hautboys, etc. On certain days I instruct some Indians in dancing . . . After that I go among the workmen, to the brick-makers and tile-makers, the bakers, smiths, joiners, carpenters, painters, and above all the butchers who kill fifteen or sixteen oxen a day.

All this was done between rising and nine-thirty. If there was time over, Sepp spent it in the garden. At nine-thirty he sent out the meals to the sick, meat, white bread and milk. Then about ten-thirty a boy rang a bell for *examen conscientiae*, 'Then I lock myself up in my room for a quarter of an hour and go to dinner.'

At table, as in Jesuit houses in Europe, a well-taught boy read a chapter of the Bible in Latin and a passage of the *Legenda Sanctorum* in Spanish; a second boy read the *Martyrology* for the day in Latin. If his companion was present, Sepp spent half an hour in recreation. At twelve-thirty both priests recited the Litany of the Saints: 'And what spare time is left after that until two, I spend as I please, for instance, in making statues, composing some musical pieces, etc.' When the two o'clock bell rang for the Indians to return to their work, he again visited the sick. 'At four o'clock we have prayers, then we bury the dead which happens daily.' After supper taken at seven, half an hour was spent in some 'diversion', then the priests retired for a rest, which was 'frequently interrupted by the urgent needs of the sick'.

The visit of priests from other townships was made the

occasion of special fare. Venison was always plentiful: deer, wild boar, goats, pigeons and partridges 'so numerous and tame that you can knock them down with a stick'; honey was used for dressing in place of oil and vinegar; fish was abundant, caught by the Indians in their hand or with a bent nail serving as a hook: European species were uncommon but there were plentiful and 'delicious Indian fish, the king's fish among the choicest'. It had no bones and could be caught only in winter.[25]

Every Sunday and Friday there was high Mass and a formal sermon, on holidays first Vespers were sung: 'Every Sunday at three o'clock I baptize infants: of these I have christened several hundred in a short time; some of them are dead, others alive.' On Saturdays marriages were performed, sometimes eight couples at a time; on the first day of the month there was a requiem Mass for deceased Indians;[26] in Lent there were additional services, and in holy week processions with floats as in the cities of Spain.

In the larger townships the children to be taught the catechism numbered sometimes two thousand;[27] but it was the care of the sick that was the most continuous burden: in a township of seven to eight thousand the priests were fortunate if there were fewer than two hundred confined to their homes.[28] Apart from the regular visiting mentioned by Sepp, medicines had to be prescribed and prepared. Three or four towns had Jesuit brothers tolerably skilled in medicine, but they were seldom able to visit other towns when most needed.

Visitors to the Reductions were impressed by the general good health of the Indians and also by their cleanliness: their washing and toilet facilities were far in advance of anything found in the Spanish towns. At Ignacio Guazú there are remains of a tunnel six feet high and three across leading down to the river: it was flushed regularly by buckets of water brought up from the stream on pulleys. In other places streams were diverted to cleanse the toilets. Danger of infection was minimal.

The only chronic trouble affecting the Indians was worms induced by the large amount of semi-raw meat they consumed. It affected them mainly in the coldest season, June. Frequently they died of it. The remedy devised by the priests was an emetic produced from tobacco leaves, 'all bitter things', noted Sepp,[29] 'being at enmity with worms'. After vomiting, the Indian was given a drink of cow's milk into which was squeezed the juice of a sour lemon, mixed with some rue and mint and then strained before it was administered.

On occasion the Indians also fell victims to measles or 'spotted fever' : it raged at intervals. At the Guaraní town of St Joaquín, out of two thousand Indians, notes Dobrizhoffer,[30] 'so many were laid up with this disorder that often none was left to supply the sick with food, water, wood and medicines'. With his companion, Padre Fleischauer, Dobrizhoffer was occupied day and night with the sick : two hundred persons died : few infants and no old men, but mostly persons 'in the flower of their age'.

Smallpox in the La Plata basin was more devastating among the Indians than any plague in Europe. In the Jesuit period the Indians failed to build up any resistance to it. Recurrent severe epidemics decimated the population : there are no exact figures for the seventeenth century,* but in 1733 the Jesuits counted 12,933 victims among children alone; in 1737 there were more than 30,000 deaths, a figure equivalent to the total population of several Reductions.[31] Among the Indians, only the tribes of the Chaco recovered after catching it. The epidemic of 1765, the last recorded by the Jesuits, 'having swept away twelve thousand people in thirty Guaraní towns,' writes Dobrizhoffer,[32] 'spread to the distant hordes of the savages scattered throughout Chaco, and though almost all took the infection, yet few died in proportion to the number of the sick. . . . In the town which I founded for the Abipones, one woman only escaped the contagion, yet out of the many hundreds who took the disease, twenty alone fell victims to it.'

In 1730, Cajetan Cattaneo, newly arrived from Europe, while making his way upriver from Buenos Aires to Candelaria, found the Indians of the forest lying sick in

* There were epidemics in 1618, 1619, 1635, 1636 and 1692.

heaps. They scarcely had the appearance of human beings. When a victim was drawn by his legs out of his cabin to be buried 'the skin slipped off from the flesh and this was all that was left in the hands of the Christians who undertook this charitable office'.[33] All savage Indians who had been abandoned in the neighbourhood of the estancias or Reductions were brought in : the dying had also to be given some rudimentary Christian instruction before receiving baptism. 'They die in their thousands,' one priest wrote, 'and whatever care is taken, they are generally carried off in a few days. Every house becomes a hospital : the sick lie on the ground, their bedding is a deer's skin and a calico coverlet or, at best, a hammock. More than once infidels have flocked in crowds to the Reductions . . . and have been brought to embrace Christianity' by the impression made on them by the priests' behaviour.[34]

While the Jesuits found remedies for most illnesses, they could do no more than meet smallpox with mainly herbal concoctions : in the place of drugs they used sulphur, alum, salt (a rare commodity), tobacco, sugar, pepper, the fat of hens, jaguars and sheep; and also gunpowder.[35] They were ineffective except in mild cases.

But when diseases other than smallpox afflicted the Indians, the Jesuits' medicine undoubtedly saved many lives. Their remedies were partly Indian, partly European, always pragmatic. Without money to pay for imported drugs, the priests devised cures from material at hand : shrubs, trees, the intestines or other parts of wild animals. No doubt a number of prescriptions had been introduced into Paraguay by the first missionary party, including Fields, from Bahia. The stimulus to research there had been given by St Ignatius : in answer to their scruple as to whether priests should practise medicine, the founder of the Society of Jesus firmly stated that charity should extend itself to everything.

It was discovered, for instance, that the intestines of the cayman or South American crocodile, dried and reduced to powder, gave instant relief from stones and quartan ague; the flesh of the *vacuna*, a species of hornless goat, with a dark-yellow silken skin, provided a cure for gout and kidney pains: the priests applied the skin externally but the Indians ate the flesh, which was unsavoury to the European palate; in the high Andes the Indians cured snow-blindness by the application of the vacuna's flesh.

The water-hog, larger than a mastiff, with ears like an ass's and a loud nocturnal roar, was fairly common in the plains near the Paraná: it had even more medical uses than the vacuna: its very soft hair was found to assuage sciatica, gout and all bowel pains; laid on the saddle it generated a heat that was 'extremely beneficial'; but some Jesuit infirmarians considered the iguana still more useful. Described by Dobrizhoffer as a kind of lizard, sometimes an ell and a half long, 'resembling the dragon St George is represented as overthrowing',[36] it often produced in its head little stones which, ground to powder and swallowed with water or even applied to the body, could dislodge blockages in the kidney. Others claimed (Dobrizhoffer is careful not to commit himself) that 'a stone, an ounce in weight, found in some other part of the animal's body, powdered and drunk in tepid water, removes obstructions of the bladder'. Dobrizhoffer recommended the iguana's white flesh as very savoury: it fed largely on a diet of honey, small birds' eggs, oranges, sweet citrons and other fruit: he also enjoyed eating the animal's eggs fried.

The anta or the great beast, a species of South American antelope, was the last animal used in the Jesuit pharmacies. In size it resembled a full-grown ass, with a snout like a pig's, short ears, sharp teeth, cloven forefeet. It was usually found asleep in the day: its stomach pouch contained a bezoar stone* which the Indians believed far more effective than the stones found in other animals: it was used by them for multiple purposes. The Spaniards valued only the anta nails which they exported to Europe as a cure for epilepsy, smallpox and measles: the belief in their efficacy was based on the supposition that the anta itself was liable to these diseases.

Both priests and Indians were surer of themselves in the practice of arboreal medicine. The discovery of quinine commonly credited to the Jesuits—it was known in Europe

* A small stone, sometimes containing calcium phosphate, formed by undigested mineral matter eaten by animals when grazing.

as Jesuits' bark—was made by the Incas: the Peruvian Jesuits did no more than make its properties widely known and introduce it to Europe in 1650.

Similarly in the Paraná region, the Guaraní had from pre-Conquest times extracted a resin from the long, thick roots of the jalap tree: it flowed copiously under a hot sun and was used very effectively to cure bile, rheum and similar troubles.

The amount of beef consumed by the Indian made frequent purges a necessity. A gentle purge, tasteless and looking like flour, and harmless for children, was made from the root of the mechoachan, easily recognizable by its convolvulus-like flower; a stronger one, which the Jesuits prescribed with caution, was derived from the *piñon de Paraguay*, commonly called the cathartic nut: it was also used to produce vomiting. Yet another purge, between these two in strength, was obtained from the rind of the tamarind, a species of plum.

Some of the most common South American trees produced a variety of medicines: for example, the sassafras, with laurel-like leaves and blackish fruit, was used to provoke perspiration and urine, also to heal syphilis, obstructions of the bowel and disorders of the womb; a hard wood from the broad, stocky holy tree was used to stop dysentery: it grew only in the Paraguayan Chaco in the areas claimed as their own by the Mocobíes; in the rest of the country the resinous bark of the guayacan tree was used for that purpose: it was hard and made up of several layers of skin and spotted grey; where this was unavailable the juice of the mangaỹ served— it was the size of a cherry tree and had a golden-coloured fruit.

The remedy for sore eyes was taught by the Indians—the *zamu*, or as the Spaniards called it, the *palo borracho* or drunken tree, that grew to a great height from a barrel-shaped trunk surrounded by thorns which were ground to a healing powder; and a similar tree, the *zuyñandỹ*, had a bark that was used in treating wounds made by the teeth of a jaguar.

The tall *cupay*, not to be confused with the *corupaỹ*, a spongy wood unfit for any use, and the *corupicaỹ*, used for dressing oxhides, found only in the northern forest of Paraguay, with leaves a foot in length, yielded an abundance of excellent oil the colour of water. It stopped very quickly the flow of blood from open wounds; it was also used to heal snake-bites and remove scars; in the form of a plaster it relieved languor of the stomach; two or three drops swallowed with a boiled egg stopped dysentery and, mixed with garlic, brightened pictures better than any varnish and without any darkening through time. In the church and sacristy its natural oil was used for giving statues a flesh colouring. Bruises and extravasation yielded to water boiled with the shavings of cedar wood and drunk with an infusion of quinine. The white Paraguayan algaroba, different from the European species, was covered with a soft yellow skin and its seeds had a pleasanter taste : pounded into a mortar and left to ferment for twelve hours it effervesced with its own natural heat and became a sharp and wholesome tonic. To this drink Dobrizhoffer ascribed the uncommon toughness and longevity of the Abipones, as well as the robustness of their horses and oxen. It was found in abundance in the Chaco near the Santiago mission, but not in the region of the Paraná. 'The algaroba', continues Dobrizhoffer,[37] 'affords not only meat, drink and medicine, but also excellent materials for building wagons, houses and ships.' The black Paraguayan algaroba served to remove stones and stranguary; and the pods of a third species produced a sudorific potion which, according to another writer,[38] would cure many persons who in England could not be restored to health without the aid of salivation.

The generation of the Irishman, Thomas Fields, knew little of pharmaceutical medicine, though sometimes the remedies they prescribed were effective. When in 1616 virtually the whole township of San Ignacio Guazú went sick with influenza, Padre Juan de Salas concocted a syrup which healed them.[39] A short time later, when Padre Altamirano was Provincial, a central apothecary store was established in the capital, Candelaria : the textbook used was the *De Medicina* of the Spanish brother, Diego Basauri, who had been infirmarian at the Jesuit College of Asunción for fifteen years. Though not a trained doctor, he acquired through practice much medical skill; he gathered Indian recipes and added others of his own. On his death in 1629, his place was taken by a Portuguese brother, Francisco Couto, an able nurse based on San Ignacio Guazú and loaned for periods to other towns which happened to be suffering an epidemic.

Among several, two other seventeenth-century infirmarians should be named: Juan de Montes and Domingo Torres. Montes seems to have studied medicine and practised surgery in Europe before becoming a Jesuit: his death in 1687, followed in the next year by Torres's, was recorded as a great loss to the Jesuits; Torres was an enthusiastic herbalist. As late as 1733 he is named in an instruction of the Provincial to all priests: 'There is available in the Archives of the Reductions at Candelaria, deposited there long ago by Padre Christóbal Altamirano, a list of medicines made out on the advice of Brother Domingo Torres.' The Provincial recommended strongly the old prescriptions of Torres.

On his arrival in 1693, Sepp was astonished at the pharmaceutical skill acquired by the missionaries, and still more by the medical services available to the Indians.

In the mid-seventeenth century each town had its own hospital, but long before Sepp's arrival permanent hospitals had been judged unnecessary. In times of smallpox or other contagious diseases, sick-bays were improvised. In some towns, for instance Mártires and Candelaria, the staff was provided by members of the Sodality, who made the beds, swept the floors, scrubbed the pots and dishes. But at other times the sick were cared for in their own houses: the Indians were attached to their homes and disliked being taken to hospital.

Infirmarians always accompanied the military on its expeditions. In another recommendation, dated February 1680, Padre Christóbal Altamirano instructed each Reduction sending a contingent to dislodge the Portuguese from the island of San Gabriel, to provide infirmarians equipped with the ordinary medicines, and also with enemas, cupping-glasses, lancets, lint, bandages, salt, sulphur, gunflint, honey and twelve hammocks for the wounded.

While each town had its infirmarian, there were only two doctors for all the Paraná and Uruguay Reductions, stationed at Candelaria and San Nicolás; there was a third for the Chiquitos. Brother Enrico Adami, a Milanese doctor, who died as the result of an attempt to find a way upriver from Asunción to Chiquitos, was an enthusiastic advocate of *yerba vara dorada* which, he claimed, had well-proven curative properties. In the same school was Brother Pedro Montenegro, probably the greatest pharmaceutical botanist of Jesuit Paraguay: he wrote several works in both Spanish and Guaraní: only two have survived, a book on surgery and another entitled *Properties and Virtues of the Trees in the Mission Provinces and Tucumán*, the most quoted work on herbalist medicine of the period.

These men belonged to the school of naturalists founded by Ruiz de Montoya, who devoted three chapters of his *Conquista Espiritual* to animals and one to herbs. But the most comprehensive work came at the end of the period, in 1773, with Padre Pedro Lozano's *Descripción Chorográfica de Gran Chaco Gualamba*: it included a historical study of the great epidemic of 1589; he noted its symptoms with great wealth of detail, charted its recurrence, and gave his opinion on the remedies proposed by the different schools of doctors. In a more practical sphere, Padre Segismundo Aperger was reckoned one of the best physicians of his day: contemporaries refer to him as the Hippocrates of South America.

In this company a curious Englishman, Thomas Falkner, more than holds his own. The son of a Manchester doctor and herbalist of the same name, and a pupil of Manchester Grammar School, he studied physio-mathematics in London under Newton and anatomy under Professor Richard Mead. At the age of twenty-four he was commissioned by the Royal Society in 1730 to visit the Río Plata and report on the medicinal properties of South American waters and herbs. At the same time the famous South Sea Company, known as *El Asiento* in Spain, named him its physician and surgeon.

The work of the Jesuit herbalists in Paraguay was already well known to the Royal Society. On his arrival in Buenos Aires Falkner frequently visited the Jesuits in the city. After twelve months he became a Catholic. On 14 May 1732 he entered the Jesuit novitiate in Córdoba on completing his task for the Royal Society.* To give him opportunities for further research the Jesuits placed him first in Santiago del Estero, then in Tucumán, Córdoba and Santa Fe. Later he joined an expedition to Patagonia. His work on South American plants owed something to each province. He also discovered medicinal properties in the meat of the *carancho*, a bird of prey belonging to the *Falconidae* family; he devoted some lines to the bird in his *Description of Patagonia*, which became Charles Darwin's guide-book when he explored the coast of South America in the *Beagle*: Darwin considered Falkner correct on all points he checked.[40]

Today, when the jaguar has been nearly exterminated, the accounts of its predations in the Reductions seem unreal. To both Indians and priests it was an ever-present source of dread. The so-called Spanish lion, a larger and stronger beast, was a curiosity to the Jesuit naturalist; unlike the jaguar, it seldom attacked a human being:† the Indians hunted it for sport.

'Jaguars', wrote Sepp from Yapeyú, 'are not only very hurtful to cattle, but also very dreadful to the inhabitants [of the Reductions] who know no other enemy but this. They are seldom far from the canton.' He and others spoke of the vast number infesting the fields, sometimes in troops, attacking calves more often than oxen or cows: 'But if a jaguar happens to catch an ox alone, he leaps upon its back and points him in the first joint of his neck and afterwards tears it open with its claws; when he has a mind to a calf, he watches it as it lies upon the ground and, advancing softly, bites off the head at once and sucks out the blood through the neck.'[41] Their strength was prodigious: meeting in the pastures two horses tied together to prevent their escaping,

* His researches were published and translated into Spanish under the title *Tratado de las enfermedades curadas por drogas amerimanas*.
† The 'lion' (*felis concolor*) was a huge tawny cat, weighing about 80 to 100 lb with a tail 72 to 90 inches long: its head and tail were small in proportion to its body: the early settlers called it a panther, the Incas *puma*; in Brazil it was known as the *onca*. The jaguar (*felis onca*) was called the *tigre* in the Jesuit documents; eight feet long with a thirty-inch tail, it was sometimes mistaken for the leopard, which is not found in the new world.

they would attack and slay one and drag him along with the other, still alive, to their den. 'I should not have believed this,' Dobrizhoffer says, 'had I not myself witnessed it.'[42]

They spared no living creature. Often they entered the townships at night, particularly after or during a storm, to shelter themselves from the rain or cold wind.[43] At Yapeyú a jaguar invaded the priests' garden and attacked a brother from behind : such accidents, Sepp remarked, were frequent.[44] Attracted by the smell of flesh, they stole at night into the Indians' houses, but always finding beef laid out for breakfast they left without attacking the occupants.[45]

At times townships were besieged by packs of jaguars. In 1637, after a plentiful harvest that marked the end of a great famine, jaguars raged through the countryside in great packs clawing and mauling the Indians; they invaded the Reductions, which hurriedly put up defences against them. The worst attack came at an outlying *aldea* belonging to Santo Tomé. Confronted with an 'army' of jaguars, the Indians erected a palisade, behind which they were besieged without respite for four days and nights. When no relief came, they took to prayer. The priest who happened to be with the Indians ordered nine days of intercession, with a solemn Mass each day to musical accompaniment in honour of Our Lady. 'On the ninth day the siege was raised, the beasts dispersed and the Indians made their way back to Santo Tomé proclaiming they owed their deliverance to God.' The respite was brief. The forest tracks and fields remained infested, the township was again attacked, some Christian and many pagan Indians were killed. More than two hundred snares laid in the neighbourhood were ineffective. The Jesuits of Santo Tomé, unable to explain the phenomenon, ascribed it to witchcraft. Only when all the Indians had made a public repudiation of dealings with sorcerers and followed this with a private confession, was the township freed of the plague.[46]

In fact Santo Tomé suffered worse than most towns because the famine had been more acute in that area. For a whole year in the wild country outside Santo Tomé 'there was nothing to be seen except burials and bodies consumed by slow hunger or rather living corpses.' The number of

Indians to be fed then was greater than at later periods, more than 1,000 families. Some 6,000 persons were recent Christians, the rest still pagans, susceptible to witchcraft.[47]

Jaguars remained a danger to the priest on his missionary journeys, although they were constantly hunted—Spaniards and Chaco Indians on horseback used leather thongs, lassooed the beast, then strangled it by dragging it along the ground; the Guaraní Indians preferred the spear and traps. Even on the rivers there was no security; the jaguars were excellent swimmers, and when there was no food to be found in the woods, plunged into the water to catch and eat tortoises; sometimes they boarded the priest's canoe.[48] On land a fire was always kept burning at night, but 'if it goes out', wrote Sepp, 'the tiger will be sure to watch his opportunity' and seize the nearest sleeper to him. This happened on two occasions to Sepp in his first year at Yapeyú.[49] In the Chaco, Dobrizhoffer travelled always with two spearmen who, if he failed to kill the jaguar with his musket, pierced the animal as it leapt to attack. Once, his Indians, passing with him through Spanish-occupied country, left their spears behind so as not to appear distrustful of their newly-won Spanish friendship. Dobrizhoffer writes:

> Travelling with six Mocobíes from the city of Santa Fe to the town of San Javier, I passed the night on the banks of the round lake, in the open air, as usual. The fire, our nightly defence against tigers, shone for a while in the midst of us as we slept but at length grew very low. In the middle of the night a tiger crept towards us. . . . Anticipating no danger, I had neglected to load my musket. At my direction firebrands were dexterously hurled at the approaching tiger. At each throw he lept back roaring, but resumed courage and returned again and again, more threatening than before. Meanwhile I loaded my musket. But as darkness deprived me of all hope of killing the tiger and left me with only the desire to escape, I loaded my musket with plenty of shot and fired it off without a ball. The beast, alarmed at the horrid thundering, instantly fled. . . . The next day at noon in a narrow path, bounded on one

side by a lake and on the other by a wood, we met two tigers which would have been caught by a noose by the pursuing Mocobíes had they not fled and hidden themselves in the wood.[50]

It was the same priest who discovered, possibly from his Indian companions, the best defence against jaguars, namely, urine. 'Direct it into the eyes of a tiger threatening you at the foot of a tree and you are safe : the beast will immediately take to flight.'[51]

9

Government

One of the more remarkable features of the Guaraní Reductions was the high quality of the priests posted there over a century and a half. Mostly they were men who in their home countries would have occupied a university chair or attained eminence in scientific research. But with all their sympathetic understanding of the Guaraní character, their estimate of the Indian's intellectual capacity was universally low. Sepp in his pharmacy found his Indian assistants 'so void of sense and judgement that without constant supervision they would quickly send the patient to the next world'. It was the same in the kitchen where he judged them 'naturally stupid'.[1] Dobrizhoffer was harsher: 'If they don't understand anything immediately they soon grow tired of examining it; sometimes, when puzzled, they cry *tupâ oiquaá*, God knows what it is': they had small reasoning power and smaller inclination to exercise it; to attempt, as the first Jesuits did, to argue from created things to the existence of a Creator, was futile: reasoning was a process 'troublesome and almost unknown to them';[2] they could not comprehend anything that was not present to their outward senses. As one cacique explained: 'Our grandfathers and great-grandfathers were wont to contemplate the earth alone, anxious only to see whether the plain afforded grass and water for their horses. They never troubled themselves about what went on in the heavens and who was the creator and governor of the stars.'[3] In agriculture the Indian was no more capable. Handed wheat seeds for sowing, he was more likely to put them in his

154

belly than the ground; given a cow to milk for the family, he would kill the animal that day and return the next for more.[4]

If the Indian had any capacity for management, the Jesuits proved unable to develop it. Living as he had done for centuries off plentiful supplies of game and fish, the Guaraní despised the Spaniard for making provision against famine. Only one writer, Muratori, questioned the Jesuit assessment of the Indian: he maintained that their skill as musicians and engravers argued that with proper training they could master the speculative sciences; he even urged that they were fit for higher studies and eventual admission to the priesthood: the Indians had 'as good heads as we and want nothing but study'; he insisted that the stigma of dullness was imposed on them.[5]

This is a unique opinion. If correct, it would imply a radical condemnation of the Jesuit missions; and, worse, a basic dishonesty in the Jesuit treatment of their subjects.

However, it was the German and Swiss priests, not the Spaniards, who put the lowest intellectual rating on the Indian; but at the same time, the same men were the first to acknowledge and in fact to develop the Indian's skill in the crafts. Sepp points out that the Indian can imitate or copy anything, however intricate in structure or pattern, that is put before him. He was speaking from his experience in several missions when he wrote to his brother in Europe:

But stupid as they are at inventing, they are happy at imitating, provided you give them a model; thus if you show one of the Indian women a piece of bone-lace, she will unrip some part of it with a needle and will make another after it, with so much exactness that you shall not know one from the other. We have two organs, one bought from Europe, the other made here so exactly after the first, that I myself could scarce discern the difference. I have a missal printed in Antwerp, which is imitated in writing by an Indian with that nicety that they are scarcely distinguishable. We have trumpets and watches made here not inferior to those of Nuremberg and Augsburg and some pictures, excellently well copied. In short, they will imitate anything very nicely provided they have the model before their eyes, without which they cannot take one step, their intellects being so dumb that they cannot form the least idea of a thing unless it is set before them.[6]

A section of an altar missal, hand-written by an Indian and preserved today at Ignacio Guazú, resembles exactly in all minutiae the printed pages from which it was copied. It belongs to the middle of the period 1655 to 1755, which is reckoned the finest in South American calligraphy: within these years the best examples are from the Jesuit Reductions. The Indians wrote with an unmatched elegance and care. When Bucareli, the Viceroy of Buenos Aires, came to Yapeyú to supervise the expulsion of the Jesuits, he ordered the new cura of the Reduction to have an Indian copy a book for him, *A Description of Man from his genesis to the moment of his death*. Nothing was said of the artistic quality of the Indian's work, but there survive from this time in Madrid archives a large number of letters in superb calligraphy sent by caciques of the Reductions imploring the king to send the Jesuits back to Paraguay.* With the aim of delegating as much responsibility as possible to the Indians, the Jesuits established schools in all the Reductions. During the later period the teaching was done by the Indians themselves. Here boys, principally the sons of caciques and the more prominent Indians, could learn to read, write and add. In this respect the Jesuits' townships were in advance of the Spanish. Boys who were particularly gifted received instruction in Latin. The Laws of the Indies did not oblige the natives to learn Spanish, nor was it necessary, for Guaraní was spoken by the settlers; in their own interest the Jesuits tried to teach the Indians Spanish, but with little success.

Simple addition proved more difficult to teach than the most complex craft: it was done through the medium of Spanish, since there were words only for the first four

* To this day the Guaraní retain the art of perfect reproduction. Given a suit to copy, they will make one undistinguishable from the model, with all its stains, darns and threadbare parts.

numerals in Guaraní: the numeral five was expressed by the
same word as hand, ten by two hands, twenty by two hands
and two feet. Beyond this there was a word, *much*, which
was repeated to form a superlative, and finally there was
simply a number 'too great to be counted'.[7]

In the early days of the missions the Jesuits, believing that
the teaching of numerals was necessary both for civilized life
and the exact confessions of sins, taught the whole population
of the township to count in Spanish up to a thousand in
public recitation; but the attempt was futile. The priests were
very cautious in crediting the figures of boys they themselves
had taught.[8]

In the spirit of the Laws of the Indies, the Jesuits tried to
preserve the authority of the caciques. It was the plan of
Philip V to make five hundred caciques of the Guaraní
Reductions Knights of Santiago, but the caciques attached
more importance to their hereditary position, and the distinction was never conferred.

By selecting the children of caciques for education, the
Jesuits attempted to give these families a prestige which was
formerly acquired through prowess in war. The Customs
Book of the Reductions insists that the priests should take
care that 'the caciques are shown respect by their subjects;
they should be honoured by offices and have some distinction
of dress to mark them off from their people'. Another instruction goes farther: the caciques, as in pre-Conquest times, can
bring back forcibly any vassal flying from his Reduction; if
his vassals should make their way to another Reduction and
the cacique wants them back, then the priests should assist,
trying gently to persuade them to return.[9]

It was largely from the caciques that the personnel of
government was drawn; its form was ordered according to
the Laws of the Indies. At the head were the *corregidor* or
burgomaster and his deputy or *teniente*; and assisting them
three *alcaldes* or supervisors, two for work in the town and
one for the rural districts; then four councillors or *regidores,*
a prefect of police, a steward, a scribe, a royal standard
bearer or *alférez real,* with several assistants. Together these
officials made up the *Cabildo* or town Council.

The teniente with his assistant alcaldes were each put in charge of a quarter of the township. On Sundays after the principal Mass they reported the occurrences of the week to the priest. Their principal function was to get to know all the families living in their districts; to relay to them the priest's orders, to visit their Indians, inspect the work allotted to them and assign awards, which included the privilege of kissing the priest's hands : as a French visitor noted, this was the first degree of assurance of the after-life. As a sign of office they carried an ebony or whalebone cane, the length of a reed, with a silver knob; the other officials carried a shorter unornamented cane.[10]

The elections to offices took place annually at the end of December from a list of candidates drawn up by the retiring officials. The Laws of the Indies gave the parish priest the right to challenge nominations. On new year's day the new officials were installed and invested with their insignia at the entrance to the church. Later the formal confirmation of the Spanish Governor was obtained. On new year's day the Jesuits also appointed their own officials, sextons, sacristans and others.

For a period in the seventeenth century the boys of each Reduction had their own cabildo : it was laid down by the Jesuit Provincial that its number was not to exceed fifteen. The experiment, an attempt to give future officials a civic sense, was later abandoned. It was found that boys could not be kept from running to the Fathers to report on their fellows.

The Jesuits aimed to give full employment to the whole township, men, women and children. One Jesuit, Ignacio Insaurralde, devoted a two-volume treatise in Guaraní to the subject of the *Right Use of Time in the Reductions* :[11] there were work, leisure and feast days. Since the Indian was naturally indolent, the economy could be maintained only by a system of well-regulated labour. Men who followed a particular trade were obliged to work two days weekly at communal undertakings either in the fields or in public building, and more frequently at harvest time. Leisure days were spent mainly in the primitive occupations of hunting and fishing:

the Indians knew well the animals and fish that had the most tasty flesh. The evenings of feast days were passed in military displays and mock warfare : the Indians' skill with the arrow amazed the European; whether they aimed at an animal in full course or a bird on the wing they seldom missed their mark. They also played a primitive form of football with a rubber ball : as Peramás explains : 'They did not play ball with the hand as we do but with the upper part of their bare feet, passing it backwards and forwards with great dexterity and precision.'[12]

The care of the home fell to the woman : she drew drinking water from the fountain or river, prepared the food, moulded pitchers, pans, plates and dishes from the clay. Every mother of a family could weave cloth : each week she was given a supply of cotton from the communal store and handed in the woven material to the *economo* : the cloth not needed in the townships was sold, and with the cash industrial tools were purchased. Usually the women also helped in the fields, accompanying their husbands to the outlying farms.

After catechism and Mass in the church, the boys had their breakfast served in the courtyard of the parochial house. If it was a work-day, those not attending school were conducted by a senior to the fields : there they were put to work clearing fields or removing rocks from the roads; always they sang at work and had with them a statue of St Isidro, patron of farmers. In the evening they returned to church for prayers that ended with the litany of the saints. The evening meal, like breakfast, was eaten in common in the courtyard of the priests' house. The girls also were occupied. Under supervision they performed lighter tasks in the fields : according to the season, they plucked the open buds from the cotton plants or frightened off the flocks of parrots and other birds from the seeding crops : they clapped hands, uttered shouts or made other noises now produced mechanically. No girl was allowed to enter the parochial house : like the boys they had their meals in common. They entered church by their own door with the women and had their own floor area allotted them. This segregation was enjoined by the Law of the Indies. The absence of children from home during the day made it possible for the mothers to give more time to their lucrative weaving.[13]

In the Jesuits' view the sexual appetites of the Guaraní were aroused early. To prevent fornication, youthful marriages were encouraged—girls at fourteen, boys at sixteen, 'it having been found by experience that when maidens and young men continue in a single state for any considerable time they have found means to pair themselves'.[14] More than an adequate livelihood was always at hand; no dowry was demanded; the marriage contract consisted simply of two undertakings— from the girl to fetch water for her husband and from the youth to provide fuel. All they needed—a home, a hammock or oxhide, a little salt, a few loaves and a cow for the wedding feast—were provided by the town. It was the girl who courted the youth : she would go to the priest and say, 'I want to marry so and so'; the young man was then called up and asked whether he cared to marry the girl. If he agreed, only the priest's blessing was needed to make the match.[15] No music or dancing was allowed at the family feast. Marriage among the Guaraní was a matter-of-fact business : as many as ninety pairs might be married together in church, always on a Saturday.[16]

The missionaries admired the way the Indians nurtured their children. Swaddling clothes were unknown; instead, the infants were covered with a loose-fitting garment that gave their limbs complete freedom of movement. 'In all the Guaraní towns I visited,' recalled one priest,[17] 'I never met an Indian who was lame, deformed or hunch-backed: all had perfect articulation of their limbs.' Foster-mothers were not used, except when a child was orphaned or a mother sick. Orphans were brought up by their relatives, but their food and clothing were provided from the communal store.[18]

The Swiss Jesuit, Florián Paucke, both artist and writer, was the only person to sketch in detail the costumes of the Indians : his drawings date from the last years of the Jesuit Reductions and refer mainly to the Mocobíes among whom he worked. For the dress of the Guaraní there exist only verbal descriptions. Like the Spaniards the men wore short loose breeches and a cotton shirt. There was nothing in dress to distinguish them from Indians in other parts of Spanish dominated America. Commonly the Indian possessed two *ponchos*, a white one for daily wear, a second usually dyed, often a prize awarded in a tournament held on festivals. All went barefoot except the caciques.

The women wore a sleeveless shift with many folds, fastened round the waist and coming down to their ankles, and over it a *tipoi* or gown of the same length with sleeves, which they took off when doing hard work. Their long hair was brought down the sides of their face like a nun's veil. Around their forehead was a tightly drawn headband to which they fastened any burdens which they might carry on their shoulders.

Before entering the Reductions almost all the Indian men wore their hair long: it was an indignity to have it cut. The men generally had little beard, and that only in advanced age. Consequently it was only with difficulty that they could be distinguished from women. To emphasize from early years the distinction of sexes the Indian males of the Jesuit townships kept their hair short: this also distinguished the Christian from the infidel and, in warfare, friend from enemy.[19]

Provincials reiterated frequently the injunction against long hair. They also forbade fancy trunks, sleeves of printed cotton, ribbons and ornamental buttons. Such 'vanities', as the Customs Book called them, once allowed, could not be controlled. Also, they would eliminate the distinction between caciques and vassals, and so weaken the structure of government.

In their eating habits the Indians remained half-savage. For the most part they lived on beef, which they ate without salt and half raw; the Fathers, who had to attend the consequent illnesses, failed to abolish the custom. Sepp complained: 'Several times I have sent meat boiled after our own way to some Indians that were sick, but afterwards they gave it to the dogs and returned to their own diet.'[20] The resulting worms meant that the Indians seldom lived beyond their fiftieth year. Their own remedy for stomach pain was to plunge naked into the river or lie with their belly on hot sand. Some preferred damp grass. When indisposed, they could not be taught to take care of themselves. Consequently 'a Reduction of seven or eight thousand souls is considered in a good state if at any time there are less than two hundred Indians lying sick in bed'.[21] Of the 50,000 oxen belonging to the township of Yapeyú (San Miguel had many more), at least fifty were slaughtered every day to satisfy the appetites of 7,000 Guaraní: 'After fasting only a few hours a Guaraní will devour a young calf. . . . Place food before him, and the rising and setting sun will behold him with his jaws at work and his mouth full but with an appetite still unsatisfied. . . . You will agree with me that Paraguay may be called the devouring grave as well as the seminary of cattle.'[22] Another priest reported seeing two Indians eat a whole ox in the space of two hours, throwing away only the head, feet and entrails.[23]

Animals were slaughtered three times a week, and rations distributed from the meat store; but neither this measure of control nor the attempt to teach the Indians to make *charqui* (meat dried in the sun and then pulverized) checked their voraciousness: there was always abundant beef to be had for the labour of lassooing. In fifteen minutes it was ready for the fire perpetually burning in the home. Ribs were the favourite portion, eaten when they had been toasted on the outside and still raw inside. Partridges were also eaten in great quantities: the Indians had only to knock them down with a stick in their walks through the fields. Adult Indians had no fixed time for meals: 'The clock is not their rule, but the calls of a craving stomach':[24] the children, who were given meals at regular times, lapsed into the habits of their parents as soon as they married.

Water was the ordinary drink of both Indians and priests; for festivities they brewed a small beer made from maize ground into meal, malted, dried over a fire and fermented for two or three days. This *chicha* was judged a better drink than cider, more wholesome than European beer, very strengthening as well as nourishing.[25] The occasions on which it was drunk must have been rare, for a European visitor to the Reductions reported that the Jesuits followed the precepts of Mahomet, forbidding 'all fermented drink that might endanger their despotic rule and make their subjects throw off the yoke laid on them'.[26]

The norms of justice were first laid down by Nicolás Durán, the Provincial of Paraguay from 1623–8 : in the Reductions where there were only a few Christians there was to be no punishment of any kind, only paternal correction; very rare cases might demand slight punishment : the utmost care was to be taken not to make the name of the Fathers odious or to associate the faith with a punitive code. In the older Reductions established in provinces still largely pagan, no punishment was to be given except under the priest's supervision; the stocks could be used only with the permission of the Provincial in every instance : all punishments were to be awarded and inflicted by the alcaldes; never were the Fathers to chastise with their own hands.

In time a penal system was formed. This was necessary. Savage Indians were constantly joining the Reductions and no communal life could be maintained unless a minimal standard of behaviour was enforced. But even the traveller Azara, perhaps the severest critic of the Jesuit system, admitted that the priests enforced the law with moderation.

The common punishment was a few azotes administered by the corregidor in the centre of the square at a stone pillar to which the delinquent was tied by his hands. Public punishment was essential as a safeguard against excess in the number or severity of the blows, given perhaps in passion or simple stupidity. According to the orders of the Provincial, Altamirano, only caciques were exempt from punishment in public.* The Provincial's permission was needed to deprive them of office after their appointment had been confirmed by the Spanish Governor. A teniente had the same privileges. Homicide was punished by eighty azotes, public indecency by thirty or sixty, dealing in witchcraft by fewer. Every crime had its stipulated penalty, which could be moderated in particular cases. Incest and similar offences, also the procuring of abortion, carried a prison sentence of two months in irons, with twenty-five azotes, never more, at three different

---

* In this the Jesuits followed Spanish custom which exempted all officials from public punishment.

times : these delinquents were also deprived of all their offices. Adultery was treated with less severity, twenty-five azotes and fifteen days in prison.

The seemingly severe penalties for stealing listed in the Customs Book help to indicate the difficulties the priests had in teaching its wrongfulness : for instance, an Indian caught stealing a horse or mule was given twenty-five azotes, and when he returned with the animal to the Reduction from which he had stolen it he was given another whipping and a month in prison, during which he was made to work.

These were the occasional offences. At times, particularly in Santa Rosa and Nuestra Señora de Fe, two Reductions in the group nearest Asunción, there were intermittent bouts of drunkenness. In fact, as well as in the eyes of the Indians, it was their own elected officials, confirmed in office by the Spanish authorities, who administered punishment on their own authority. By the Laws of the Indies they were the ruling body, although the supervison of priests was always needed both as a safeguard against brutality and as an aid in adjudicating more complex cases. In no instance did priests take disciplinary action in their own name.

A further safeguard against abuse was the control exercised by the higher Jesuit authorities, the General in Rome, the Provincials and Visitors. In 1718, for example, the Jesuit General, Michele Tamburini, warned the Provincial of Paraguay against cruelty in the punishment of delinquent Indians. There is evidence that at intervals abuses did occur in one or other of the townships—cases of negligence, impatience or excess. On one occasion at least, a priest who had been immoderate in the punishment he had ordered was given a term of imprisonment in a Jesuit house. The incident may have resulted in the order given by another Jesuit General, Francisco Retz, that 'any missionary who was excessive in punishing Indians should be removed instantly from the Reductions'. The ruling was incorporated in the Customs Book that was read regularly at the Provincial's visitation.

Certainly mildness was the Spanish Jesuit tradition. The Indians, so reluctant at first to forgo the freedom of their forests, in the space of a century and a half did not once rise

in revolt against the priests, while in the same period there
were frequent risings among the encomienda Indians. Only
a gentle enforcement of law could account for the fact that
two priests in each township were sufficient to control up to
six or seven thousand Indians.

Boys were punished by those in charge of them with three,
four or five azotes according to their age. Adults were beaten
by adult Indians. The punishment of women was adjusted
to their sex. No woman could be given more than twelve
azotes, except in very grave cases. The sentence was always
to be carried out by women : a pregnant woman was always
excused.

Priests on their first arrival in the Reductions were struck
by the simplicity of the Indians who underwent punishment.
As Sepp remarked, they were treated as 'we treat our
children, only that instead of a birch, we use a scourge. . . .
This correction they take very patiently, without any cursing
or swearing, nay, without making the least noise. . . . The
correction being over, they kiss the missionary's hand and
return him thanks into the bargain.'[27]

The night between 9 p.m. and 6 a.m. was divided into
three watches during which officials patrolled the township :
their task was to keep the sick under observation, report mis-
demeanours, guard against attacks of hostile Indians or
Mamelucos and against incursions of preying animals. Before
the Swiss and German missionaries introduced clocks and
campaniles, the end of each watch was beaten on a drum.
The night watchman, along with the daytime police, formed
a preventative force, domestic and paternalistic rather than
coercive.

As early as 1645 the Jesuits were debating how to deal with
cases of murder. In that year the Provincial Congregation
recorded their far from unanimous views in a letter to the
General in Rome, seeking his guidance. Should murderers be
handed over to the Spanish authorities? Banishment from the
Reduction was not a deterrent, still less an exemplary punishment : moreover it would bring a bad name on the Reductions at a time when the Jesuits had enemies in Asunción
ready to make capital of their problems. To take no action

would be asking for more trouble. Up to that date there had been ten to twelve instances of murder: the punishment awarded had been thirty or forty azotes.

In his reply the General was inclined to favour 'perpetual' imprisonment with good commons, but he left the ultimate decision to the Provincial in consultation with the more experienced missionaries: there were some who favoured the introduction of a Spanish magistrate, dependent on the ordinary Spanish judiciary, into the Reductions or at least a group of Reductions, but objections were made that the Spanish officials did not understand the Indian mentality; they had all the haughtiness of petty judges and acted as lords and masters of the Indians. In the end the General's recommendation of 'perpetual' or 'life' imprisonment was followed.

It is not certain when prisons were first built for grave offenders. A system of incarceration is first referred to in the General's, Tirso González's, *Reglamento de Doctrinas* at the end of the seventeenth century. It seems that, by then, groups of Reductions shared a communal prison over which an Indian constable was given charge. After a lapse of some years, a plausible excuse would be found for releasing a 'life' prisoner, though in the mind of the simple Indian the sentence, when passed, was regarded as perpetual. In his 1718 instruction the General Tamburini laid down that 'life' imprisonment was never to exceed ten years: during that time gentleness was to mark the treatment of the prisoner. If irons were used they should not prevent the prisoner walking about his cell; stocks should be restricted to criminals who would have received a capital sentence before a secular judge. What was inexcusable, wrote the Jesuit General, was the abuse of retrenching little by little the prisoner's food until he was in danger of dying from hunger: 'Nor do I understand', he added, 'how such an excess can be committed without the taint of homicide or without incurring an irregularity.'* In the eighteenth century the question of capital punishment arose again in a different form. In 1741 and in the year

* Irregularity: a term from the vocabulary of canon lawyers to denote an action which incapacitates a priest from carrying out his functions.

The grandeur of the ceremonial varied with the size of the town. Yapeyú, which had close on eight thousand, about a third of the population of Buenos Aires in 1767, led in splendour for most of the period. With its mixed Indian population it could call on a wider range of native talent and tradition.

I O

Chiquitos

The first encounter of the Jesuits with the Chiquitos Indians occurred in the early days of the Guairá mission: their request for priests was turned down for lack of men. At the same time it seemed certain that their turn would come, for the natural line of expansion was from Guairá through Itatín to the west. However, it was not foreseen that the Mamelucos would drive the Itatín missions south and at the same time block the approach to Chiquitos from the east. After this the Cárdenas affair made further commitments impossible until the arrival of German, Swiss and Czech priests at the end of the seventeenth century.

The Chiquitos stretched from the eastern foothills of the Andes to the frontiers of present-day Brazil to the north-east, and of Paraguay and Argentina to the south and south-east. It was an area of thick tropical forest broken with open plains of rough pastures, swamp and scrub drained by the Mamoré and its tributaries. The people belonged to the Guaraní family. They had been first discovered by Martínez de Irala when he sailed up the Paraguay in 1542. In the following year Alvar Núñez Cabeza de Vaca had organized a large expedition in search of El Dorado, actually the Inca empire described to him by Indians of the upper Paraguay. Pushing west from Puerto de los Reyes, he had come across Indians who wore silver discs on their lower lip and gold earrings. A second expedition organized by Irala in 1548 had crossed the northern Chaco plains and entered the southern part of the province of Chiquitos.

Between 1557 and 1560 Nuflo de Chaves had conquered the province. Near the San José range, he founded the city of Santa Cruz de la Sierra which was moved south in 1595 to near its present site. It was then that the Chiquitos who had been under Spanish influence for forty years reverted to their primitive life. From time to time they raided Spanish settlements mainly with the purpose of gathering iron tools.

In 1690, nearly a century later, the same year that the Jesuits established a College at Tarija, north of Jujuy, some of the Chiquitos sued for peace with the Spaniards. They were being harassed both from the north and the east by the Mamelucos, and some entire tribes had been carried off into slavery. With the help of a small Spanish contingent, the Jesuits undertook to hold back the raiders.

The Chiquitos were still a restless people, moving about in the forest in search of game and fish, going often forty miles to a good hunting ground: there they would construct a temporary village, then move on again; they wore no clothes, but their various tribes were distinguished by different body paints. Sometimes they slung a jaguar skin across their back or covered their loins with a cloth of twisted cotton.[1] Penetrating their country Padre José de Arce, a native of the Canary Islands, met a group of Chiquitos caciques at the site of the present settlement of San Ignacio: they had summoned a general assembly of their people to decide whether they would accept Christianity. On a July night the meeting began with their traditional dance. 'In groups of six or seven they gathered round a musician who played a kind of panpipes. Other musicians used hollow pumpkins in which small stones had been inserted, while the rest hummed on one note. The whole dance was a slow measured stamping, a mechanical movement that was more terrifying than amusing for the onlookers.'[2] As the dance progressed, the caciques proposed the question for debate. Views were expressed as the movements continued. After dancing they fell to drinking. Although it was winter, they went off to bathe in a nearby stream and, on emerging, put on their finest plumes and painted their faces and bodies all over. At dawn they sat down to a banquet and only after long preparation did the caciques announce

the unanimous decision : they would accept Christianity on
two conditions—first, that those who did not come over would
not be obliged to leave the country, and second, that children,
even if their parents were Christian, should not serve at the
altar : such a practice, it was feared, would impair their
manliness.

The terms were accepted. On the last day of July, the feast
of San Ignacio, the foundations were laid of the first Chiquitos
Reduction.

The Jesuits then began to penetrate the country in pairs.
High hills interspersed with marshy valleys made it harder
terrain to work than the Paraná or Uruguay. Different
methods of attracting the natives had to be devised. The
jungle was thick, the rivers few, the people scattered in small
groups in clearings that hardly provided a sufficiency of
arable soil. The Indian guides who accompanied them helped
to dispel the suspicion that the priests were Spanish agents.
The Chiquitos watched them with curiosity. 'The beginnings
were happy,' wrote one of the priests. 'We were received well
by the Indians and loaded with fruit and the produce of the
earth. In return the natives were given glass beads, small bells,
needles and hammocks. It was our rule to take nothing without returning something of equivalent value.' This diplomatic
exchange of gifts merely took a stage further a custom well
established among the Chiquitos, for 'if one tribe had success
in fishing and another in hunting . . . the first would approach
a predetermined spot, lay down supplies of fish and then
withdraw. The second tribe would then take up the fish and
leave in its place an equivalent amount of meat.'³ The Jesuit,
assuming the role of ambassador, would introduce himself
with a simple speech. An example has been recorded :

It is for your sake, my children, that I have left my parents
and brothers who live over there where the sun rises. I
learnt that you were without hammocks and I have come
to bring them to you. Here they are. Take them. They are
yours. (He would then distribute three hundred hammocks.)
Listen to what I endured on my travels. My little boat
dragged its moorings and I was almost drowned. Tree

trunks obstructed my passage and forced me to wade in the water up to my chin. I really do not know how I am still alive. I should like to be able to visit you more often and bring you tools and clothes, but you live so far away . . . and the Indians of my mission do not like it when I leave them. But here are some axes I brought with me. There are enough to make a clearing . . . I am going to hand them to your cacique so that you can cut down the trees.[4]

From the first days of the Conquest these Indians had searched for iron with the same zest that the Spaniards had searched for gold. The Mojos, peaceful agriculturist neighbours of the Chiquitos to the west, became slave hunters in order to sell their captives for cash with which they could buy hatchets and knives. To the north the Conibo of the river Ucayali, a tributary of the Amazon, threatened to rise against their priests who had proposed to give other tribes the iron implements which they considered their monopoly. Even to-day the Tsirakua Indians of the Chaco attack travellers to rob them of knives. The tools brought by the Jesuits achieved among the Chiquitos what song and dances had done among the people of the Paraná.

This covetousness was natural enough to Indians who had to live by their agriculture and possessed only hardwood sticks with which to till their fields. The clearing of the jungle had always been a painful task for these Stone Age people : first they had to burn the tree trunk, then cut out the carbonized wood with a stone axe, and finally set the tree to fall at an angle that would uproot others on its way to the ground. With these new implements the Chiquitos were able to clear and sow three times the area they had previously cultivated. To supplement their diet of maize and bitter mandioca they had hunted the tortoise in the woods and rocky hills. It supplied for them the place of beef among the Guaraní of the Paraná.

After establishing San Ignacio, Padre Arce pushed west and founded San Javier on 31 December 1692. San Rafael followed in 1696, San José, today the most impressive of them all, in 1697; this last was the work of Padre Suárez, who was responsible also for San Juan Bautista in 1699. Still more foundations came in quick succession, ten in all within an area of some 6,600 square leagues, in places which, sometimes after a failure or two, were found best suited to support the largest number of families. The site chosen was always on a long elevated ridge of land, and in each place a different tribe or sub-tribe was concentrated. One German missionary explains how the Paraná system was adapted to Chiquitos. 'The first step', he writes, 'is to find a suitable site immune from floods. Then the forest is cleared and a large square formed in which the houses are arranged in rows with three sides for the Indians and the fourth for the church and the missionaries' houses, the workshops and the school. The houses are poor, made of wood thatched with thick grass, but the church is well-built.'[5]

The search for safety from the Mamelucos greatly helped the priests to gather the Chiquitos into towns. The threat of slavery continued long after the establishment of San Javier.

'At a certain time every year,' writes one of the Fathers,[6] 'each Christian community sallies forth in turn in search of Indians.' It was in his last excursion, in 1704, that Padre Lucas Caballero, Arce's first companion, made for the territory of the Puraki Indians, a branch of the Chiquitos, with whom he was already on terms of trust. In one of their villages he ran into a troop of Mamelucos who ordered him back. Caballero continued. Every village was deserted. The Puraki had fled to denser forest leaving a few small boys perched high in the trees to report the advance of the raiders. Eventually Caballero caught up with the Indians and found them on the verge of starvation : there had been a devastating drought in the province. A cross was erected and encircled by Puraki praying for rain. It came and saved the crops. Caballero continued on his way. In his absence the Mamelucos spread the report that he was one of their number disguised as a priest and was out hunting Indians to take them as slaves to Santa Cruz. The ruse failed. Catching up with Caballero, the Mamelucos leader now claimed that he was officially authorized to conduct an exploration of the country.

Threatened with death, Caballero stood his ground and secured himself further in the confidence of the Indians.

The coming of the Jesuits worked a social revolution. Large tracts of forest were cleared for sowing, sizable groupings of people into towns became possible, the population increased. Between 1731 and 1766 the ten townships grew from 14,925 to 23,788. These figures are remarkable because, as Dobrizhoffer pointed out,[7] deaths among the Chiquitos far exceeded the number of births. 'Whether the paucity of issue', he reflects, 'is to be attributed to the climate, the water, the food, especially the land tortoises they eat in such quantity, or to natural sterility in the parents, let the learned judge. I have frequently heard it said that had not the Jesuits brought a multitude of savages from the woods, the towns must have long since been depopulated.'

Like the Guaraní the Chiquitos in their woods had been unaccustomed to regular work. Their crops, sown in October, were harvested in February. The land was suited to rice, but the Indians did not care for it. Sugar cane was eaten by children, adults sucked it only when water was scarce. Chicha was made by the women : at work or idle they chewed corn, then poured boiling water over the chewed mass and left it to ferment for eight days. In the absence of currency, the chicha was used for barter. To curb quarrelsomeness, the priests forbade fermentation for more than three days.

Starting from these practices, the Jesuits undertook a vast agricultural programme that was needed for a stable life. Lack of pasture made it impossible to introduce cattle on the scale they had developed in the south. But by patient cutting down of the forest, moderate-sized herds could be maintained. Ponds were made to retain water in the dry season. 'Peruvian sheep, the size of deer' were introduced : they could stand the cold climate and also be used as beasts of burden. Beans, lemons, and pumpkins were grown, but no apples, pears or peaches. The towns, though they attained a period of prosperity never reached later, were still far less thriving than the Paraná Reductions.

In the temporary Chiquitos villages the hall of the cacique had been the only large structure. This was now replaced by

the church. Poor soil, lack of lime and stone and river transport left no alternative to the hardwoods that had been used
in the construction of the early Guairá churches. Like the
cacique's hall which was built to contain the entire village,
the house of God, the *ypoohti tupa*, was planned to accom-
modate the entire population of the town, sometimes over five
thousand, or the numbers to which it was hoped the settlement would eventually expand. Each of its three naves was
supported by a line of six to eight carved pillars; the main
altar, the confessionals and the altars of the Virgin and patron
saint were similarly carved; the walls were of adobe, and both
inside and out they glistened white in the sun from a substi-
tute for lime extracted from burnt snails. The tower was a
simple structure standing away from the church, its bells cast
from metal brought from as far away as Potosí. Various
animals provided gut for string instruments. In all essentials,
church practices were the same as on the Paraná. The
Chiquitos gave up painting their bodies, the women at work
now wore their hair tied back, but on approaching the church
they loosened it as a sign of respect for the Blessed Virgin, the
Nupaquina, their mother. On festival days the men dressed
in their feathers carried to church their bows and arrows,
indicating that they were prepared to fight for the honour of
God. Often two organs accompanied the singing, fourteen or
more violins, three or four bass viols, double-bass fiddles,
harps, flutes and a few trumpets. All but the last had been
manufactured in the Reductions by German Jesuits. The
favoured music was the compositions of the Jesuit Zipoli.*

The language presented the priests with problems they had
not met on the Paraná. The male and female vocabularies
had no points of resemblance: even phrases like *I shall go*
were different on the lips of a man and woman; a boy would
use a different word from a girl for 'mother'. In church a
priest, after preaching in the male language, had to repeat
his sermon in the female language.

Among dramas performed on festivals their favourite was

---

* The old organ built by Padre Schmid for the Reduction of San
Rafael is still in the loft of the church with musical scores copied by
the Chiquitos Indians.

the story of St Eustachius. According to legend, the saint when out hunting saw the picture of the crucified Christ between the antlers of a stag. The woodland country of the Chiquitos formed a perfect setting for the performance. Games followed. Their most characteristic contest was shooting: 'Eighty or a hundred men would attack each other with blunted arrows which were often very painful. Yet no man would show pain on his face for fear of being mocked. Another pastime was a game with a ball made from rubber which they got from the bark of a tree: they smeared the liquid rubber on their arms and, as it dried, stroked it off and put on more, working it with their hands until they had a ball of the required size. They were very skilful at this game and kept the ball in motion with their heads.'[8]

The Indians now became conscious of a new security. The forges established by the Jesuits drew to the towns Indians from remote places and often kept them there. Sometimes they travelled as much as six hundred miles to get instruments of iron. Still untamed tribes were held back from attacking the new Christians for fear of losing the benefits of iron. The fishing of the Chiquitos was revolutionized by the metal hooks; when an attack was made on a Reduction the forge was always spared; the Piro Indians to the north decided to murder a Padre Ricketer only after they felt certain they had sufficient knowledge to maintain the mission forge without his help. Another priest noted that he had to be parsimonious in distributing metal goods, otherwise the Indians would believe that iron could be gathered in the fields.

With the iron brought laboriously from Potosí, planes and saws were made as well as axes: in the end almost every kind of instrument could be found in the mission workshops: one priest arranged a device for holding a cross-cut saw, clocks were manufactured, several lathes set up for making rosaries. The women were employed mainly in spinning: they held the cotton skilfully in a thick rope round the left arm and manipulated the spindle so that it never touched the ground. 'A happy and busy community was formed in which all were equal,' wrote one priest.[9] Eventually every Chiquitos male possessed, apart from his bow and arrow, a knife, a tinder box, a fish hook and several needles. Scissors remained a luxury. The use of the lancet which the priests taught the Indians kept in check the influence of the witch-doctors who, as they sucked wounds, claimed also to draw out small stones, which in fact they had held all the time in their mouth: they were feared because it was thought that they had the power also to insert them.

To finance the purchase of iron ore the Jesuits developed a wax industry: the wax which the Chiquitos purified was obtained from a bee no bigger than a gnat. From Potosí, where the wax was bartered, it was distributed throughout Peru. A smaller trade, mainly with the south, was done in the vanilla plant which flourished in the moist areas of the missions, where it grew entwined with palm trees: its triangular sheaf, full of small seeds, was sought after by Spaniards for the manufacture of chocolate. Only towards the end of the Jesuit period was its use widely exploited.

Most Jesuits did not delude themselves about the motives of the Chiquitos in becoming Christian. The historian Padre Chantre y Herrera admits that their reasons were seldom spiritual: 'We could have done nothing without the axes we distributed,' he confesses.[10] On the other hand, it would be wrong to explain the success of the Jesuits in this district of South America exclusively in economic terms. There were mystical factors also at work.

In many instances, the influence and ascendancy of the Jesuits rested on the character the priests acquired in the eyes of the Indians. They were a species of shamans, particularly popular because they practised their arts gratis. Certainly the neighbouring Mojos under the Peruvian Jesuits believed that their priests exercised authority over nature: thanks to them the rivers did not overflow, the jaguars did no harm, the carnivorous fish spared their sting. On their side, the Jesuits did not discourage these simple beliefs. In fact, to enhance their prestige, they interpreted disasters to their ends. Padre Caballero's behaviour is an example. A witchdoctor asked the cacique of a village to deliver the priest into his hands. The cacique, who had been given knives and hatchets by Caballero, declined. Soon afterwards the witchdoctor died.

Caballero did not hesitate to claim a connection between the two events and in this way enhanced his prestige. To the Indians of the Ucayalí, Ricketer boasted that he possessed relics more efficacious to aid women in childbirth or to heal common maladies than any herbs of the magicians. Not unnaturally, the shamans saw in the priests rivals who would supersede them. The Aizuari Indians of the upper Amazon attributed an eclipse of the sun to the magic of Padre Samuel Fritz, a Bohemian Jesuit: they asked him in tears whether he had killed the sun to punish them for some offence.

At first the Chiquitos feared baptism. Since in the early days of the new Reductions the sacrament was given only to the dying, they believed that it contained some malevolent power. Much later, they came to regard it as beneficial and asked to be baptized every time they fell sick.

The interpretation which the Indians gave to sacred images sometimes surprised even the Jesuits. When a figure of the Crucified Christ was set up for the first time in a church, they feared that the priests had put it there under their eyes to remind them that their clerical masters, if provoked, were capable of fierce reprisals.

As might be expected, the Jesuits in Chiquitos did not hesitate to use a theatrical *mise-en-scène* to impress the Indians: they entered their villages in priestly vestments bearing a cross in their hands and followed by neophytes chanting catechetical hymns. When called upon to make peace they sat in front of the church flanked by caciques of the warring factions. But the high point of the Jesuits' mystical appeal lay in their authority, which resembled that of a superior cacique: from the first they claimed a comparable position. Among the Chiquitos more than the Guaraní the cacique's authority was sovereign: his lands were tilled for him, his buildings raised at public expense; he punished severely and abitrarily; all paid him a tithe of their hunting and fishing. The priest's pre-eminence, like the cacique's, was marked by acts of generosity, by powers of eloquence and by force of character. The ambition of both was identical, to assemble the largest number of families and care for them. At almost every point the comparison held.

It was the same in the Chaco. A spokesman from the numerous Tobas tribe, with whom the Jesuits were remarkably successful, asserted that a good cacique was one who constantly thought of the welfare of his people and protected them against epidemics.

When faced with hostility from savage tribes, the Jesuits resorted to means of pacification that might have been inspired by the Mamelucos. Like the slave-raiders they organized man-hunts. At the head of a party to convert Indians a Jesuit would penetrate enemy-held territory. The expedition might last three or four months. A path had to be cut through the forest and each day a portion of corn and mandioca left in the hollow of a tree for the return journey, protected against the depredations of the monkeys. Morning and evening prayers were said and a cross erected at the night's resting-place. After several days' journey, one of the party would climb a tree in the hope of catching sight of smoke on the horizon, a common sign that there were Indians in the neighbourhood. When finally smoke was seen, the party formed a circle and closed in on the village. The next step was to isolate a handful of heathen Indians and take them captive. Then the priest would come forward, try every dialect he knew till he hit on one that was understood, then offer the heathen Indians peace, security and ample food if they would accompany him back to his Reduction.

It was a dangerous strategy because an alarm might be raised in the village and the priest killed. Nor was smoke always the sign of an Indian village. In 1766, Padre Knogler, who describes these hunts, came on a group of runaway slaves armed with guns and sabres. It never occurred to Knogler or others that this forcible conversion of Indians was not justified by its benefits.

As the hunting party drew near the Reduction with their captives, it was met by a procession that conducted it to the church. A *Te Deum* was sung and the newcomers were distributed among the families of the mission Indians. They were treated with great kindness, subjected to Christian instruction and forced to learn the dialect of the area. Only when their attachment to the mission was no longer in doubt were they sent back to their own villages loaded with presents. These neophytes had much success with tribes that until then had been considered intractable. With their long tradition of warfare the Chiquitos found these raids attractive; often they grew restive in the peaceful atmosphere of the Reductions and were happy with the illusion that they were on the war-path again. They also wanted servants, which the Jesuits would not allow them to acquire in any other way.

By the middle of the eighteenth century these expeditions had become highly organized. The report on them sent to Rome in 1756 describes them for Jesuit eyes only. 'These new converts', the anonymous writer explains,

have caught from our Fathers their evangelical spirit and zeal for converting infidels to the orthodox faith. They go out in search of their barbarian relations and friends, even sometimes their enemies, up to three hundred miles away. If they find any recalcitrant they terrify and subdue them with a show of arms but do not actually attack them. Then they lead them home . . . From Santiago in the course of the last six years they have gone out twice against the Tunachi, an extremely savage tribe reared on fighting, and once from San José with great labour and unequal results against the Caipidi. They brought back nineteen Tunachi and seventy Caipidi to their Reductions. The second expedition to these tribes came off better : nearly all the Tunachi and more than three hundred Caipidi were brought to the Christian faith thanks to Padre Gaspar Troncoso.*[11]

In an early excursion of this kind, the Jesuits came in contact with the Manasí tribe, just two days distant from San Javier, the most westerly Reduction. Caballero was un-certain whether they were a branch of the Chiquitos people : many of them were brought into San Javier and their customs studied. In several points they resembled the Incas. Tolerably prosperous, they lived in neat symmetrical timber houses that

* These tribes mentioned in Jesuit writings would seem to have dis-appeared without trace.

formed long streets and sizable squares. The largest square was reserved for the cacique's residence; even the smaller houses contained several rooms. The settlements were close to each other; the principal building was a large hall in which they worshipped. Like the Incas, they used for constructional work a hatchet made from a large stone with a firm edge.*

But it was the religious tenets of these people that fascinated the Jesuits. 'They believe according to a tradition from their ancestors that a lady of supreme beauty once conceived without the co-operation of man, that she brought forth a most charming child, that the child, having attained a certain age, filled the world with admiration of his virtues and prodigies, that one day in the presence of a numerous crowd of disciples he ascended into the air and immediately transformed himself into the sun which shines upon us. They add that were it not for the vast distance his features would be visible.'[12]

These quasi-Christian beliefs may have owed something to the preaching of the early Augustinian friars among the Incas. Unlike the Incas but like the Chiquitos, the Manasí did not actually worship the sun; they gave it, along with the moon, a measure of veneration and when its light failed through an eclipse, they would say that it was cruelly torn by dogs with which they believed the sky abounded. 'Accordingly to defend their dear planets from those aerial mastiffs at the time of an eclipse they would send a shower of arrows into the sky amid loud vociferations.'[13] They believed in two gods and one goddess, Quipoci, the spouse of the first god and the mother of the second : all three appeared from time to time behind a curtain when the people were gathered in the great hall of the cacique; only the priest or *mapono* was allowed to see them, speak with them or ply them with drinks. Sometimes the *mapono* would put questions to the gods on behalf of the people and then emerge from behind the curtain with answers

---

* Cf. *Redación de las costumbres y religión de los Indios Manasicas*, written in 1706, the only study of the Manasí, a tribe now extinct, which was discovered that year. It is also the only detailed ethnological work on any group in the province of Chiquitos. The religion that Caballero describes is, in the words of the American ethnologist, Alfred Métraux, 'a blend of shamanism with a pantheon of gods of Peruvian origin'. Cf. *Mid-America* (July 1944), p. 189.

so ridiculous that even the crowd laughed mockingly at them.

Sometimes, from her place of hiding, Quipoci was heard singing songs, at other times she would address the Indians making the point that she was their true mother who protected them from the wrath and cruelty of the two gods. On their side of the curtain the Indians invoked her help in their misfortunes.

These and similar beliefs that had partial parallels in the Christian faith, made the conversion of the Manasí a task largely of adaptation. To their credit the Jesuits studied with precision the beliefs of the tribes they met and made them the starting-point of their catechesis. From their reports written on the Chiquitos, it is clear that there had been a great advance in their scientific approach to missionary problems since the days of Fields and Ortega; they now noted religious tenets with the same accuracy that they did linguistic variations or social customs. Among the Chiquitos they found a more circumstantial structure of an after-life than was held by other Guaraní: when the soul left the body it was conducted by the *mapono* to heaven, there to live in eternal joy. However, it took the *mapono* some time to do this: he first disappeared deep into the forest for several days, crossed a bridge perpetually guarded by one of the gods whose business it was 'to purify the souls of the dead from all stains contracted in this earthly life; if the souls failed to pass the process of purification they were thrown over to sink in the stream'.[14] As they fell, they caused floods and rain. This was always a man's fate if as he crossed the stream he rejected the command to cut his long, dishevelled and scabby hair. Should the soul succeed in crossing the bridge, he found the land of the dead an agreeable country with quantities of honey and fish and large trees that exuded a delectable resin on which the souls subsisted. There were black monkeys about and an eagle soaring in the sky. The land in this world was allotted to people according to the district in which they had died.[15]

The *maponos* were respected by the Jesuits; they abstained from game and fish in order not to lose their shamanistic powers; they were to be distinguished from the *chupadores* or suckers, a low class of trickster who made a livelihood from witchcraft. The *mapono* was given the same privileges as the cacique: if he lived in the village, the community built his house; if he preferred the country, his property was protected against thieves; like the cacique, he was supported by the faithful.

From their base in Chiquitos the Jesuits now made a further attempt to convert the Guaycurú, among whom Roque González had preached unsuccessfully in 1610. In 1756 hopes ran high. The Jesuits from the Chiquitos Reduction of San Corazón reported:

Not far away are the Guaycurú, notorious for their ferocity and great numbers. Everyone fears them and they fear none. Since they are so cruel all agreed that it would be foolhardy for a small party to approach them, so Padre Francisco Lizardi, Visitor to this mission, gave an order that a force of a thousand picked Christian men from the Reductions of San José, San Juan and San Corazón, strong and well-armed men, should advance against the Guaycurú with two priests, Antonio Guasp and José Chueca: they were not to give battle but to tame the barbarians and bring them to a better way of living.[16]

This expedition had a twofold purpose: 'We hope', the writer concluded, 'to win over to God a very savage people and at the same time to make safer the approach to the Chiquitos from the Guaraní towns.'

From the opening up of the province of Chiquitos in 1690, the Jesuits of the Paraguay Province had been troubled by the difficulty of communication with Asunción and with their stations on the Paraná: they had even proposed handing over to their Peruvian brethren the area they had recently civilized. The decision was referred to the Jesuit General, Tirso González. In spite of the difficulty of the route between Asunción and Chiquitos, González was in favour of leaving the mission in the care of the men who had pioneered it. At the same time he urged that they should search for a new and shorter route between the capital and Chiquitos.

The established line of communication lay through

Tucumán to Santa Cruz de la Sierra. If Buenos Aires was the starting-point, as it often was, the distance to the nearest Chiquitos Reduction was 1,640 miles; from Asunción it was further, for the priests had first to travel south to Santa Fe to join the trail from Buenos Aires to Córdoba. From Córdoba it ran through forest to Tucumán, then through desert to Tarija and Santa Cruz, and from there through dense jungle to the nearest mission still 135 miles distant. However, it was known to be possible to travel from Asunción to Chiquitos up the Paraguay river which, in its upper reaches, formed the southern boundary of the Chiquitos province. The route held unknown hazards from untamed tribes, but it was shorter and less fatiguing. The difficulty lay in finding the way and marking it once it was found. Between the thirteenth and eighteenth parallels, the Paraguay passed through a vast region of swamps and marshes in a labyrinth of channels that changed their contours and direction every year—the famous swamps of Xarayes, which in the rainy season looked like a great sea of smooth water covering as much as three thousand square leagues with low islands, marshy tracts and plantations of trees, but in dry weather dwindled to a multiplicity of small rivulets. In both seasons the area formed the main obstacle in the search for the short route that was known to exist between Chiquitos and Asunción.

It took the Jesuits seventy years to find and chart a passage and it cost them many lives. The first attempt was made in 1691, the year following the foundation of the Chiquitos mission. Setting out by river from Asunción with the object of joining Padre Arce in San Ignacio, a party of seven priests got as far as the hills called Ibitiratis after a month's sailing, but they were forced to return for reasons never recorded. The next attempt eleven years later was made from north to south. In 1702 two priests from Chiquitos reached what they believed to be the Paraguay river and erected a cross as a marker on what they took to be the river bank. They then returned to their base. The plan was for another party starting the next year from Asunción to sail upstream until they reached the cross, then strike west for the Reduction of San Rafael. It was an ingenious design, but took no account of

the seasonal flooding. The composition of the party formed
to make the journey north indicates the importance given to
the exploration by the mission Superior: Padre J. B. de Zea,
who died in 1719 as Provincial of Paraguay, Padre Bartolomé
Jiménez, elected in 1710 to represent the Province in Rome
and Madrid, Padre Francisco Hervás, a pioneer missionary
among the Chiquitos, and Brother J. B. Neumann, a Viennese
well known in the country as the founder of the first printing
press in the Río Plata region. Each of these men took charge
of one of the five balsa rafts which sailed from Asunción with
a small pilot boat: Itapúa, Loreto and Concepción had each
contributed a raft, the fifth was the joint gift of Santo Tomé
and San Borja, the pilot boat came from San Cosme. The
wind failed and only twenty-one miles were made in the first
fortnight. After weeks of sailing they failed to find the cross:
it had been swept away by the rising waters. Soon after the
return of the expedition, Brother Neumann died.

There was a further failure the following year, 1704. And
then the project was allowed to rest until 1715 when, after
he had studied the reports drawn up by the 1703 expedition
a new Provincial, Padre Luis de la Roca, decided on a fresh
attempt.* Again it was led by Padre de Arce, now a man of
sixty-four. With him was Bartolomé Blende, a Fleming.
Travelling three hundred leagues from Asunción, de Arce
reached Lake Manioré, which lay to the west of the Paraguay
and ran parallel with it for more than twenty miles. It was
in flood. From its shores he cut his way for another two
hundred and ten miles through virgin forest to San Rafael.
This was country he knew: he was the first European to
work in the area. At San Rafael he was welcomed by his
companion of the earlier expedition, Padre de Zea. But after
months on the water and in the forest, he stayed only long
enough to change his clothes and bandage his sores: he left

* These reports are printed with annotations in an Appendix to an
article by G. Furlong, 'De la Asunción a Los Chiquitos por el Río
Paraguay' in AHSJ (1938), pp. 54–79. Both were written ten years after
the expedition. There are inconsistencies in detail: the first is by Padre
Arce, the second by an unnamed member of the party. Yet a third
report, printed in the same place, is taken from the Annual Letters of
the Province.

at once to bring aid to his companion Blende whom he had
been forced to abandon sick in the marshes in the care of a
party of Guaraní. When he reached the place on his return
none was alive. At an unknown date and place de Arce also
died. Laconically Dobrizhoffer notes: 'Padre Bartolomé
Blende, a Fleming, and Padre de Arce, a native of the
Canaries, were slain by the Payaguas anno 1715.'[17]

However, the 1715 expedition had confirmed the existence
of a short route: had Padre de Arce spent more than a night
at San Rafael, he would certainly have recorded it. It was left
to others to make the discovery afresh. All that was known
was that it lay through Lake Manioré.

Opposite Asunción the river Pilcomayo branched west from
the Paraguay. It was now thought worthwhile going up this
river, then unknown, to Lake Manioré and perhaps on to
Chiquitos.

In 1721 a new two-pronged expedition was mounted
designed to meet in the area of the recent martyrdoms. From
Asunción Padre Gabriel Patiño and Padre Lucas Rodríguez
set out in a long boat with sixty armed Indians. They
travelled seven hundred miles mainly in a northerly direction,
but turned back unable to navigate further owing to obstructions in the stream. They failed to find Padre Felipe Suárez
who had travelled from Chiquitos via the Zamucos. He too
turned back with nothing accomplished. The same held of
three more attempts made between 1738 and 1740. The
danger from the Tobas Indians accounted in part for their
failure.

It was only with the establishment of a Reduction among
the Mbayá Indians of the northern Chaco that this long
series of explorations met with enduring success. In 1760
Padre Sánchez Labrador, one of the most outstanding priests
at work at the time of the expulsion of the Jesuits, founded
a Reduction for the Guaycurú and Mbayá Indians a hundred
and thirty miles north of Asunción on the river Ipané, one of
the eastern tributaries of the Paraguay. From here he made
many excursions. The most notable began on 7 December
1766. On 9 January the following year he reached Corazón,
the most easterly of the ten Chiquitos Reductions. He left a

detailed account of the journey which seemed to open a new epoch for the Chiquitos.[18] 'The iron wall, so to speak, has at last been breached,' wrote a Jesuit friend.[19] Labrador's journey was destined to be one of the last recorded adventures of the Paraguay Jesuits.

From a wild group of tribes, the Jesuits shaped the Chiquitos into a nation. Their success was due in large measure to the respect with which they treated the culture they found in the forests. They did not enter the province like men extending an embrace to an inferior race. From the day Padre de Arce watched through the night the dances and debate at San Ignacio, they knew they were being closely observed by caciques, shamans, hunters, women and children. In turn they observed the Indians' ways. Their method was to retain and redirect as far as they could their primitive customs and reorientate their equally primitive impulses. The Christian culture they established has remained to this day although the economic prosperity of the province has long passed. The stone church at San José stands with many timbered churches as a memorial of their enduring work. Possibly their secret is best expressed in the phrase of a modern American contemplative writing in a different context: 'Our communication with primitives and with primitive society demands an ability to communicate also with something deeper in ourselves.'[20]

I I

The Chaco

Although punitive expeditions had penetrated the Chaco
from Asunción in the first twenty years after the foundation
of the city, it was not until the 1570s that the first attempt
was made to subjugate the countless savage tribes that
occupied this vast unexplored area of swamps, dry plains and
long, sluggish rivers. Entering the Chaco from the north-east
in what later became the province of La Laguna, a Spanish
soldier of fortune, Andrés Manso, crossed the cordillera of the
Chiriguanos and laid the foundations of a town in the plains.
Threatened with annihilation by savage Indians, he was
rescued by the Viceroy, Francisco de Toledo, who came up
with a heavy army. Already in 1571 Toledo had struck terror
into the Indians of Peru by executing Tupac Amaru, the last
of the Incas, in the public square at Cuzco. Now after frightful slaughter of the Chiriguanos Toledo withdrew, leaving
behind him a proud, maddened people, irreconcilable to the
Spaniards. Pilaya, Paspaya and other Spanish settlements
were totally destroyed.

Then in 1612 there was the failure of Griffi's mission to
the Guaycurú from Asunción. However, the Jesuits never
abandoned the hope of subduing the Chaco. Their next
attempt was made in 1638, this time from the west. Using
Jujuy as an advance base they followed successfully the wake
of a force led by Martín de Ledesma, Governor of Tucumán,
east into the territory of the Chaguas. Ledesma built a town
on the river Lobo and here Padre Gaspar Osorio, a Castilian,

looked after the troops while he completed his plans for an
Indian Reduction : it was reckoned that more than 50,000
Indians could be found in the area. Osorio also made a comparative study of the languages of the Tobas, Mocobíes 'and
other very numerous nations, both because many of them
desired to become Christians and because there were hopes of
making a way through them to other populous nations'.*

The vision of fresh conquests now fired Osorio's imagi-
nation as it had done Montoya's in Guairá, González's in
Uruguay and van Suerck's in Itatín. The soil was rich, the
Indians appeared friendly. 'Some up country were so tall that
Osorio could scarce reach their heads with his outstretched
hand.'[1]

In their early excursions Osorio and his companion Padre
Medina crossed a mountain range and came on the Ocloia
Indians, among whom the Franciscans had once worked. The
first Reduction was established among them some thirty-three
miles from Jujuy. Six hundred Ocloia were baptized, but the
Franciscans claimed the area as their mission territory and
the township was handed over to them.

Osorio and a newly-arrived Italian from Cremona, Antonio
Ripario, then struck out in the direction of the province
Jauja. Their route took them through thick forest : 'Provisions
fell short and they sent back Sebastiano Alarcón, a youth
born in Paraguay who was anxious to enter the Society, with
some Ladradillo Indians to Jujuy. The second day after
leaving the Fathers, these Indians murdered Alarcón and took
his skull along with them to a place where Osorio and Ripario
were passing the night. They then plundered the Fathers'
baggage and the next morning murdered them, cutting off
their heads which they carried off as trophies.'[2] This happened
on 1 April 1639.

Osorio's plans had been authorized on the assumption that
they would be backed by a fresh supply of European priests
already on their way to Buenos Aires. However, the three
deaths in three days led to the abandonment of the Chaco
mission for the second time. But not for long.

* Del Techo, p. 63. All other accounts of the first attempts to open
up the Chaco are based on this early Jesuit historian of Paraguay.

In 1641 Padre Juan Pastor, the Rector of the Jesuit College at Esteco, set out for the Abipones.* Striking east from Tucumán, he came on the Matará some two hundred and forty miles from his starting-point. Their almost permanent state of intoxication made it difficult for him to achieve anything among them : on the death of any member of the tribe they feasted and drank for three days continuously, at the end of which they devoted one hour to weeping.

Pastor continued another hundred and eighty miles.

No sooner were they out of the village of the Matará than they fell into thick woods frightful for the many dens of wild beasts, the tracks of jaguars and other things that threatened death. The prickly boughs of trees sometimes lashed their faces and tore their garments. Their greatest hardship was want of water, for though they were dried up with heat and weariness there was only rainwater in the ditches and it was stinking and more a plague to the nostrils than a comfort to the parched mouth.

About half way the thick woods were succeeded by lakes and marshes caused by the flooding of the Red River over an area of twelve miles. After passing the lakes the road through the plain improved until they pitched their tents six miles from Abiponia.[3]

The Abipones were to be made famous throughout Europe more than a hundred years later in the writings of Martin Dobrizhoffer. The first historic encounter of the Jesuits with these curious people is described by del Techo.

Pastor went on alone. His Matará guides remained behind through fear. On his way he was met and encircled by two hundred Abipones on horseback : 'They were naked and their horses bare, the men tall, broad-shouldered, showing their inconstancy by the rolling of their eyes and the fierceness of their long flowing hair. When they levelled their

* Esteco was a city founded from Tucumán in the southern Chaco. The attacks of savage Indians compelled the founders to abandon the site, which was on the east bank of the Salado, and transfer it to the other bank, where it was destroyed by an earthquake.

arrows at him, he addressed them in the Tonocoté language.'*
The priest explained his motives. The Indians threw down
their arms and saluted him courteously. While the cacique
conducted the missionary to his village, his son went to fetch
his companion. Caliguila (that was the cacique's name) was
ready to consider Christianity provided the youth of the
nation was not compelled to go to church morning and evening. It was thought that such piety might impair their virility.
The boys also should be allowed to enter the church with
their bows and arrows.†

A cross was erected, a church built of sticks and straw,
Pastor began to compile a dictionary of the language and
teach the catechism. The account he gives of the Abipones is
one of the finest pieces of anthropological writing of the
seventeenth century:

Generally they are of large stature, well-built and brawny.
In summer they go naked, in winter they cover themselves
with skins. They hang clubs from their necks and quivers
from their shoulders. In their left hand they always carry
a bow, in their right a spear. To appear more frightening
they stain their bodies different colours like a jaguar. The
men who bore most holes in their bodies and stick ostrich
feathers in them are given the greatest honour: they wear
these feathers in their nostrils, lips and ears as if they
intended to take off in flight. A beard is thought dishonourable and therefore they pluck out the down that
grows when they are young. They cultivate baldness as an
ornament. None can let his hair grow until he has killed

* Dobrizhoffer says that Padre Gaspar Cerqueira, the Paraguayan companion of Pastor, who knew the Tonocoté language used by many of
the tribes, made the first contact with the Abipones, leaving behind
Pastor with the Matará guides. *History of the Abipones*, III, p. 110.
† Dobrizhoffer found that resistance to religion among the Abipones
came mostly from young men and old women, the women because they
were the priestesses of the tribal rites, the young men because they had
an inordinate passion for cutting off the heads of Spaniards and
plundering their wagons. The young women were in favour of
Christianity because it promised to make their marriages stable. *History
of the Abipones*, II, p. 153.

an enemy in war or in a duel. Manslaughter is the only proof that they are soldiers.

They also have their nobility and heroes and they advance to these honours by stages of excessive cruelty. Anyone wanting to become a hero must endure most horrid tortures, having his legs, thighs, arms, tongue and other parts of his body not be mentioned pierced and the skin of those parts torn off with a rough stone. Five elders perform this butchery on the candidate. If he gives the smallest indication that he is suffering pain even by the slightest movement, he is not admitted into the order. If he bears himself resolutely and rolls himself in his own blood as a sign he is satisfied, the honour is conferred on him.[4]

All Abipones, men and women, were decorated with a cross on their forehead, with two smaller lines at the corner of each eye extending towards the ears, besides four transverse lines at the root of the nose between their plucked eyebrows. After these tribal markings had been pricked with thorns, ashes were sprinkled into them and, mixing with the blood, made the markings indelible. The pattern most favoured by the women resembled a Turkish carpet. On becoming Christians, the Abipones gave up the custom of piercing their lower lip with a hot needle.

To train themselves for this ordeal, young Abipones pricked and flayed themselves from childhood. It was common to see boys run thorns or briars through their tongue, lips or other parts, concealing their pain under false laughter. The women painted their bodies, naked above the waist, and adorned their breasts and faces with stones. The back of their head was shaved bald. Commonly families were limited to two children; the father carried one, the mother the second as the tribe moved from place to place setting down their mats in the outline of a town. Only after these two children were able to take part in a tribal migration without parental care did custom allow other children to live after birth.

Nevertheless Pastor and Cerqueira made progress among these Spartans of the bush. 'Within a few weeks they happily saw something resembling Christianity beginning to flourish

among these savages.' Then suddenly Pastor was recalled to
Esteco : he had been chosen by his brethren to do the business
of the Paraguay Province in Madrid and Rome. A company
of Abipones with Caliguila at its head accompanied the
priests on the first ninety miles of their return journey, hunting food for them in wild country. They begged them to
return quickly.

In Europe Pastor did not forget the Abipones. He gathered
in Cadiz enough foreign Jesuits to make permanent and
extend his settlement in the Chaco. It was then, as they were
on the point of embarking, that letters arrived from Madrid
restraining their departure. Cárdenas's first blow had fallen.
As Dobrizhoffer writes : 'If those German, Italian and
Flemish Jesuits had arrived in Paraguay, doubtless by their
labours the Abipones, Tobas, and Mocobíes would have been
induced to receive the Catholic religion; whilst, left nearly a
century in their savage state, they overran the whole province
with hostile and generally victorious arms.'[5]

Towards the end of the seventeenth century, with the
arrival of the first German priests, another attempt was made
to penetrate the Chaco, this time in the territory of the Yaró,
a branch of the Guenoa, in the neighbourhood of Corrientes.
A settlement, San Andrea, was formed, but the Indians,
unable to shake off the influence of their witch-doctors,
reverted to their wild life. They protested : 'We do not like
to have a god who knows and sees all we do in secret.' The
massacres they continued to commit in the territories of
Corrientes, Santa Fe and Montevideo 'exceeded belief and
calculation'.[6]

But the main advance came later, initiated by the Jesuit
College of Santa Fe, one of the most prosperous cities under
the jurisdiction of Buenos Aires : it had rich pastures beyond
the complex network of rivers on both sides of the city and
behind it. Trade from the interior passed through here on
its way to the Atlantic. But in the hundred years after the
withdrawal of Padre Pastor, the city more than once was
almost razed to the ground by the Abipones and their allies
the Mocobíes and Charrua : 'The more valuable and remote
estancias were entirely destroyed, slaughters were committed

in the market place at midday and it was ordered by law that
no one should enter church unless armed with a musket.'
Other smaller towns and hundreds of Spanish settlements
around Rioja, Santiago del Estero and Corrientes disappeared
almost overnight; even the Guaraní Reductions on the Paraná
did not escape. In the neighbourhood of Córdoba, three
hundred miles to the north-west of Santa Fe, the Abipones
were on the warpath, killing all Spaniards within a radius of
eighteen miles of the city; at San Miguel they murdered them
in their own homes and stayed many months in sight of the
city, virtually besieging it. A short distance from Salta, the
Tobas slew more than three hundred persons in a single raid.
On one occasion the Jesuits of Santa Fe lost the estancia on
which the College depended for its support. At this time, the
priests answering calls from the sick in outlying districts
exposed themselves regularly to the risk of assassination.

But the fighting was spasmodic and there were times when
the Indians came off worse.

At intervals of peace the Jesuits had tried to preach the
gospel. Small missions would be started among the tribes and
then warfare would break out again : the Indians would
scatter and, as often as not, the priest would be murdered.
Desire for vengeance against the Spaniard was always
smouldering. There was also the suspicion that the priests
wanted to make them Christians in order to enslave them to
the Spanish Crown.

During one more prolonged truce with the Spaniards of
Sanda Fe, the Abipones along with their allies the Mocobíes
came regularly to the market to dispose of the goods they had
taken from the slaughtered Spaniards of other cities still at
war with them. Frequently they visited the Jesuit College in
the plaza across from the Governor's residence. Eventually
in 1732 two regular visitors, the Mocobíe caciques Alentin
and Chitalin, agreed to receive Christian instruction. A colony,
San Javier, was founded among them no great distance from
Santa Fe. Under Padre Francisco Navarro it grew fast. Other
Mocobíes to the north were induced to join. Two schools were
opened, one for writing, the second for music. Later under
the Silesian Jesuit, Florián Paucke, Mocobíe musicians and

choristers gave frequent concerts in Santa Fe itself and on one occasion in Buenos Aires.

Dobrizhoffer, who knew the cacique Alentin, describes how, 'standing by the little chapel with a brazen bell he called to the performance of their religious duties the very people he had formerly animated by the sound of the trumpet to the slaughter of the Spaniards'.[8] Alentin and Chitalin were joined by a third cacique, Domingo, with a troop of horse with which he had spread terror in the neighbourhood of Córdoba.

The Mocobíes made excellent Christians. Their custom, shared with the Abipones, of slaughtering unwanted children, was renounced and their practice of polygamy also. In Lent they scourged themselves with the frenzy of fourteenth-century Florentine penitents. Despite smallpox their number increased. A second colony, Pedro y Pablo, was founded for them. Among their priests were Miguel de Zea, the explorer, later Provincial of Paraguay, José Cardiel, the historian and pioneer missionary of the Pampas, and Martin Dobrizhoffer, until he was transferred to the Abipones.

But in material prosperity the Chaco Reductions were poor even in comparison with those of Chiquitos. When the governors of Santa Fe and other cities had been under siege from the savages, they had promised the Jesuits every assistance, but after a site had been chosen and a few mud huts built, they would withdraw their men and then despatch letters to the Viceroy and to Madrid declaring that they had subjugated several wild tribes. None of the things on which the stability of the towns depended was provided—no axes, or agricultural implements or even looms. Without this aid the Indians still had more to gain from war than from peace.

In the end the Guaraní towns until recently terrorized by the Abipones supplied their needs: what they could not find was donated by benefactors of the Jesuit College of Santa Fe. Dobrizhoffer declares that no European swineherd would have lived in the hovels occupied by the priests in the early days of these colonies, and his statement is supported by the official inventories drawn up for the Madrid government on the expulsion of the Jesuits a quarter of a century later. Their

rough houses were made of wood and surrounded by a
stockade, both to guard them against sudden attack and to
provide a refuge for women and children while the men were
out fighting. For further protection there were no doors, but
only narrow slits in the walls. Inside there were five or six
sections which passed for rooms, almost unfurnished except
for a plentiful supply of firearms. Sometimes there was a sofa
slung between four stakes, religious books, medicine bottles
and wine for Mass. A priest who had established a mission
among the Toquistines had also copies of Cervantes and
Quevedo.

Visiting Abipones were always liberally entertained at San
Javier. Eventually they also asked whether their people living
in the province of Santa Fe could have Jesuits. The first site
offered them by the Governor as a settlement was wide open
to attack and rejected outright by the Abipones, who suspected a trap of the Spaniards. Years passed before the
tribesmen made a second approach. This time the choice of
position was wisely left to them. They selected a fine site on
the north shore of the river Rey, a tributary of the Paraná,
about two hundred miles from Santa Fe in the centre of the
territory which they had long claimed as their own. It was
flat country with superb pastures on all sides, ample fuel, fine
soil and wild animals in plenty. It was also an excellent
defensive position should trouble break out again with the
Spaniards: in winter it was protected by water and in
summer, when the water receded, by mud flats. Some years
later when peace with the Spaniards seemed secure, the
Abipones asked to have the town transferred to a pleasant
hill on the southern shore.

This foundation was first made in 1748. The intrepid José
Cardiel and another Castilian, Francisco Navalón, were
chosen to organize it. As Padre Pastor had done a century
earlier, they built a small mud chapel and a hut for themselves and another for the cacique. Here once more other
Abipones came and put down their mats in the form of a
town. Two more colonies followed, but the priests had no
illusions: 'The greater number were attracted by the desire
of novelty rather than by religion. The expectation of trifling

presents, the beef that was distributed free every day, and security were the main magnets.'⁹ Later Rosario was served by José Brigniel, who summoned a great convention of all the Abipones. Dobrizhoffer, then his assistant from 1650, witnessed it. So far the tribe had made peace only with the Spaniards of Santa Fe : the assembly was called to discuss a general peace with the other Spanish cities. Abipón caciques came from every part of the Chaco each accompanied by a picked troop of horse, 'figures frightful to behold'. At the start, conflicting opinions were expressed. Many wanted Corrientes and Paraguay excluded from a peace settlement : they feared a universal peace would cause a decline in their military prowess; they argued : 'War with at least one Spanish province is necessary for us if we are still to enjoy the opportunity of plundering the things we need for our daily use.'¹⁰ The other side was represented by an influential cacique : he spoke in this sense : 'Haven't we got lions, jaguars, stags, emus and all the feathery and scaly creatures to train our weapons on, to say nothing of our enemies in the Chaco?' He carried the day. A general peace was agreed on, but on condition that the Abipones and their allies captured by the Spaniards and Guaraní were sent home without a ransom, while the Christian prisoners of the Abipones should have to purchase their release. In San Jeronimo forty-seven Spaniards were held by the Abipones. The Fathers were glad to be rid of them.

These curious savages won the affection of the Jesuits more than any other Chaco tribe. In the hundred years since Pastor they had changed little. Handsome men with thick raven black hair, they still spent their lives roving the plains under the sub-tropical sun, the women rather fairer than their men because they rode under the protection of a parasol. Dobrizhoffer completes Pastor's ethnological account. Living with them and riding with them as he did for two years, he admired more than anything their almost indestructible physique. Both men and women possessed acute eyesight, fine aquiline nose, sound teeth, 'never with a hump, a wen, a hare-lip, a monstrous belly, bandy legs, club feet or an impediment of speech'.¹¹ And yet they were always in motion like the monkeys. They never suffered from jaundice, epilepsy, the stone or other maladies that afflicted the European; even smallpox and measles were rarely fatal with them. They never experienced headaches; they could pass many days and nights in the rain, drink large quantities of stinking, marshy water without ill-effects; with ease they could digest half-roasted beef, jaguar or emu flesh; for weeks on end they could sit on their hard leather saddles without stirrups, or perch themselves high up in trees without giddiness; they recovered quickly from war wounds; they fell victims to musket shots only if they were struck in the heart or head; 'in extreme old age they can hardly be said to have grown old', men of almost a hundred would leap on a fiery horse like a boy of twelve and sit it for hours.[12]

Even after they had become Christians, the Abipones confessed regretfully that animal flesh tasted flat and insipid compared with that of men. Both their allies the Mocobíes and their enemies the Tobas continued to enjoy their prisoners of war. Dobrizhoffer tells of a party of Tobas who fell suddenly on his friend the cacique Alaykin as he was drinking at daybreak in a distant plain with a troop of his followers. He and six of his men were slain and then roasted and devoured by their victors. The Jesuit adds wryly : 'An Abipón boy of twelve who used to eat at our table was killed at the same time by these savages and added to the repast . . . but an old woman who had been slain there with many wounds they left on the field untouched, her flesh being too tough to be used.'[13]

The Chiriguanos who had visited the College of Santa Fe shortly after the Abipón caciques, now after a hundred years asked for the Jesuits to return to them. The large force Francisco de Toledo had brought against them was an acknowledgement of their claim to be the most important tribe in the Chaco; they were also the most numerous, some 50,000 settled mainly in the furthest point north-west from Santa Fe bordering on the provinces of La Laguna and Santa Cruz. But now their influence spread to all parts. In organization they were not unlike the Chiquitos, living in villages under a hereditary cacique and meeting for the discussion of grave topics that concerned the whole people. Their energy, cunning and warlike spirit made them perhaps the most feared and respected by the Spaniards. In their wars they took so many captives that they formed slave villages called *chanés*. More than any other tribe, they took pride in their liberty.

By 1733 two Reductions had been formed for the Chiriguanos, Concepción in the upper part of the valley of Las Salinas, and La Virgen del Rosario, lower down. Both were due to the enterprise of the Jesuit College of Tarija, and both faced constant threats of destruction from still savage members of the tribe. On 16 May 1735 the end came for Concepción when Padre Julian Lizardi, temporarily alone, was caught at the altar, dragged three miles out of the Reduction, pinned to a rock and found dead the next day with thirty-two arrow wounds in his body : his church was destroyed and his Christians who had not escaped to the woods made captive. Rosario survived. In 1762 it numbered 262 Indians or some sixty families.[14]

This number represented a fraction of the nation. But in the thirty years that followed the first pivotal foundations in the Chaco, there was scarcely a tribe in the vast area that had not at least one Reduction among its people. These primitive missions formed a cordon round the eastern and western boundaries of the Chaco and thus protected the Spanish cities. The work of the Jesuits brought to an end nearly two hundred years of spasmodic warfare and butchery.

Geographical features aided the Jesuits. At Santa Fe the river Salado flowed into the Paraná. It was up the line of this tributary that took its rise in the regions of the Andes bordering on the main body of Chiriguanos that most of the mission stations were established.

Apart from Rosario for the Chiriguanos, there was San Ignacio de Ledesma, also in the north-west, for the Tobas, four small tribes reckoned no more than 5,000 in all, cruel and each with a language of its own. Mingled with them at San Ignacio were some Mataguayos, whom the Jesuits judged a mean and cowardly people ready to betray any man's trust and plunder him for material gain.

Following the Salado downstream was San Esteban for the Lules. In 1762 there were seven hundred and three Indians in this Reduction, some hundred and ninety-three families.[15] In contrast with the Chiriguanos the Lules were a handsome race, pacific but at the same time brave. Ranging across the dry plains from the Salado to the Rio Grande, they made their livelihood from hunting, theft and cannibalism. For drink they used rainwater. Among them the Jesuits established two Reductions both on the Salado, San Juan Bautista which counted 1,300 and Pilar among the Pajanes, a subdivision of the tribe.

Also on the Salado were San José and Nuestra Señora de Buen Consejo for the Vilelas, more pacific than the common run of Chaco tribes and consequently few, some 1,600 in all their ten branches, and the last of the six on this river cordon Concepción for the Abipones. The remaining three Abipón colonies, Rosario, San Fernando and San Jerónimo, lay on the eastern borders of the Chaco either above the Paraná or near it. The figures for San Jerónimo at this time did not differ greatly from other Abipón settlements: 450 Christians, ten widows, and 272 catechumens. The large number under instruction would indicate that the Jesuits were in no haste to make Christians of these noble savages. In the same area as this cluster of Abipón missions were San Javier and San Pedro for the Mocobíes.

The geographical siting of these thirteen missions made communication between them comparatively easy. It was also possible for one to give warning of attack to another and to bring up military aid in the event of a sudden assault.

Separate from these two groups of containing missions were two in an isolated position north of Asunción among contrasting tribes: San Juan Nepomuceno was established for the Guanas who were discovered living in three large villages on the river Yabebiri, a western tributary of the Paraguay: they were reckoned to number 30,000 and were perhaps the most docile of all Chaco tribes; they were not nomadic. And in the same area Belén was founded for the Mbayá who, with a smaller number of Guaycurú, were finally brought into a Reduction. Still, the Guaycurú remained a fierce people at enmity with all the Chaco tribes except the Guanas, whom they treated as vassals.

For seven years Sánchez Labrador, one of the most distinguished scientists of Paraguay, worked among the Guaycurú and Mbayá. He was the explorer of the Chaco Boreal. At heart a naturalist, he was also a remarkable ethnologist. Unlike nineteenth-century writers who had only a superficial interest in Indian life, Sánchez Labrador wrote descriptions of native customs as exact and minute as his classifications of plants and beasts. His account of the rigidly stratified Mbayá society with its warriors, aristocrats and serfs, is among the finest works of its kind. It was from Belén that Labrador set out in 1760 on the historic journey that took him in two months to Chiquitos.*

Sánchez Labrador's account, for instance, of the drunken órgies of the Guaycurú is far from a self-pitying groan of a pious missionary; it is a fascinating piece of reporting from the field. 'The two gods of this nation', he writes,[16] 'are Venus and Bacchus. Their propensity to drink is inherited rather than acquired. The only thing that can be said for them in the state of intoxication is that they don't fight among themselves or with strangers. Their drinks consist of *chicha* and *aloja* strengthened by unpurified honey.' Several days were passed in the preparation of the orgies. First, search was made for wild honey which they gathered in abundance from hives built underground or in hollow trees. While the beverage was fermenting a bell was rung, a signal to the participants in the orgy to refrain from food that evening until they gathered at sunset the following day.

The orgy lasted twenty-four hours. While they drank, a horn was sounded continuously. Its hoarse note made an infernal and monotonous din, always the same bass note

---

* His *El Paraguay Natural Illustrado*, with his own numerous illustrations of plants and animals, is in the Archives of the Jesuits in Rome where it awaits publication. His other principal work, *El Paraguay Católico*, was printed in 1916 at Buenos Aires in four parts: the first two deal with the ethnology of the Mbayá and give a geographical and botanical description of their milieu, the third contains his grammar and dictionary of the Mbayá language, the fourth is an ethnological and geographical account of the Province of Buenos Aires and of Patagonia.

violently blown. At intervals they played a plantillo made of terracotta, wood or bone which produced a whistling sound to summon to the tent any who might not yet have drunk. A boy in fancy costume played a tamboril or sang of the prowess of the drinkers.

An order was observed among the participants. Each was given his chicha in turn, drank as much as he could, then started talking. All became their own panegyrists. There was always need to slaughter something, even if it was only a hen. Heads grew weak with the drink, noise and tobacco smoke. Some Indians became nauseated, others provocative, but they all went on drinking until the dregs were drained. It was the old people who indulged in the greatest excess.

As the number of missions grew, there was a fair prospect that the pacification of the Chaco would be complete by the end of the century. But always there was the danger that one or several missions would be overrun. Dobrizhoffer describes an attack made on Rosario in August 1765. Savage Tobas, joined by some pagan Mocobíes and Guaycurú, six hundred in all, were reported by Abipón scouts to be gathering in the area for an assault. Many Abipones fled, only to be driven back to the mission by hunger. Help was sought from the Spanish authorities. Four soldiers arrived who looked 'as though they had come to die, not to slay the enemy': the captain was so afflicted with gout that he could hardly lift his hand to his mouth, a second soldier was a consumptive, the third a melancholic while the fourth was almost made incapable of walking by a large swelling in his groin.[17] When the cacique of Rosario saw them he judged defence out of the question and left the Reduction, pretending that he was going out to hunt. Most of the people crowded after him. Only these four Spaniards and four Indians were left to give battle.

Dobrizhoffer's pride was aroused. He watched the smoke of the enemy encampment as he made preparations for defence. Fortunately, the evening before the attack eight Abipón warriors returned to double the strength of his forces. At two in the morning he was relieved from his watch by an Indian who soon fell asleep: 'While this man was snoring

and the dogs were mute (at other times they would bark at a
strange fly) about 4 a.m. six hundred savage horsemen drew
near . . . in the profoundest silence by the light of the full
moon.' With his unfailing sense of absurdity Dobrizhoffer
continues :

In the first attack the savages carried off, without opposition, sixty ploughing oxen which I had confined in stalls
near my house. Part of them besieged the houses of the
Abipones that, being engaged in the defence of their
property, they might not be able to come and assist me.
The rest of the savages, leaving their horses at the border
of a neighbouring wood, surrounded the paling of my
house, and filled the courtyard with a shower of arrows.
The soldiers, awakened at last by the screams of the
women who were flying to the palisade, instead of instantly
discharging the cannon and all the muskets at hand upon
the assailants, stupidly wasted time in collecting their
luggage, and after they had deposited this trash in a place
of safety, the captain comes, with a snail's pace, to awaken
me, and after much circumlocution announces that we are
surrounded by enemies, with just as much composure as
if he had only been wishing me good day. When the
captain perceived that I had armed myself and left the
apartment, he fired his musket but hit no one; from where
he stood he could neither see the enemy nor be seen by
them. Spying the smoking musket directed towards the
moon which appeared right above my house, 'What injury
have you received from the moon, good man,' said I, 'that
you are firing at *her*?' He, however, not a little elated at
his musket's having made so unusually loud and ready a
report, said pompously to one of his companions, 'Come
brother, do you discharge your musket also?' but this
soldier, a remarkable tall lean man, betook himself to a
corner of the house, shaking in every limb, like a person in
a fit of the ague.'

Dobrizhoffer was frightened but he advanced alone :

I ran towards the savage host, aiming a musket in a

threatening manner, and as I went along the ground was
strewed with arrows which rattled under my feet. The
savages, ranged in a triple row, stuck to the palisade like
flies, and were defended by its thick and lofty stakes
through the interstices of which they were able to shoot
arrows at us, but could hardly be reached by our bullets;
on which account I did not think it advisable merely to
fire the musket, thinking that if they heard the report and
saw none of their companions fall, they would cease to fear
and boldly quit the palisade. I therefore walked straight
towards the paling, intending to take a more certain aim
at the savages with four pistols, and a gun to which a
bayonet was prefixed. But an unlucky accident discon-
certed this fine scheme; for when I was about ten steps off
the palisade and was just going to fire, an arrow an ell and
a half long, made of the hardest wood and barbed with
five hooks, pierced the shoulder of my right arm, wounded
a muscle by which the middle finger is moved, and stuck
fixed in my side. On receiving this wound, I took hold of
my musket with my left hand, and entered the house, so
that the captain, who was lying hid there, might pull out
the arrow; and in order to do this, he twisted it quickly
round and round with his hands, just as you mill chocolate,
by which the flesh was sufficiently torn to open a way for
the hooks to be taken out. What torture this caused me,
no one that has not felt the same himself can possibly
imagine.[18]

Dobrizhoffer's arm was useless, but the savages withdrew,
frightened by the musket that he pointed at them from a
distance of ten paces. As they ran to their tethered horses
Dobrizhoffer pursued, firing his musket into the air. The
Indians scattered. Three hundred went to round up the
Abipón horses grazing by the river, the other three hundred
formed a semi-circle round the mission. At two in the afternoon Dobrizhoffer saw the plunderers reappear driving 2,000
horses. For them this could be reckoned a victory. Dobrizhoffer was happy to be alive. The sheep were saved by an
Abipón boy, who from a safe place shot arrows at the

marauders as they attempted to drive them off. One Spaniard had shot at the moon, another did not even know how to load his musket.

The only casualty among the Abipones was a lady whose wounds Dobrïzhoffer attended. He himself suffered greatly from thirst after losing a lot of blood. Within sixteen days his wound had healed by the application of hens' fat. When the cacique returned with his hunting party, he pursued the Mocobíes and recovered four hundred horses.

The raiders moved on. The Governor of Asunción mounted an expedition against them but they were not to be found.

Even when the Abipones were left in peace, they had little time or taste for Christianity. War and hunting interested them more. The majority of boys and young women attended church in the evening for instruction, but hardly any male adults. The priests found it impossible to wean them from drinking orgies and superstitions. Even the dying were reluctant to receive baptism. Because Rosario was then made up of 'energumens more than catechumens', Dobrizhoffer was without the small pension given to the missionaries by the Crown.

Illness followed. Relieved by his old friend and teacher Padre Brigniel, Dobrizhoffer made his way upriver to Asunción. Then, after a short convalescence, he was posted to the Guaraní Reduction of San Joaquín where he had begun his missionary career. The cacique of the town had begged to have him back.

But even with the strategic siting of the Chaco missions, communication between them was sometimes difficult. The German missionary and pioneer botanist of Paraguay, Florián Paucke, has left an account of his journey from Córdoba via Sante Fe to the Mocobíe colony of San Javier.[19]

He was at Córdoba when he received his posting. Before starting out, he was taken by the Rector of the Jesuit University there to visit some *estancieros* who were ready to offer him some financial support for his colony which, like Rosario, got no grant from the Crown. With a large wagon and eight good horses he took the dangerous road, three hundred miles long, to Santa Fe. His luggage consisted of a hectane of wine, a bag of yerba, another bag of charquí or dried meat and, of course, his flute, espineta and trumpet. He was passing through the area which the Abipones and Mocobíes considered their own hunting ground. Some months earlier they had attacked Jesús María, a Jesuit estancia now almost a suburb of Córdoba, killing several adults, taking children prisoners and leaving the priest there with six lance wounds in his body.

At Santa Fe Paucke delighted two Mocobíe youths sent to escort him to San Javier by his eccentric method of playing the flute, holding it to his upper lip and blowing from beneath. His esteem among the Mocobíes was quickly established, for they thought he was blowing through his nostrils.

It was some hundred miles from Santa Fe to San Javier, three days in a country cart, twenty-four hours on horseback or as little as thirteen hours if a change of mounts was available. On this occasion it took Paucke eleven days. He had with him about eighty horses for the mission and wagon oxen as well. The rivers were swollen, the rain incessant and a storm never far away.

In the day Paucke rode on horseback, at night in the wagon, while the Indians took care of the animals and prevented them scattering. One night, owing to lightning, the Mocobíes were forced to abandon their horses; they spent the whole of the next day rounding them up: two-thirds of them were lost.* The same evening they reached the river Saladillo, a small stream now swollen to sixty yards in width. Using the Indian method Paucke crossed first. His craft was a *pelota*, an undressed bull's hide made square by cutting off feet and neck and turning up the four sides like a hat to the height of two spans, holding them erect with a thong. Saddles, musical instruments, the personal belongings of the priest, were thrown in for ballast. In the middle sat Paucke precariously maintaining his balance. Through a hole in one side of the pelota a strap was inserted which the Indian held in his teeth and one hand, while with the other hand he paddled

* Their method was to send a tame mare among them with a bell round its neck. Normally the horses scattered on a plain would gather round her and be retrieved.

his way across. In rivers wider than the Saladillo the swimmer held to the tail of a horse while he clung on to the strap with his other hand. Paucke's navigator was a Mocobíe youth of fifteen.* But the oxen could not be got across. They turned back as the waters rose. Paucke and the boy found themselves stranded for the night on the far bank. There was a sub-tropical downpour. The boy handed the priest two hides, one for a mattress, the other for a covering. Soaked and shivering Paucke remained awake all night.

About one in the morning the sky cleared. The moon came out. The boy shouted, 'Look, see how the monkeys have eaten the moon.' It was the night of an eclipse. Paucke laughed. A moment later he was scared. Behind him there was the howl of a jaguar. His only hope was to remain still. Slowly, as the night advanced, the jaguar withdrew.† The crossing was resumed at dawn and continued to midday. The following night camp was pitched beside a long lake. A stockade of yuya was thrown up against wild animals. During the half-hour crossing of the lake the next morning, Paucke noticed a dozen different kinds of duck. He shot a few down and the Indians like dogs retrieved them instantly.

On his arrival at San Javier, the church bell was rung. Here Paucke was joined by a London-born Jesuit, Peter Pole, who had put into Buenos Aires as a sea captain, become a Catholic and in 1748 joined the Paraguay Province.[20]

The language of the Mocobíes and Abipones presented as many hazards as journeys through the country they occupied. Normally it was extremely difficult for a European to get his

---

* Dobrizhoffer, who also describes this method of crossing rivers, writes: 'At first it appeared very formidable and dangerous to me, but instructed by subsequent practice, I have often laughed at myself and my imagined danger and always preferred a hide in crossing a river to a tottering skiff or boat' (II, p. 121).

† At this time the Spaniards who hunted jaguars on the more civilized east bank of the Paraná and La Plata sent every year to Europe about 40,000 skins. In the Chaco the jaguars were not hunted except by Indians and were far more numerous. For one skin an Indian would receive from a Spaniard a badly made knife. The Spaniard would re-sell the skin for a florin or twelve silver reals. Cf. G. Furlong, *Entre los Mocobíes de Santa Fe según las noticias de los misioneros* (Buenos Aires 1938), p. 52.

tongue round the words which they pronounced fast and indistinctly, 'hissing with their tongues, snorting with their nostrils, grinding with their teeth and gargling with their throats'. The total effect was similar to that of ducks quacking on a pond.[21]

Both the Mocobíes and Abipones had the custom of suddenly abolishing words and substituting new ones if they chanced to gather unfortunate associations. This added to the difficulties of compiling a dictionary, for even common words like 'alligator' suffered this change. A further complication arose when a person was promoted to the rank of a noble : he then added or interspersed new syllables in words that made them unrecognizable. Moreover, nobles had words peculiar to themselves for objects which occurred in daily conversation. Finally, each subdivision of each group of Indians had its own dialect.

Nevertheless Padre Brigniel, Dobrizhoffer's companion for a period, who was already fluent in Guaraní, compiled a dictionary of the Abipón language which eventually occupied a hundred and fifty sheets and was enlarged by his successors. Every sheet had to be kept up to date.

The Abipones partially understood Tonocoté, which Pastor's companion had used when the first contact was made with them early in the seventeenth century. It was a language still better understood by the Lules. The Chiriguanos, like the Chiquitos to their north, spoke a version of Guaraní although they occupied a country fifteen hundred miles from the Paraná Reductions. But all the Chaco Indians had the same problems as the Guaraní over numerals. When asked how many horses they had rounded up, they might answer that they would stretch from the river to the priests' house. Counting was an unnecessary and tedious process. For the priests it was no less tedious to introduce into their language abstract notions that were needed for Christian instruction. The work was still in its initial stages at the time of the expulsion of the Jesuits.

Paucke's sojourn among the Mocobíes has rightly been judged one of the most remarkable episodes in missionary history anywhere. On his arrival in 1748, San Javier was five years old. Already it had experienced many setbacks, raids of savages, fire and floods. Paucke's inventiveness and genius in devising profitable occupations for these savages led San Javier into a prosperity comparable to that of the Guaraní Reductions. Instead of teaching them agriculture, to which they were temperamentally unsuited, he instructed them in trades. Soon there were forges, tanneries, mills, carpenters' shops and brickyards. The women turned to weaving and dyeing. Within three months he had bartered seventy-three fine blankets produced by the Mocobíes for forty-eight hundredweight of tea and fifteen hundredweight of sugar and tobacco. Idlers were induced to work, a factory was built to house the blanket industry when it became too big for the homes. His organ was the admiration of Santa Fe; his choir gave concerts there and on one occasion at Buenos Aires.

But it was the Spaniards who prevented Paucke from going more deeply into the Chaco. Thanks to his work among the Mocobíes, an area of the country extending to an average of ninety miles round Santa Fe was now occupied and farmed by Spaniards; and these lands were among the best in the La Plata region. Hitherto few Spaniards had ventured beyond the immediate surroundings of the city: as one of them wrote in 1734: 'The cattle must be kept under guard; the Indians lurk in the fields, along the rivers, on the islands and at the least sign of negligence waylay the Spaniards with impunity.'[22] Now the Mocobíes threatened to return to their old life if Paucke was removed from San Javier. Only in 1763 was a solution reached and a site for a new Reduction for the Mocobíes, San Pedro, finally chosen, a wooded elevation which was quickly cleared of four thousand trees, and had an extended view on all sides, with a clear, well-stocked stream at its foot and fertile land beyond. Paucke describes the dedication:

The mounted Spaniards and Indians assembled on the square on both sides of the church. The commandant stood in front of the church with me on his right and the cacique Elebogdin on his left. Taking both of us by the hand he stepped forward and said, 'I, Francisco Antonio de Vera y de Muxica, with lawful delegation from the Crown, do surrender to you, Florián Paucke and the Elebogdin here present, in the name of his Majesty this territory for your own in the name of the most Holy Trinity.' We thus became proprietors of an area two miles to the south, four miles to the north and to the east and west as much as we might need in such manner as no foreigner could settle within these boundaries without our agreement.[23]

The new mission did well. Orchards were planted with saplings given by the citizens of Santa Fe. By the end of the first year twenty-five hundredweight of cotton had been produced. Paucke then 'begged' seven hundred head of cattle, fifty-two horses and more than two hundred sheep from the Spaniards. In 1765 he was visited by another cacique who wanted a similar Christian village for his people.

For their undertaking in the Chaco the Jesuits paid their price in lives. The maps of the period mark the approximate site of their murdered men. Dobrizhoffer gives succinct details of some of his contemporaries, for instance, Padre Augustín Castanares, a South American from Salta, slain with a club by Tobas and Mataguayos as he was travelling through their country. This was on 15 September 1744. Then there was Padre Francisco Ugalde, a Basque, first pierced by a shower of arrows, then burnt to ashes in a church which was set on fire by the Tobas with arrows headed with flaming tow. And Brother Alberto Romero, who had his head cloven with an axe by the Zamucos in 1718. But their spirit is best expressed by Dobrizhoffer when, at the end of his list, he makes mention of himself : 'Padre Martin Dobrizhoffer, whilst defending his own house and the chapel against six hundred savages in the town of Rosario had his right hand pierced with a barbed arrow, the muscle of his middle finger hurt and one rib wounded by a savage Toba at four o'clock in the morning on 2 August 1765.'

12

Song, Dance and Church

Many priests in all these Reductions had been formed in the Jesuit theatrical traditions. From their first days in the Colleges of Europe they had taken part in classical, religious and allegorical plays and in live tableaux and symbolic processions. Others, as young teachers, had composed plays for performance by their pupils on academic occasions. Transferred to Paraguay, they saw that the instructional role of the theatre was more important there than at home. From the beginning they found it the best method of explaining to simple savages the complex truths of religion as well as the principles of Christian morality: the Indians, with the mentality of children, could take in only pictorial instruction.

Although it was not until 1660 that the first Spanish theatre in the new world was opened at Lima, religious plays had been performed in the open air in Peruvian cities before civic and ecclesiastical authorities for nearly a century earlier; in addition there was a small and private theatre in the Jesuit College at Lima, where plays were staged before unsegregated audiences of black, white and creole. The Jesuit Letters of 1582 speak of a most successful production of *Dives and Lazarus*; in 1604 *Joseph of Egypt* was put on for the benefit of the new Viceroy, Montesclaros, and still others in 1624 to celebrate the canonization of St Ignatius Loyola.

It was the Jesuits sent in 1586 from Brazil to Paraguay who first saw the role processions and music might play in the conversion of the Indians. Fields, Ortega and Saloni reported that the Guaraní had the musical instincts of birds, and a sense of tune far more developed than that of Indians in other parts of South America. 'Give me an orchestra,' wrote one Jesuit, 'and I shall conquer at once all these Indians for Christ.'[1]

The priests were unable to penetrate the forest on foot: there were too few of them and, in any case, the Indians persisted in fleeing in fear from the white man. But the Fathers noticed that when they sang melodies from their canoes, the Guaraní crept to the river banks and surreptitiously watched them pass. This determined their approach. On all their travels they took musical instruments with them and played as best they could. Chateaubriand in his *Spirit of Christianity* writes poetically: 'The Indians descended from their hills to the river banks in order the better to hear the enchanting notes, while many cast themselves into the water and swam after the boats. Bows and arrows fell unheeded from the hands of the savages and their souls received the first impression of a higher kind of existence and of the primitive delights of humanity.'[2]

Although the Jesuits used music to ingratiate themselves with the Guaraní in a systematic manner, they were not the first to observe that it was the most effective way of engaging Indians. The missionaries who landed in Veracruz in 1523 had asked that the men sent from Europe to assist them should be able to play an instrument. In 1527 the Flemish Franciscan, Pedro de Gante, founded in Mexico a school which concentrated on musical education; another Franciscan, Jodoco Ricke, had already in 1568 in his school at Quito many Indians who were able to read and write music and play the flute, the flageolet, organ and keyboard instruments.

Even in pre-Columban times all Indian ceremonial had been accompanied by the music of shell and clay trumpets, flutes of pottery or reed, various kinds of drums, singing and dancing. All that the Jesuits did was to develop the musical potential of the Indian to a degree that had not been reached in Inca days.[3] Their General Aquaviva was quick to see the importance laid on music in reports to Rome and gave every encouragement to the employment of music in the

Paraguay missions. The two pioneers of the first Guaraní
Reductions, Cataldino and Maceta, were ordered in 1609 to
gather the Indian boys every morning to learn to read and
sing, and to instruct them in the playing of musical instruments. Three years later dances were performed by these
Indians carrying torches before the Christmas crib. From
1614, if not earlier, theatrical pieces were staged on Sundays
in the Guairá Reductions, but curiously it was in the short-
lived Guaycurú mission that the most startling progress was
made. In 1611 a group of Guaycurú were taken across the
Paraguay to the Jesuit College at Asunción, where they
celebrated a fiesta with some pieces they themselves had
composed in their own language.

Hymns written in Guaraní by the Franciscan Padre
Bolaños in honour of the saints were taken up by the first
Jesuits in Guairá. Before 1619 a whole Christian catechesis
through sensible symbols and pictorial dances had been
developed. From the forests, Indians came into the settlements drawn by the magnificence of divine worship and
slowly penetrated the veil of drama to the truths of the
Christian faith. Religious dogma was reduced to verse and
sung as a preamble to the mysteries of the Rosary. Simple
melodies, adapted to the Indian taste, were used both in
church and in processions through the streets and fields. The
climax for the neophytes came with the solemn administration
of baptism in a chapel set aside and specially ornamented
for the ceremony.

Music and dance festivals were already the feature of the
Guaraní Reductions when Diego de Torres made his visitation
in 1613. At San Ignacio Guazú, the Indians trained by Roque
González arranged, 'as was their custom', triumphal arches
under which the Provincial proceeded into the town; boys
and girls, in two columns, led the way 'singing in harmonies
the praises of the sovereign Virgin and the adults with their
musical instruments played jolly airs and dances'. Later,
González carried to the east bank of the Uruguay the music
he had developed on the west. In 1623, when news of the
canonization of St Ignatius and St Francis Xavier reached
South America, Roque González brought some of his Indians

from the Uruguay missions into Asunción for the entertainment of the city.

They were divided into two troops, one in Indian, the other in Christian dress, and performed a battle, dancing very dexterously to music. The Indians, distinguished by the variety of their feathers, were armed with clubs and bows, the Christians with long crosses. It was diverting to see them sometimes all mingling together and then presently parting, sometimes fiercely attacking one another, sometimes falling into two ranks and then mixing again. And after they had fought in this way for some time the Christians gained the day and led off the Indians as prisoners and presented them to their bishop and governor, to indicate that they were now subject to the church and the Catholic king.

By 1628 the Indians were such skilled musicians that a party of twenty went down river to Buenos Aires for a concert in honour of the new governor, Francisco de Céspedes. In a letter to the King, the Governor described how the Indians played the organ, violin and other instruments at Mass with great precision and executed dances before the Blessed Sacrament 'as professionally in all ways as if they had been trained in the court of your Majesty'.[4] Commonly there were thirty to forty musicians in every town. Training started at the age of nine or ten; boys with a better timbre were selected to form a choir. The office of chorister or musician was highly esteemed. Every kind of instrument was introduced. Probably in the first days of the Reductions, choirs were even larger. From time to time the Jesuit Generals in Rome urged retrenchment: 'In no Reduction', ran one order that was incorporated into the Customs Book, 'shall the choir exceed forty and an effort should be made to reduce this number especially in smaller places.' Choir boys were allowed to sing the epistle at solemn Masses.

By stages the simple dances developed into dramatic pieces influenced by the biblical plays still popular in the towns of the Hapsburg Dominions from which the missionaries were

drawn. By 1642 when the first centenary of the foundation of
the Society of Jesus was celebrated in Paraguay, drama was
well developed. Each Reduction put on its individual festival
for the entertainment of its neighbours: at San Ignacio Miní
a military tournament was followed by a mock naval battle
under torchlight on the Paraná. At Itapúa, after a play, there
appeared a vast old giant with white hair, followed by a
hundred boys in different coloured garments, singing the
Carmen Saeculare; they were met by a hundred oxen, and
with them passed under a hundred festal arches into the
church; at the porch a hundred loaves of bread were distributed to the people, who then filed through to find the
building illuminated by a hundred lights; laudations of the
Society of Jesus numbering another hundred were then sung.
In the cities where the Jesuits had Colleges, even more
unabashed self-praise was organized. At Tucumán, at the
crossing of the main streets, a statue of St Ignatius darted out
fire from a cane on to a hydra and a giant, signifying the
victory of the Jesuits over heresy and paganism; plays were
acted, the tower of the church illuminated and 'all manner
of sports performed on horseback'.[5]

Entertainment on a smaller scale was regularly organized
for the reception of new priests in the Reductions. When
Sepp arrived in 1691 at Yapeyú he was solemnly greeted by
the corregidor 'in the name of the whole nation with a short
but very good speech'. The next day was spent 'in mirth and
jollity'. Four different dances were performed that evening.
'The first by eight boys; managing their pikes with great
dexterity whilst they danced. The second was by two fencing
masters, the third by six seamen, and the fourth by six boys
on horseback. . . . Afterwards they gave us the diversion of
a kind of tournament on horseback. As it was then night,
they illuminated the place with ox-horns filled with suet, for
there was no oil or wax in the place.' All did their part with
a grace that would have honoured an audience of kings and
emperors.[6]

Later, the solemnity of receptions was regulated by the
Customs Book: no Superior, not even the Superior of the
Reductions, was to be received with the blast of bugles, the

rolling of drums and clarinets, nor with any military pomp. These demonstrations were reserved for bishops, governors and for royal or ecclesiastical visitors, and among Jesuits for Provincials.

But there was no restriction on the pageantry for the feast of Corpus Christi. The procession at the close of the solemn Mass was as magnificent as anything seen in Europe. In the days preceding the feast the Indians went out into the forest, cut down boughs of green trees, and with them formed two parallel walls through which the procession was to pass. Between these walls were erected triumphal arches with cupolas thirty feet high decorated with flowers; the decoration of each arch was entrusted to a cacique and his vassals. Meanwhile, others who had gone hunting brought back parrots, ostriches, monkeys, armadillos, deer, jaguars and lions which were chained to the arches; fruits, odoriferous vegetables, basins filled with fishes were laid along the route. The whole of creation, animal, floral and vegetable, was made to do homage to the Blessed Sacrament carried solemnly between four altars erected at the four corners of the square.

When the priest came out of the church with the monstrance, he was met by four companies of soldiers who guarded him on the processional route; he was then greeted with a fanfare of music—organ, harps, trumpets, zithers, flutes and drums. After incense had been offered and the Collect of the Blessed Sacrament sung, the priest sat down and the dancers came forward: ten or twelve youths in Asiatic dress, each swinging a thurible with burning incense, bowing down to the ground in native fashion. Two choristers then intoned the *Lauda Sion*: each verse ended with the offering of incense and was repeated to the accompaniment of a dance; a second pair intoned the second verse, song, incense, and dance alternating until the hymn was concluded.

The dramatic peak occurred at a corner altar where four dancers dressed like four kings, each with crown and sceptre, intoned the *Sacris Solemniis* and then executed a dance in adoration of the Blessed Sacrament. In succession each king prostrated himself, laid his insignia on the altar, and withdrew. Finally, the Blessed Sacrament was taken back to the

Church. 'Provident priests', wrote Fr. Dobrizhoffer,[7] 'hung up in the tabernacle a small part of crocodile glands, to which musk adheres, wrapped up in a piece of gold or silk stuff in order to keep off worms, which in so moist and hot a climate are otherwise bred in the sacred wafer.'

Second only to Corpus Christi in solemnity were the celebrations of Holy Week. The ceremonies were accompanied only by 'graver' instruments. Tenebrae on Wednesday evening opened the sacred triduum, and when at the end of the final psalm of Lauds the last candle was carried away, there was a noise throughout the church of the male members of the congregation voluntarily beating themselves in penitence with azotes. This was repeated on the two following evenings. On the night of Maundy Thursday there was a Passion sermon and on Good Friday a Passion procession, led by thirty or more boys in cassocks, each carrying an instrument of the Passion and escorted on either side by a torchbearer. Passing in front of the priest seated in the porch, they entered the church and in turn each held up the instrument and in a tone of lament sang in Guaraní, 'These are the bonds with which our Saviour permitted himself to be bound for our sins. Ay, ay, my Saviour and Lord'; a second boy carried a carved wooden hand, chanting, 'This is the hand, etc.' and so the rest. The procession then left the church to go round the square with the people following and the choir singing the *Miserere*. Floats of the Passion were brought out and carried through the streets in the Spanish manner; a large number of *disciplinantes* accompanied the procession on either side. At the central cross, a Passion hymn was sung and the procession dispersed.

On Holy Saturday morning, as soon as the flame had been struck from a flint in the ritual manner, a huge fire was lit at the door of the church and all the congregation snatched a brand and carried it off to their homes.

On Easter Sunday morning the township woke to the sound of flutes and timbrels. On two thrones inside the festooned church sat statues of Christ and the Virgin. The men on one side came out bearing the Christ in procession, the women and girls on the other side with the Virgin. Taking different sides of the square and led by the militia, the male and female columns met in the town centre. This was their way of enacting the meeting of the Virgin with her Son after the resurrection : her statue was made to bow three times to him. Acolytes then rang their bells, the militia waved their banners, the instrumentalists struck up and, after the *Regina Coeli* had been sung a dance was performed before the statue of the risen Christ. The processions then returned to Church for solemn Mass and sermon.

The foundation of the musical tradition of the Guaraní Reductions was the work of two Jesuits, a priest Jean Vaissau and a Brother Louis Berger, who was also an artist. Vaissau, a native of Tournai, had been a chaplain at Brussels at the court of Albert and Isabella before becoming a Jesuit. In answer to Diego de Torres's request, three other musicians accompanied him to Paraguay in 1618, an Italian, Pietro Commentale, a Frenchman, Claude Royer, both skilled amateurs, and the more professional Jean Berger, a native of Abbeville. Vaissau was sent to San Ignacio in Guairá. He had only been there six years when he died of the plague, but he had already formed the first academy of music in the La Plata area. His period and his place of origin would make it probable that he introduced choral chants for which Belgium had been distinguished from the beginning of the sixteenth century. One of the early historians of Paraguay says that from his school in San Ignacio the 'use of music and symphonic instruments spread to the new towns'. Berger's desire had always been to proceed to China or Japan, but at the personal request of the Jesuit General, Mutio Vitelleschi, who sent him from Rome strings for the construction of his violins, he stayed on in Paraguay. For a period of two years he was loaned to Chile to teach music to the Indians there, but neither in Chile nor in other parts of the Paraguay Province, even in the district of Tucumán, did he find the same musical talent he had done among the Guaraní. Only the Chiquitos and Mojos Indians belonging to the same national group had comparable gifts. There the tradition of dance and music built up by the Jesuits from Paraguay and Peru continued into the second half of the nineteenth century.

Writing in 1874 the traveller, Franz Keller, described his visit to the former Reduction of Exaltación in Mojos about a hundred years after the expulsion of the Jesuits:

A dozen swordsmen [*macheteros*], on the day of the consecration of the church, went singing and dancing and brandishing their broad knives and wooden swords, from cross to cross [standing in the square], headed by their chieftain, who carried a heavy silver cross and was followed by the whole tribe. They wore dazzling white camisetas, rattling stag's claws on their knuckles, and fanciful headgear composed of the long tail feathers of the aránas and of yellow and red toucan's breasts. At every cross and before the altars of the church they performed a sort of allegorical dance, with a great show of brandishing their inoffensive weapons, which they, at last breathless and perspiring, laid down together with their savage diadems at the foot of the crucifix, the whole evidently representing the submission of the Indians and their conversion to Christianity.[8]

In their main movements the dances had remained unchanged. Here and in other former Reductions they had been kept alive by the authority of the caciques who, when there was need, forced the younger members of the tribe to participate.

The Jesuits had among their number critics of the expense involved in clothing the Indian dancers. On information from Paraguay the Jesuit General, Charles Noyelle, wrote to the Provincial calling his attention to excess in dress and to other abuses: costumes, he had been told, were too costly and often pagan or at least profane, the movements in certain dances were unbecoming, if not indecent, often too faithful to native gyrations; it was hardly right that the Provincial and his staff should be the first to applaud these measures when he went on visitation. He had been told that in the Reduction of San Nicolás the dress of one dancer had been cut from an altar frontal; an order given to the previous Provincial that all the dancers' costumes cut from silk should

be adapted to make cassocks for torchbearers had been
ignored, and worse, new costumes for dancers had been made.

Noyelle's successor, Tirso González, extended these restrictions to include the costumes worn by the mayor and cabildo
of the Reductions. On 11 June 1694 he wrote to the
Provincial, Lauro Núñez: no new dresses were to be purchased; an intolerable burden was already being borne by
simple and poor people; there was need for moderation and
modesty: henceforth no silk was to be bought; there were
to be no beaver hats, either for daily use or for fiestas;
costumes, even for fiestas, should be made of simple materials;
the purchase of cloth from England and Holland, and *finos
de Segovia*, previously sanctioned by the Provincials, should
cease; materials had to be more in keeping with the humble
condition of the Indians.

Clearly the Indians resented this curtailment of their finery.
At their request representations were made to Rome. It was
argued that silk was harder wearing than cotton and in the
long term was an economy. The General admitted 'some
force' in the argument and, bowing to the experience of the
men on the spot, rescinded the prohibition on silk, ordering
a watch against too steep a rise in the price of silk materials.

Other practices liable to abuse were closely watched in
Rome. In 1684 Charles Noyelle called the Provincial's attention to the alleged bad example of certain priests, who on
festal days sat with their back to the Blessed Sacrament talking and laughing while they watched dances in church. Later
the custom grew up of transporting Reduction Indians to
Córdoba to entertain the Jesuits gathered for their triennial
meetings: this added greatly to the expenses of the Province;
often Indians died on the journey—twelve, for instance, on
one occasion out of a hundred and forty-seven; several
musicians and dancers on another occasion had not returned
home: some had run away, others had stayed on in Córdoba,
leaving their women neither married nor widowed and their
children orphaned: 'With fasting and prayer the success of
the Congregation should be awaited from God. I order that
such festivities should never be held except on the occasion
of a canonization.'

In spite of the Indians' instrumental and choral skill, no Indian, not even a master in the Reduction schools of music, was ever found who could compose a single line of music. None could be taught to produce a song, even in his own language; the instrumentalists never departed from their score, whatever instrument they played, nor added or altered anything by harmonies or trilling; they usually held the score in front of them, but they played or sang equally well whether they looked at it or not. The results astonished Europeans. 'I have travelled throughout Spain,' wrote Peramás, 'and in few cathedrals have I heard better music.' Padre Cattaneo wrote back to Italy in amazement after listening to an Indian boy of twelve play the most difficult motets a priest had brought from Bologna.

Unfortunately, while the dances remained Indian in inspiration, the music was European. There are many accounts of music in the Reductions, but they are not written with professional precision: the main sources are letters of Provincials, memoirs or private letters of priests to their families overseas. Certainly there was a prodigious flow of music into South America, particularly from Spain and Italy, but practically nothing was salvaged from the decline of the Reductions. When the Jesuits were expelled, no instructions were given for the disposal of musical papers, though every other scrap was gathered, classified and searched in the hope of finding material for charges against the Society. It is most likely that the musical papers left behind in the Reductions were lost at the time the churches were pillaged.* The musical instruments probably suffered the same fate.

The greatest loss was the dispersal of the musical scores written by Domenico Zipoli, considered by some historians one of the most brilliant Italian composers of the eighteenth century. Born at Prato near Florence in 1675, he had been organist at the Gesù and the Lateran, as well as master of music at the Roman College, before he joined the Jesuits in

---

* Only at the Chiquitos Reduction of San Rafael is there an unsorted heap of musical scores written out by Indians and bundled into a wooden box that was shown to me in the loft of the church, with the remains of an organ built by Padre Martin Schmid.

the Paraguay Province in 1716, the year he published in Rome his *Sonate d'intavolatura per organo e cimbalo*, dedicated to the Princessa de Forano. At Seville, while waiting embarkation with a party of fifty-three other Jesuits, which included the architects Primoli and Blanqui and the physician Aperger, he was offered the post of master of the chapel there. He declined and on reaching Buenos Aires in April 1718, joined the noviceship at Córdoba. There while preparing for ordination, he composed much music that has been lost.* His scores were sought after in the Reductions, particularly Yapeyú, which thanks to Sepp had become, after the Jesuit church in Córdoba, the main centre of music in the La Plata Viceroyalty. Zipoli's fame spread to Peru and Chile, where his works were performed in Jesuit churches. Eight years after his arrival in the new world he died, not yet a priest, at the estancia of Santa Catalina. According to one historian,[9] 'If Zipoli had remained in Rome, the *caput orbis* might perhaps have never heard a more accomplished musician.'

At Córdoba Zipoli had been *maestro de capilla*, which at this period involved three tasks, the composition of music, the playing of the organ and the direction of the choir. He also taught music in the university. When dances and theatrical pieces were performed in the Reduction of San Borja to celebrate the accession of Charles III in 1760, three operas were staged, *King Orontes of Egypt*, *The Shepherds at the Birth of Christ* and *Philip V*; the date of composition of all three was 1725 and, since no other musician was at work in the Paraguay Province at that time, they were almost certainly the work of Zipoli. Right up to the end of the Jesuit period in Paraguay, his brethren wrote with almost unlimited enthusiasm of his compositions. Compared with him, Antonio Sepp, in other respects a major figure, is unimportant. A statement of D'Orbigny, the early nineteenth-century traveller,

* Apart from a Mass recently discovered in the cathedral library of Sucre, only a *Tantum Ergo* and Litany found in the Mojos missions have so far been recovered from all Zipoli's South American compositions. Cf. Samuel Claro, *La Música en las Misiones Jesuíticas de Moxos* (Universidad de Chile 1969), pp. 25–7.

might be taken to prove that the Indians, unable to read musical scores, were content to preserve from memory the songs taught them by the Jesuits. In his travels in the Chiquitos area D'Orbigny was astounded at the musical attainment of the Indians, who mingled with their native songs some of the most famous work of European composers.

The inventories made at the time of the expulsion contain complete lists of all the musical instruments found in the Reductions down to a description of the workshops in which the instruments were made. In all the towns there is mention of at least one organ. In Ignacio Miní, Apóstoles and Santiago, there were spinets or primitive pianos. Martin Schmid, who found himself in 1717 in Chiquitos without any instruments for his choir, at once established a workshop where he produced flutes, harps, lyres, trumpets, violins and organs. He even made a monochord. His companion and collaborator, Juan Mesner, a Bohemian, founded a school in Chiquitos for the transcription of musical scores and was later deputed to go round this group of Reductions to establish choirs. When he was unable to leave his own mission, pupils were sent to him for instruction. Thanks mainly to these two priests, the music of Chiquitos was only a little less developed than that of the Guaraní missions at the time of the expulsion.

Every garment and item of foot or head wear in each Reduction was also listed in these inventories, extending often to many columns—Persian, Moorish, Spanish costumes made of silk or taffeta, and the costumes of officials worn on ceremonial occasions. The equipment is lavish and probably more extensive than in most theatres of contemporary Europe. Certainly the orders of the Jesuit Generals would seem to have been loosely interpreted, possibly because the Viceroys gave every encouragement to the theatrical talent of the Indians.

For long periods both in Chiquitos and on the Paraná, large numbers of Indians were engaged in the construction of the church which, as in Europe in the Middle Ages, became once again the assertion of a new-found faith. It was sited and planned to dominate the settlement and inspire the natives with Christian awe. The first churches to be built were simple wooden structures; though homely they impressed the Indians, who were unfamiliar with the most rudimentary architecture. They were low but spacious, with aisles supported by timber beams : until stone was used, the roof could not be raised in proportion to the length and breadth of the building. However, these first churches still had a stately appearance against the rows of one-storied houses. Unglazed windows perforated the adobe walls decorated with paintings on linen and framed with a cloth fringe or wainscoting. The columns and corniches were highly finished, and particular care was given to the decoration of the baptismal chapel. The three or four side altars were set off with artificial or natural flowers and were strewn with sweet herbs. Garlands decorated the body of the church : the cedar wood, particularly the paler species, never lost its strong fragrance; the *anguaỹ*, preferred for its hardness by native carvers and used in Peru and Brazil for the manufacture of balsam, was burned at services in place of incense; the natives were accustomed to its sweet smell, for the witchdoctors perfumed their huts with it when they received their clients, so as to create the illusion that they were breathing in a divine atmosphere.[10] On greater solemnities other perfumes were burnt and the floor sprinkled with scented waters : in fact all the senses were marshalled to assist the simple devotion of the Indians in their first years of settled Christian life.

José Cataldino, the founder of San Ignacio in Guairá, was responsible as much as any other priest for this early emphasis on church building. Though not an architect, he built in the forests more magnificent churches than existed in any Spanish settlement in Paraguay. Of the thirteen Guairá Reductions, San Ignacio and Loreto, the two oldest, possessed the finest churches : on either side of the nave ran a row of cedar columns with carved pedestals and capitals; the portico, tabernacle, the benches, confessionals and other furnishings were already finely chiselled.[11] Although no trace of these churches remains today, the descriptions given by the missionaries make it clear that in structure and ornamentation they resembled the churches that still stand in the province of Chiquitos.

The Jesuits were quick to discover the value of the native cedar which grew exceptionally high, straight and broad in Guairá and in the north of Tucumán : its beams were broader than those obtainable from any other and they never decayed under water. They were laboriously cut with a handsaw and conveyed on wagons to the construction site. They served also for the larger canoes : from a single cedar a canoe for thirty oarsmen could be hewn. Later, cedar trunks became so prized in Buenos Aires that they were conveyed there from the forest round Asunción nearly a thousand miles away. For shorter planks and smaller canoes the timboỹ was used, but it proved less valuable.[12]

The height of the cedar, together with the lack of lime, largely determined the style of the early Reduction churches. The first part of the building to be raised was the roof, supported, not by the walls, but by the two, sometimes four, lines of pillars. Sockets to take the pillars were first dug, twenty-two feet apart, each socket about eight feet deep and five and a half in diameter. Selected stones were embedded in the base and sides of the cavities to receive the cedars, which were felled with parts of the roots still adhering to the base : these were scorched to resist dampness and pressed into the cavity, which was then filled with broken tiles or bricks compressed together with mud. Sometimes twenty or thirty yoke of oxen were used to transport the cedars from the forest when they could not be conveyed by river. After the rods, entablatures, beams and roof had been constructed, the heads of the pillars were carved into round or square patterns to form ornate capitals.[13]

Within twenty years of the foundation of the first Guaraní Reduction, the first notable architect of the missions was at work. It is not certain whether Bartolomé Cardeñosa was an amateur or a professional. By 1634, when he wrote to Fr Vitelleschi, the General of the Jesuits, for a Roman textbook on architecture and design, he had already built the church at San Nicolás and probably others. Clearly some of his Jesuit brethren considered him too large-minded in his conception of what the Indians required. There is a letter from Vitelleschi, dated 16 October 1637, to Diego de Boroa, Provincial of

Paraguay, urging moderation in style : he had been told that
the Guaraní churches were too grand and costly and imposed
too heavy a burden of work on the Indians.

The Provincial refuted the criticism. The scale of building
begun by Brother Cardeñosa continued. At the end of the
century Antonio Sepp wrote to Europe : 'Each canton has a
handsomely built church and steeple with four or five bells,
one and sometimes two organs, a gilt high altar besides two
of four side altars, a richly gilt pulpit, diverse painted
images, eight, ten and sometimes more silver candlesticks' as
finely made as any in Europe.[14]

The progress was due to several Jesuits, both brothers and
priests, from many nations. In general the brothers excelled
the priests as architects, contractors and instructors of the
Indians : in the work of decoration they used to the full the
skill of the Indians as copyists. But the Indians' inability to
master mathematics prevented them from supervising any
constructional work. In the first period of the Reductions,
three men were mainly responsible for the advance made on
the primitive methods.

Brother Philippe Lemaire, a Fleming, joined the Paraguay
Province in 1640, some ten years after the destruction of the
Guairá missions. He had previously worked as a carpenter-
joiner in naval dockyards in France, Portugal, England and
Brazil. His handling of the cedar has given him a notable
place in the history of Spanish-American architecture. Unfortunately none of his work in the Reductions remains, although
his period of activity (1640–71) coincided with the increasing
grandeur of the mission churches. However, the Jesuit church
at Córdoba and the chapel belonging to the adjacent Jesuit
house, now national monuments, stand intact. The roof of
the church is a unique architectural feat. Lemaire took charge
of the building in 1660 when the walls, 104 feet apart, were
already in place. As the span was too great for a stone roof,
Lemaire made designs for a vaulted roof of cedar, resembling
the inverted hull of a contemporary galleon. He himself
supervised the felling of the cedars and their transportation
nine hundred miles dówn the Paraná, and across the desert
regions of central Argentina. Over 3,000 wooden pins were

used in the construction, which took nearly twelve years. The principles he followed had been developed in the French dockyards by the naval architect, Philibert de l'Orme:[15] they were used again later in the Jesuit churches of Salta and Santa Fe, while the more general experience Lemaire gained at Córdoba benefited the Reduction churches.

Antonio Sepp and Brother Juan Kraus, a Czech from Pilsen, who arrived together in Buenos Aires in 1691, succeeded jointly to the position occupied by Lemaire. In 1698 Sepp began what was then the most spacious of the Guaraní churches, at San Juan. Kraus, a pupil of the European architect Ruberto Blank, was his clerk of works; they co-operated also on the church of Santo Tomé. Sepp's contribution to mission architecture was twofold: he discovered a method of extracting a small quantity of iron from stones called *ytacuru* by means of a fire kept burning for twenty-four hours, and, towards the end of his mission career, in 1732 he laid down a book of building instructions which were followed in the second and more ambitious building period of the missions. The extraction of iron, in the judgement of a number of the priests, did not repay the labour spent on it, but at the turn of the seventeenth century, after seven years had passed without a load of iron reaching Buenos Aires from Spain, his discovery proved a boon. It was the time he was building up San Juan from its foundations. Although the quantity of iron was small, its quality could compare with any in Europe 'so that the hoes and chisels I give my Indians are of pure, net steel. The same goes of all other tools.'[16] Without Sepp's help the Guaraní would never have carved the millions of cubic feet of stone and hardwood used in the later mission churches. In fact Sepp's discovery made it possible to rebuild in stone all the old churches of cedar and adobe: the remains of the walls and arches are testimony to his genius. Later, Sepp's iron works at San Juan were put in charge of two Germans, Carlos Franck, a blacksmith and mechanic, and Juan Wolff, a carpenter, both of whom were also competent architects.

The original copy of Sepp's rules is now in private hands. The book deals with the qualities of various kinds of timber, their use and treatment and the time they should be felled.[17]

In his instructions for making roof tiles he writes: 'The mud has to be kneaded like bread and kept in the pit for three days, to be trodden on by oxen morning and night.' In another place he remarks on the advance made: 'Formerly they used to bring tiles from Potosí, but since we have begun to make some of our own, I have no less than six long streets in my town the houses whereof are roofed with tiles.'[18]

In place of glass, which was extremely dear and scarce, the Jesuits both in the Colleges and on the missions used talc, a softish white stone found in the mountains near Córdoba. It had slender laminae which could be divided with a knife into small plates. Out of its numerous leaves, most of them darkened with black or yellow spots, a few were white and transparent; these served in place of glass in windows and lanterns.* Unfortunately, they were brittle and were often torn away in storms. 'But in the last years of my residence in Paraguay,' writes Dobrizhoffer,[19] 'a quantity of glass was brought thither in Spanish ships and the price being reduced the houses and churches shone with glass windows.' In church windows facing south, in place of glass the Jesuits used a hard, white, and transparent stone, not unlike alabaster, which they brought from Peru, 'for the south wind, which is excessively violent in South America, breaks all the glass that opposes its fury, often levelling whole houses, breaking the enormous masts of ships and tearing up lofty cedars by the roots.'[20]

Although it is much altered, Kraus's work can be seen in the church of San Ignacio, the oldest colonial building in Buenos Aires. In 1710 he was certainly engaged on it. Like many Reduction churches, it has three entrances, all the same size, leading into a porch. On the second storey of the façade, the two panels to the left and right of the window contain vases of flowers in stucco relief in true rococo design. Although the belfry with a balcony below the arch has been dwarfed by the later addition of two towers, the church remains an impressive reminder of the lost grandeur of the Reduction churches. None of Kraus's work there survives.

* Examples of talc used for glazing can be seen in the colonial church of El Pilar in Buenos Aires.

When Kraus was transferred from San Juan to Buenos
Aires, he was replaced by a Milanese architect, Brother José
Brasanelli. The churches at Itapúa, Loreto and San Borja
were all built by him, and it is probable that he had a share
also in construction of San Javier. With Brasanelli the
German and Bohemian architects gave way to Italians and
Spaniards, who utilized the techniques discovered by their
predecessors. Grand stone churches could now be built, and
among the new generation of builders Brasanelli was perhaps
the most remarkable, for he was also a skilled sculptor and
painter. The church at Itapúa with its transepts and three
naves was 194 feet in length and 104 feet at its widest; its
thirty-two windows were all glazed and surmounted by
sculptured arches decorated in gold and varied colours. Seven
large doors, a portico and line of columns formed the façade.
Loreto was only twenty-seven feet shorter, but was perhaps
more striking with its vaulted timber roof and cupola decorated with scenes from the life of the prophet David. It was
Montoya's foundation and his grave was there. San Borja,
the third of Brasanelli's churches, was equally spacious. It
cannot be proved that Brasanelli was responsible also for the
church at San Ignacio Miní : when in 1724 the Provincial
visited this town, the number of Indians was increasing
at such a pace that a larger church was required. Since
Brasanelli was the only recognized architect working at the
time in the Reductions, it may well have been his work. He
was called in also to extend Santa Ana and built a cupola
and new tower there.

Contemporary with Brasanelli were two other Italians,
Juan Primoli, a professor of architecture from Milan, and
Andres Blanqui from Ciampioni in Isubria : they first worked
in Buenos Aires and Córdoba before being transferred to the
Reductions. There they continued building both separately
and in co-operation : for about thirty years from the time
they joined the Paraguay Province in 1716 and 1717 respec-
tively they were the dominating influence in Argentine architecture. At Alta Gracia, today almost a suburb of Córdoba,
then a Jesuit estancia, the church finished in 1762 after the
designs of Blanqui is a fine example of this brother's work,

with its curving stairway, long nave covered with a barrel vaulting, massive dome and tall lantern. Two undecorated pilasters rise the whole height of the façade. Unfortunately there are only ruins of his and Primoli's work in the Reductions. But the scale of their building can be seen in the ruins of San Miguel, the work of Primoli and the most monumental of the Jesuit churches. Built of large square-cut stone and without lime or mortar in the outside coursing it was more than 220 feet in length; a portico with seven arches formed the façade. With the churches of Trinidad and Concepción, also Primoli's work, it marked the high point of Jesuit architectural achievement in Paraguay.*

With Primoli must be mentioned Anton Hals, a German who had a hand at least in the final stages of the church of the Jesuit estancia at Santa Catalina in the hills outside Córdoba. The twin towers of the façade, with the imposing approach to the atrium, give it the appearance of a small baroque theatre. Its balustrade, decorated belfry and quatrefoil windows make it one of the most elaborate South American churches of the period. It stands still isolated in almost perfect condition. Here round Córdoba, but still more in the Paraná and Uruguay Reductions, and on the far-flung estancias in the province of Rio Grande, there were scores of chapels, halting places on the main cart routes from one town, or even one estancia, to another. They are marked on some old maps, and it is known from the minutes of the Provincials' visits that they were the work of these distinguished architects. In the region of the Paraná none survive, but in the Sierra Chica at Candonga there is a fine example again in a perfect state, a halting place on the track between Jesús María and Alta Gracia, built in 1730. Perhaps the care lavished on this and scores of other chapels led to the ruling from Rome that 'moderation is to be observed in the chapels: they are to have no façades, steps, towers, balustrades or cupolas'.[21]

Both in the Reductions and in the cities, the Jesuit archi-

---

* Primoli's work can best be judged from two of the finest colonial buildings in Buenos Aires, the old Cabildo or town hall in the Plaza de Mayo, and the church of El Pilar, partly Primoli's, in the Calle Junin.

tects trained in Europe used European ground plans but colonial structural methods. Most of their surviving works, as one historian of South American architecture points out, have 'an individuality of detail and a rugged rusticity which sets them apart from the architecture of the old world and differentiates them from the buildings seen in Mexico and central America'.[22] At times, decorative motifs of the Paraná Reductions are drawn from Guaraní folklore, like the bat that adorned the entrance of San Cosme: it is depicted flying from the church, a symbol of the spirit of darkness that cannot abide the light.*

In the Chiquitos missions most of the churches stand. The style of building developed there continued to influence parochial architecture in Bolivia and Paraguay long after the departure of the Jesuits. The churches of Caacupé, Capiatá and Valenzuela built after the expulsion show the continuity of Jesuit constructional methods and make it possible to speak of a mode rather than a style of Jesuit architecture, stretching from the province of Corrientes as far as the Beni in Bolivia. It is seen in the churches of Santa Cruz de la Sierra and the surrounding district which belong, so to speak, to the family of the Chiquitos and early Paraná missions. The decorative motifs used in Chiquitos spread to the Altiplano, and explain the profuse sculptured ornamentation of the churches around Lake Titicaca—the papaya, grape, pine cone, avocado and other fruits, also the monkey, humming bird, congar and chinchilla that are not found in the Peruvian plateau. These motifs, seen perhaps at their best in the extremely ornate façade of San Lorenzo in Potosí, are all foreign to the area, which lies 12,000 feet above the sea.[23]

At the time of the expulsion of the Jesuits, a comprehensive inventory was made of the statues and church ornaments in all the Jesuit towns. It is reckoned that some two thousand

---

* I am grateful to Bartolomé Meliá of Asunción for showing me the ancient creation legend of Apapokuva-Guaraní: it opens, 'Ñandeuvuçú (the god) came alone. In the midst of darkness he was unable to see. The eternal bats were already there and fought with him in the darkness. Ñandeuvuçú held a sun on his breast' and so scattered the bats.

statues had been carved in wood or stone by Indians trained by Jesuit priests or brothers. The list for the town of La Cruz is typical of the interiors: its church, which could contain a thousand Indian families under its vaulted timber roof, had five carved and gilded altars and a pulpit to match, comparable to the splendidly carved pulpit seen today in the church at Jujuy, considered the best example of colonial carving in the Argentine. The saints that were given niches in the altars or elsewhere in the churches are typical of those found in Jesuit churches all over the world—Ignatius, Javier, Gonzaga, Stanislaus, Francis Regis, Roque, protector of the sick, Anthony, Isidro, the agriculturist, Michael and Joseph; also there were statues of Christ, three Doctors of the Church and Our Lady of Mbororé, a title given by the Indians to the Madonna to commemorate their victory over the Mamelucos: it is found also in the inventories of other churches. These were only part of the sculptural store of La Cruz: there was a complete set of representations of Christ and his mother used in Holy Week, Christ at the pillar, the *Ecce Homo*, Christ stick in hand, prostrate in the garden, carrying the cross, in the sepulchre, risen, ascending into heaven and a figure described as the 'Nazarene'. The lists of other churches are fuller. The statues are sometimes crude, occasionally tender, as can be seen in those that survive, perhaps equivalent to the total collection of three Paraná churches: many are in private hands, others in public collections or small museums on the mission sites.

Even fewer paintings are preserved, although a school was established in the early days of the Reductions by Luis Berger, the brother from Abbeville who joined the Paraguay Province in 1616. The 'Virgin of the Miracles' in the church adjoining the Jesuit College at Santa Fe is his work. But perhaps more remarkable is Brother Grimau's 'Virgin of Tears', now venerated in the cathedral of Salta. Only one signed work by an Indian survives, the 'Mater Dolorosa' painted on wood by J. M. Kabiyu, a pupil of Berger, formerly in the town of Itapúa. The paintings on cedar from the ceiling of the destroyed church of San Ignacio Guazú, now in the Gancedo museum of Santiago del Estero, are other examples of

Berger's school. But neither Berger nor his successors could find a solution to the problem of obtaining pure colour: climatic conditions and the long distances over which the paints had to be carried spoilt their vividness.

13

The Guaraní War

The withdrawal of the Indian towns from Tape across the Uruguay in face of the Mamelucos assault had been intended as a temporary strategy. Once the Portuguese found their advance towards Asunción effectively barred by the Guaraní Reductions, they lost interest in the area. They concentrated instead on securing Colonia del Sacramento, a fortified Spanish town across the estuary from Buenos Aires. Three times it had fallen and been retaken by Spanish and Guaraní troops. To the Portuguese, Colonia was a valuable depot for goods smuggled in from England, Holland and Germany. It served also as a base for offensive operations against Spain.

While Portugal was preoccupied with Colonia, the Jesuits established themselves again in the lands from which they had been forcibly evicted by the Mamelucos.* San Nicolás was taken back across the Uruguay in 1687; originally founded by Roque González in 1626, it had fused with Apóstoles and still contained the descendants of the first settlers. In the same year Luis Gonzaga was founded and San Miguel returned to its original site. These three with San Lorenzo which followed in 1690 were all on the Piratini, a tributary of the Uruguay. San Borja, also settled in 1690, was located at a strategical ford over the Uruguay itself opposite Santo Tomé. The last two of the seven towns were on the Yyuy: San Juan, made famous by the iron works established there by its first cura, Antonio Sepp, and Santo Angel, today a thriving little provincial capital.

These towns, fewer than the first Tape missions, grew

* Cf. chapter 3.

quickly prosperous, thanks to the uncounted herds of cattle that roved the countryside, estimated in 1750 at something over a million head: they had multiplied on the rich lands from the cattle collected by the Jesuits to support the original missions and had been left behind in the retreat across the Uruguay. Other herds for which there was insufficient pasture west of the river had been driven back to form a reserve for the Reductions in the event of a famine.[1] In a short time the lands of these seven Reductions covered the whole present-day province of Rio Grande do Sul apart from a narrow coastal strip claimed by the Portuguese. All this territory lay to the west of the dividing line drawn between the claims of Spain and Portugal by the Treaty of Tordesillas signed in 1494.

Now after nearly two centuries of mainly undeclared warfare, which had persisted even when the two Crowns were united, Spain and Portugal agreed to settle their differences. This was achieved at least on paper after three years of negotiation in the Boundary Treaty signed in Madrid on 13 January 1750. The impulse came from the peace-loving Ferdinand VI of Spain who had a Portuguese wife, Maria Barbara.

Certainly there was need for a more realistic settlement than Tordesillas. Spain also was anxious to develop her La Plata trade without Portuguese rivalry; moreover she feared that her operations against Portugal might at any time involve her in a war with England. On her side Portugal was prepared to renounce her claims in the La Plata region at a price: Alexandre de Gusmão, the Portuguese negotiator, demanded in return, besides recognition of Portugal's claim of the coastal strip, a large expanse of hinterland that embraced the rich pastures of the Jesuit missions, their great herds and the seven towns with more than 30,000 Indians. Gusmão believed that Brazil's future lay not in La Plata but up country, both in the province of Rio Grande do Sul and north of the Río Negro towards the Amazon, where a new frontier was also to be drawn. The demands were high but Spain, anxious for peace, consented. Clause sixteen of the Treaty reads:

From the *doctrinas* or villages which his Catholic Majesty

cedes on the eastern bank of the Uruguay river the missionaries will leave with all their movable property, taking
with them the Indians to settle in Spanish territories. The
said Indians may also take their movable property and the
arms, powder and ammunition which they possess. In this
way the villages, with their church, houses, buildings and
property and the ownership of the land shall be given to
the Portuguese.[2]

Two preliminary boundary Commissions, one for the Río
Negro and the second for the Uruguay, were appointed. But
as soon as the terms of the treaty became known, controversy
broke out. The Spaniards considered the treaty a sell-out, the
Portuguese an unnecessary compromise. In Lisbon, merchants
objected that their interests would suffer if Colonia was
surrendered. The Jesuits also made their objections known
immediately : the treaty was in conflict with the spiritual and
temporal interests of the Spanish Crown; it was unchristian
to order the Guaraní to give up their homes; and no guarantee could be given that they would not fight.

The Indians were incredulous. Although they had no sense
of nationhood, their attachment to the place of their birth was
intense. They could not understand why the Portuguese in
Colonia were permitted to remain while they had to vacate
the east bank. Moreover, the treaty insisted that their towns
had to be in Portuguese hands before Colonia was surrendered.

The crisis came at a time when the Jesuits could expect no
support from the Spanish community in Buenos Aires. The
city merchants believed that the Jesuits prevented them
trading with the Indians; they complained that the Reductions sold better products in a better market and were
insufficiently restricted in the amount of yerba they could
deliver to the city. Although the treaty was unpopular in
Spain, this influential section of Buenos Aires regarded it as
an opportunity to steal the advantage over the Reductions.
Rumours were started that the Jesuits had built up an
independent state, and that the only article of faith they
instilled into the Guaraní was hatred of Spain and Portugal.
Facts were distorted, never to be corrected until the Jesuits

were eventually driven out : it was said that tens of thousands
of Indians had been taken from the encomenderos only to be
subjected to a harsher servitude; already the Jesuits had
twice 'led' the most powerful army in South America against
Asunción, first to depose a bishop, then a governor, both of
whom were opposed to their independence : this was proof
that they were guarding immense treasures. Further, the king
received from the Reductions only a token and derisory
tribute, which was spent entirely on pensions paid to the
priests. Maliciously, some spread word among the Indians
that the king had given his consent to the treaty only because
he had received a substantial share of the large sum paid by
the Portuguese to the Jesuits for the sale of the seven towns.
As a result of this last slander, several priests narrowly
escaped death at the hands of their own frenzied Indians.

On the side of the Jesuits, the crisis showed up the weakness of their centralized system of government in an age of
poor communications. In spite of frequent letters, the Jesuit
Generals in Rome were ignorant of the real situation; for
this they were only in part to blame. The two priests of the
Paraguay Province chosen in May 1750 to visit Rome with
a report on the state of the Reductions had been held by the
Portuguese at Rio de Janeiro and sent back to Asunción.
Francis Retz, the General, was left without personal contact
with the Province. In a letter which reached Paraguay in
January 1751, he exhorted the Fathers to unquestioning
obedience. It would be better, he said, that when the Commissioners arrived they should find the Indians already settled
on the west bank of the Uruguay. If this could not be done,
then it might be possible to negotiate for them to remain in
their own towns as Portuguese subjects.

This unrealistic letter must be put in its political context.
All over Europe people were beginning to speak and write
about the mysterious missions of Paraguay. The Jansenists
had long been preoccupied with them,* the French phil-

* Cf. Antoine Arnauld, *Morale Practique des Jésuites*, vol. 5, '*Histoire
de la persécution de deux saints évêques par les Jésuites*' (1691). The
first of these 'holy bishops' was Cárdenas, whose charges against the
Society lost nothing in their re-presentation by the Jansenists.

osophers were now interested; even those who admired in the Reductions 'the loveliest days of a new-born Christianity' or saw in them, as the rationalists did, a perfectly regulated socialist state, wondered whether or not this was the result of incalculable ambition or humanitarian zeal. Retz knew that the Society of Jesus all over Europe would be judged by the behaviour of the Jesuits in Paraguay.

On receiving Retz's letter Manuel Querini, the Provincial of Paraguay, summoned an extraordinary meeting of the mission priests, for 2 April 1751 at San Miguel. Seventy attended. Querini read publicly Retz's letter. The suggestion that the Indians should stay on as Portuguese subjects was ridiculed. Then the priests were asked whether they considered the transfer of the Indians practicable. All but two gave a negative answer. It would be impossible to find on the west bank the three principal requisites for the new towns, sufficient timber for construction and fuel, sufficient water, or sufficient land for crops and pasture: the Spaniards had occupied all that might have been available some years earlier. It was decided, therefore, to seek a revision of the treaty. Letters were to be despatched to the Viceroy, the Council of the Indies and Padre Rábago, the king's Jesuit confessor. Padre José Quiroga, already established in the king's esteem by his part in the exploration of Patagonia, was chosen to address the letter to José de Carvajal, President of the Council of the Indies and the Chief Minister of Ferdinand. It was a compelling statement, dated 14 April 1751 and incorporating the views of the meeting.[3] His points illustrate the almost total lack of understanding in Madrid of what was involved in redrawing colonial boundaries. His appeal was addressed mainly to Spanish interests.

Quiroga argued that the treaty, far from ending the smugglers' trade, would facilitate it: now it could be carried on, not as before through a single port, but via the seven towns. The Portuguese, moreover, would be given a territorial base for raids on the provinces of Buenos Aires, Santa Fe and Corrientes: the horses they rounded up would increase their war potential while the loss of mules would ruin the trade with Potosí and the Pacific towns. The Spaniards would now have to construct on the Uruguay and Paraná a line of fortresses to check the Portuguese advance. In the province of Charcas the redrawing of the boundary would expose Potosí to the Portuguese, particularly if they allied themselves with the rebel Indians, followers of the Inca Pretender : the Indians there had only recently revolted and had established intelligence with the Portuguese, who would be brought much closer to the mines by the treaty; there was reason to believe that the Inca Pretender was still in touch with them : he had boasted that, unknown to the Spaniards, his messengers had got through to Brazil in a few days.

The new frontier in the Amazon area was also going to bring the Portuguese close to Chiquitos and give them a complete stranglehold on these missions : it would deprive Indians of the mountains and lakes on which they depended for game and fish, their staple diet, and also of their wax which they sold in Santa Cruz in exchange for agricultural implements. And, of course, the Portuguese would be brought within dangerous distance of Potosí.

Even before the end of the first quarter of 1751, suspicions had been aroused by the military-style preparations of the Portuguese for taking over the seven towns. Once they were in possession of the east bank of the Uruguay there was nothing to prevent them continuing their advance; they would also be in a position to build fortifications on the Paraná, threaten Corrientes and stop trade between Buenos Aires and the interior. In any case the proximity of the Portuguese in the seven towns would lead to constant disputes; with only the Uruguay between them, it would be impossible to hold back Spain and Portugal from war. Even if the remaining Reductions were not attacked, their economy would be ruined. Some would lose their estancias, others their woods, others their yerbales : not only would the best of them fall into Portuguese hands, but the remaining ones would be in jeopardy : the Indians would have to work them from a greater distance, their rafts have to pass close to the Portuguese bank and there was no guarantee that the Indians plucking yerba would not be surprised and killed. It was on the sale of their yerba that most towns depended for the purchase of firearms and the payment of their tribute to the king. The surrender of the estancias would bring starvation : even if new pastures could be found, it was impossible to transfer all the cattle across mountains, rivers and dry plains without losing a very large number. The horses would also fall into Portuguese hands for lack of grass.

The most forceful argument was kept to the end. If the Indians were to hand over almost everything they possessed to their ancient enemies they would turn their arms against the Spaniards, their trust in the missionaries would be destroyed and this, among other things, would put an end to the pacification of the Chaco. The Jesuits would be unable to clear themselves of the suspicion of being in league with both Spaniards and Portuguese.

On top of all else there could not be a worse time for such a large-scale migration. A bad harvest was expected in the Reductions on the west bank, which would hardly be able to feed their own population. Even if they stretched their help to the furthest point, they could at very most support two of the transferred towns : and the Indians of all seven towns would have to be fed for twelve months while they built homes, planted their mandioca, found pastures, cleared the forest and built up their herds.

Inspired by the theological faculty of Córdoba University, the letter to the king's confessor, the Jesuit Padre Rábago, put the case with extreme bluntness. The transfer of the Indians went against their right to be considered free persons, against their natural right to property and even against their right to life : the treaty condemned them to perpetual exile, loss of fields and farms, and to a fresh start in life from virtually nothing. The letter concluded : 'There exists a contract binding in conscience between the king and his subjects : on the one side the subjects owe obedience to the king, on the other the king owes them protection of all their natural rights. Hitherto the Indians have never failed the Crown in their loyalty and the sovereigns have testified to this on many occasions.'[4]

By way of a note the Faculty added that, since the Indians were indisputably lawful owners of all that was being taken from them, a sovereign could dispossess an innocent subject (granted the common good required this) only if he provided adequate compensation. In this instance the compensation proposed was absurd, 4,000 pesos to each of the seven Reductions, when it was estimated that the poorest of them was worth at least a million.* In view of this the Faculty did not see how it was lawful in conscience to approve the treaty or how the execution of the royal command could be reconciled with the 'sacred obligations' of granting compensation. 'Nor do we consider it safe for us', its final words ran, 'to obey a civil and human law that is so plainly in contradiction to the laws of nature, God, the Church and the State.'

Before this letter reached Europe the Jesuit General, Retz, had died. His successor, Ignacio Visconti, elected in July 1751, continued his policies. Only seventeen days after his election he sent orders to the Paraguay Jesuits to obey promptly all arrangements made by the Spanish authorities: 'If they did not obey, the Portuguese Government would come to believe that the Jesuits in Paraguay were so wealthy in treasure and commerce that they were reluctant to hand over their Guaraní Reductions unless compelled by force.' And he continued in panic: 'I impose on every member of the Province a precept in virtue of holy obedience and under pain of mortal sin that none impedes or resists directly or indirectly the transfer of the seven Reductions. . . . And I order in the same manner every member of the Society who has anything to do with the said Reductions to use his influence and efforts to get the Indians to obey without resistance, contradiction or excuse.'

In defence of Visconti, it must be remembered that he had not yet received the letter of Quiroga or seen the protest of the theological Faculty of Córdoba University. From his central position in Rome he saw that the Jesuits had enemies in high places in most countries—chief ministers, royal mistresses and Jansenists—poised for an assault on the Society.

---

* One priest set the combined wealth of these seven towns at more than double, viz. 16 million pesos. As it was in the interests of the Jesuits to put the figure as high as possible, there is here an indication of the comparative poverty of the Jesuit towns.

Among the host of enemies, Ferdinand VI stood out as its friend. Understandably, both Retz and Visconti were anxious to do all they could to please him. Both considered their orders morally justifiable.

To the priests on the Paraná and Uruguay neither prudence nor the interests of the whole Society took precedence over the natural rights of the Indians. It was only the moral certainty of far worse consequences that in the end determined them to obey. Disobedience would have been interpreted by all thirty Guaraní towns as an encouragement to revolt. It was this prospect of a general bloodbath that decided them to counsel submission. And in doing this they hoped also to attain an amelioration of the treaty's terms.

In Madrid Padre Rábago gained some support for his brethren in Paraguay although he incurred the charge of fomenting rebellion; in Rome Visconti behaved in a manner that exasperated them. For inscrutable reasons at this moment of crisis he appointed as Provincial Padre José Barreda, a man in poor health and a newcomer to the mission. Fortunately Barreda, who assumed office on 8 December 1751, appreciated the calibre of the men over whom he was placed, defended them and leant for advice on the experienced mission Superior, Padre Bernardo Nusdorffer. Visconti's second blunder could not be righted. He appointed Padre Luis Altamirano Visitor Plenipotentiary to South America.

A Jesuit from Andalusia, Altamirano, represented the worst type of court priest. He had been appointed by a weak general to please the King and was given absolute authority in all matters concerning the treaty. He landed in Montevideo in 1752 along with the Marqués de Valdelirios, the chief boundary commissioner, convinced that the Paraguay Jesuits were actively opposing the treaty or at least doing nothing to further its execution. He had no knowledge of the situation, was too proud to acquaint himself with it and too imperious to seek advice from his brethren in the field. When the missionaries pleaded for time to resettle the Indians, Altamirano interpreted this as evidence that they were working for a stalemate. To Visconti he reported shortly after his arrival: 'There are two reasons for the inaction and oppo-

sition. . . . The first is the Fathers' excessive and blind
confidence that the treaty will come to nothing, the second,
the firm and erroneous conviction confirmed by our theologians
at Córdoba that your precepts do not bind in conscience and
consequently neither mine.'[5]

Well before Altamirano's arrival Padre Nusdorffer had in
fact visited the seven towns seeking ways to gain the Indians'
acceptance of the treaty: he reported that they could not
understand how they had been condemned to lose everything
by a king they had served faithfully for a hundred years: a
large number of their families had fallen in assaults on
Colonia which was now to be handed over to Portugal in
exchange for their own lands. In a letter to the viceroy they
pointed out that, when they embraced Christianity, 'we swore
allegiance to God and the Catholic king, and in return the
priests and royal governors promised us the king's friendship
and protection.'[6] They recalled that not very long ago letters
from Philip V, Ferdinand's father, had been read from the
pulpits of the seven towns, instructing them never to allow
the Portuguese to approach their lands.

Using his mastery of Guaraní and his prestige as a former
Provincial of Paraguay, Nusdorffer tried every kind of argument. Public prayers would be said in the square, the majority
would promise obedience, a party set out to mark limits of a
new town, but when the time for migration came the Indians
went back on their word; even when they set out, love of
their birthplace made them return. In a letter to Altamirano
Nusdorffer instanced what happened at San Luis: 'I spoke
to the Indians and they placed themselves at his Majesty's
disposal. The next day the corregidor came to my room with
other caciques and the cabildo, knelt and laid his staff of
command at my feet, saying he fully submitted himself to
the king and his wishes. He then questioned me about the
land to which they might migrate. They agreed among themselves on a certain place but I pointed out that another town
had asked for it. I told them that they might go and explore
for themselves.'[7] Nusdorffer had already sent out his own
search party, accompanied by a priest. Many places were too
exposed to the attacks of savage Indians, others too rocky,

some infested with ants, many either waterless or too swampy, none was comparable to their present sites. It was the same story at San Juan. The exceptions were San Borja and San Lorenzo : both these towns were already partially resettled across the Uruguay when the first skirmishes took place.

Against Altamirano the Indians directed a special hatred. Escorted by the Commissioners he visited Yapeyú, San Borja and Santo Tomé : of these only San Borja was among the seven towns : at Santo Tomé he lost his nerve. 'The Indians would not acknowledge him as a Jesuit because he wore lay dress; they believed he was a Portuguese and threatened to throw him into the Uruguay. . . . Terrified at the report that the Indians were approaching . . . he consulted his safety by flying in the night and soon after I found him in Santa Fe, out of danger.'[8] Dobrizhoffer, on business in the town from his mission among the Abipones, does not record the words exchanged between them.

After his experience at Santo Tomé, Altamirano was more convinced than ever that he was up against determined opposition. He now issued detailed orders to the Reductions for sermons, church ceremonies, processions to win over the Indians : he then ordered the missionaries about as delinquents under threat of expulsion from the Society. With exemplary patience men like Paucke, Nusdorffer and veterans of the Chaco endured calumnies and distortion of their motives. From now on, an even closer bond was formed among these priests that gave a fresh inspiration to their work in their last decade in South America. Left to themselves without interference from their headquarters in Rome, it is likely that they would have secured a reversal or at least a revision of the treaty. But Altamirano's high-handedness and his desire to retain favour with the king by seeing it implemented with all its injustices rendered their efforts futile : they were unable even to secure a delay in its execution which they argued was necessary for resettlement. Altamirano declined the only honourable course open to him, namely, to inform himself of the true situation and resign his commission.

Over a year after landing in Montevideo, the Spanish Commissioners met the Portuguese at Castillos on the Atlantic coast north of Montevideo in August 1752. They made soundings of the harbour, examined the terrain, then in December returned to their bases, Valdelirios to Montevideo, Gomes Freire, the Portuguese, to Colonia. A survey team made up of astronomers, cosmographers, engineers, chaplains and physicians then got down to the task of establishing a boundary as far as the river Ibicuí. With an escort of dragoons they made good progress until they reached Santa Tecla, an estancia belonging to San Miguel and fortified against the Mamelucos. Here they found their way barred by sixty-eight armed Guaraní under an Indian cacique, Sepé Tiarayo, corregidor of the Reduction. Sepé, suspecting a Portuguese trap, refused to go to the rendezvous proposed by the Commissioners. Altamirano offered his services as an intermediary. Sepé also refused to have dealings with a priest dressed as a courtier. He proudly designated the estancia chapel as a safe meeting-place. The Spaniards consented.

The meeting took place on 27 February 1753. The Guaraní troops agreed to allow the Spaniards to pass, but not their old enemies, the Portuguese. To avoid bloodshed the joint force withdrew. When news of the incident reached Europe the Guaraní force had swollen from sixty-eight to 80,000. It was said to have been equipped with artillery and officered by the Jesuits.

The deflated Altamirano then discharged a battery of excommunications against his own brethren. Again under threat of expulsion from the Order, he imposed on them twenty-four precepts: they were to bring the Indians to prompt submission by depriving them of the Mass and sacraments, their churches were to be closed and the chalices destroyed for fear they might fall into profane hands; the priests themselves taking only their breviaries were to go to Buenos Aires and make their submission to the Governor.* All priests of the seven towns, torn between loyalty to Altamirano and to the Indians, placed their resignations in

* G. Furlong, the historian of the Reductions, and Antonio Astraín, the historian of the Spanish Jesuits, join in outright condemnation of Altamirano, and find no incident in Jesuit history comparable to his behaviour on this occasion.

the hands of the Governor. They agreed to continue work until replacements were found but refused to accept the Crown stipend.

Eighteen months later, the Portuguese and Spanish forces took the field again. The interval had not been wasted by the Guaraní. In order to be free for war, they had worked intensely sowing and harvesting; every piece of scrap metal had been turned into an arrowhead; the women had busied themselves rounding stones for slings: they declared they wanted to die with their husbands and practised shooting; the caciques ordered special prayers; as Altamirano had closed their churches, they built chapels in honour of Our Lady and the Angels, patrons of the Guaraní army; banners were woven and inscribed, *Quis ut Deus*, processions of penitents organized, special litanies composed and sung.

In February 1754 a Guaraní force besieged Santo Amaro, a small Portuguese fort which they captured after a month's siege. An attack on a second fort failed. Then in July the allied army consisting of 2,000 Spaniards and 1,000 Portuguese began its advance. The Spaniards under Don José Andonaegui, the Governor of Buenos Aires, followed the Uruguay, making for San Borja, with the object of cutting off supplies and reinforcements from the Reductions on the west bank. Simultaneously the Portuguese, under the Commissioner, Gomes Freire, setting out from their base at Río Pardo, founded only two years earlier, took the line of the river Yacuí towards the more northerly towns. Bad weather, shortage of provisions and water, and desertions forced Freire to retreat. On 14 November 1754 he signed an armistice with the three Guaraní caciques opposing him and returned to base.

The revolt now spread. The Guaraní of the seven towns made an alliance with the savage Charrua. Valdelirios, the Commissioner, to justify the retreat, declared the rising the work of the Jesuits. In support, Altamirano wrote to the king accusing his brethren of instigating the rebellion.

As far as Ferdinand was concerned the affair might have ended there, but the Portuguese pressed for the application of the treaty. Preparations for another campaign were made.

The new plan was for the two armies to meet at Santa Tecla
and from there advance jointly against the seven towns.
Reinforcements had already been sent from Spain. Eventually towards the end of 1755 1,600 Spaniards and 1,200
Portuguese took the field under the same captains.

Facing them were 1,680 disorganized Indians under Sepé.*
They had a few firearms, including at most eight cannons
made of bamboo cane reinforced with rawhide in which they
placed pathetic trust : the cannons could fire at most three
times before they became useless. This force was joined by
hundreds of Indians flying from other Reductions determined
to aid their fellow Guaraní.

The campaign began with a number of skirmishes in one
of which Sepé, the Guaraní General, was killed.† In his place
Nicolás Neenguirú was appointed commander.

After joining forces the Spanish and Portuguese advanced
north-west in the direction of the seven towns across the
rolling hills of Rio Grande do Sul. At Caaibaté, an eminence
on the estancia belonging to San Juan south of the river
Yacuí, the Indians drew themselves up for battle on 10
February 1756. There was no overall command, for each
contingent obeyed its own cacique. They had chosen the hill
thinking it was a vantage-point from which to fire their
artillery; there they dug trenches and raised ramparts. As at
Santa Tecla, about fifty miles to the south-west, they declared
again that they would allow only Spaniards to pass. There
is an account of the battle written in heroic phrases by a
Spanish officer, Captain Francisco Graell, which unwittingly
shows that the slaughter of the Indians could have been prevented by a slight understanding of the Indian mentality.[9]
Graell writes that Nicolás Neenguirú, finding himself surrounded, despatched an ensign to the Spanish commander
stating that his Indians were prepared to obey the orders
given them. 'His Excellency reprimanded them in moderate

---

*San Miguel contributed 300 men, Santo Angel, Concepción, San
Nicolás 100 each, San Luis and San Juan 150, San Lorenzo 50. Those
already on the frontier brought the number up to 1,680.
† Dobrizhoffer (I, 27) describes Sepé as 'active and courageous, but as
ignorant of military tactics as I am of black magic'.

terms for the wrongs they had committed and ordered them immediately to give up the position they held and return to their towns and evacuate them, taking with them their baggage and possessions.' He promised that 'they would not be ill-handled but that, on the contrary, the king would give them all the land they needed; and he demanded that when his army reached their towns, the caciques, curas, corregidores and justices should come out unarmed and make their obeisance.' Anyone obstructing his officers would immediately be put to the sword.

Nicolás agreed to the terms. But he asked for time to round up his horses and gather his equipment before withdrawing. He was given an hour. After an hour and a half, according to Graell, all that the Indians had done was to extend their left flank. The opposing Spaniards extended their right.

There was no further parleying. Drums were beaten for the attack. 'The artillery shot first, the enemy fell into disorder and the army advanced with such valour and ardour that the infantry strove to keep up with the cavalry which on both right and left wrought fearful destruction.' Graell continues his description as though the Spaniards were facing a disciplined European force. 'The infantry, attaining the eminence, hurled itself courageously on two deep trenches and rushed some caves and a small wood into which some four hundred Indians had fled.' The slaughter lasted an hour and a quarter. The trenches dug by the Indians as part of their defences were used as burial pits. 'Among the 154 prisoners was a Paraguayan from whom it was learnt that all day the Indians had been waiting help from 200 infidel Mimianes and Charrua.'

The Indians killed comprised the greater part of their army, 1,511. On the other side three Spaniards and two Portuguese fell. The total of wounded, which included the Spanish commander Adonaegui, was thirty. Among the spoils were eight cannon, two standards, arrows, lances, a few firearms, four statues of the saints and musical instruments.

Caaibaté was known to some later writer as the American Numancia because of the stoicism shown by the Indians who stood to die rather than yield their lands. It was compared with the attempt to retake Cuzco by Manco Inca. The Jesuits had at least restricted the massacre by holding back the west bank towns from coming to the aid of the seven. When war had become inevitable, they had advised the Indians to retreat across the Uruguay as they had done a hundred years earlier before the Mamelucos, leaving behind only guerillas to harass the allied army. This strategy would have given them some hope of wearing down an enemy who had no enthusiasm for the war and found the climate fatiguing.

After Caaibaté the Guaraní became more obstinate. First, they attempted to raise another army, but there was no one who had the authority to replace Sepé. Instead, they contented themselves with ambushes and lightning raids. The Spaniards and Portuguese advanced with extreme caution. On 20 February they reached the estancia of San Luis consisting of seven *ranchos* and one large corral. On the 22nd a party of engineers was sent ahead to build a bridge over the river Jacuí. On 1 March they encamped on the estancia of San Borja, then on the 4th made preparations to cross the Monte Grande. It was not until early May that they came in sight of the first Reduction. Dobrizhoffer writes : 'Joachim de la Viana, Governor of Montevideo, sent forward with a detachment of cavalry to explore the country, having leaped from his horse on the summit of an eminence and examined through a telescope the city of San Miguel (a place inhabited by 7,000 Indians and famous for its magnificent church and fine row of buildings), in his astonishment at the size of the place, exclaimed to the horsemen about him, "Surely our people in Madrid are out of their senses to deliver up to the Portuguese this town which is second to none in Paraguay." '[10] Dobrizhoffer points out that Joachim de la Viana had supported the treaty in the hope of ingratiating himself with Barbara, the Portuguese Queen of Spain.

At Chamiebi on 11 May the Indians fought a small engagement that went against them. Then they fled to the woods taking from the great church at San Miguel their treasures which they gave to a venerated hermit living on the banks of the Piratini. When the allied army entered the town on the 17th they found it deserted. For lack of carts the

Indians had been able to salvage only a few of their goods. In the remaining towns, lying very close to each other, the cabildo, caciques and priests made their submission as the army entered. By the end of May all seven had been occupied. At San Juan, in spite of the confusion, the Corpus Christi ceremonies were carried out impressively. The Spanish captain of dragoons wrote in his diary (16–17 June): 'The spiritual organization of the pueblos is very edifying, especially in these days of preparation for Corpus Christi; the church functions have been splendid, Vespers, the offices, and procession.' Then he testified unwittingly to the enduring work of Padre Sepp. 'And especially at St Juan, where the musical corps has played and dances have been performed with great precision'; he speaks with admiration of the altars erected in the plaza, and adds that at the procession their army paraded and made repeated salutes to the Blessed Sacrament to the accompaniment of salvos from the artillery.[11]

Some Indians who fled to the mountains died of hunger, others were killed by jaguars, many fell into the hands of the Portuguese, who went to great lengths to treat them with consideration. Before the fighting had started, fifteen thousand from the seven towns had been taken in, fed and lodged in straw huts by the Guaraní between the Paraná and Uruguay.

As soon as the futile war was over, quarrels broke out between the Spaniards and Portuguese. The new Spanish Governor, the Marqués de Cevallos, arrived in Buenos Aires on 4 November 1756 with reinforcements to stamp out a rebellion that had long ceased even to smoulder. Freire was in no hurry to take over the seven towns when he had established there were no gold mines belonging to them; he insisted that all the Indians should first be evacuated across the Uruguay; when Cevallos with great tact had accomplished this by August 1758, Freire complained that the Guaraní were too near their former homes for his own security. Cevallos retorted that there was nothing in the treaty on the re-location of the seven towns: he also demanded that Freire should return the Indians he had taken into captivity at his headquarters at Río Pardo. Then there was further dissension over which of the two branches of the Ibicuí was 'the principal, origin and headwaters' designated in the treaty as the southern boundary between the Spanish and Portuguese territories. Colonia had still not been handed over to Spain. In fact, the Portuguese there were strengthening its fortifications.

Fortunately for the Paraguay Jesuits, Visconti died in 1758. With his death Altamirano's commission came to an end. Cevallos now instituted an inquiry into the conduct of the Jesuits. His predecessor, military and civil officers, seventy Indians and others were called as witnesses. The Fathers were declared innocent of any disloyalty to the Spanish Crown. In forwarding the verdict of the enquiry to Madrid, Cevallos described the charges of Altamirano and others as gross lies. He recommended that the Fathers' knowledge of the country should be used to settle the boundary question peacefully.

When the news that Colonia was still in Portuguese hands reached Madrid, opinion in favour of scrapping the treaty grew stronger. Carvajal, its chief supporter, died in 1756, Queen Barbara in 1758, and then Ferdinand himself in the following year. His successor, Charles III, had never shown any enthusiasm for the treaty. Portugal's conduct in Colonia was made the pretext for rescinding it. This was done on 12 February 1761. The seven towns were once more Spanish. Cevallos made preparations for taking Colonia by force.

The scorched earth policy of the Guaraní had made it impossible for the Portuguese to revictual their army adequately. Before the treaty was rescinded, Freire had been forced to retire to his base. As he withdrew, the Indians had stealthily reoccupied their towns : 'They found them stripped of cattle, their fields overrun with brambles and insects, their houses either burnt down or miserably dilapidated; they were sometimes terror-struck by the dens of jaguars and the holes of serpents.' The same writer describes how the Jesuits, after the restoration of the *status quo*, sought out the homeless and stray Indians : 'Crossing rivers and mountains in frost and excessive heat, they brought back a great multitude to their homes.'[12] In 1762 there were 14,000 Indians in the seven Reductions, 16,000 had been lost. It was natural that both in Spain and Portugal the Jesuits should have been made

scapegoats for the failure of the treaty. Ministers in neither
country were prepared to acknowledge their initial error.
While the Jesuits in Paraguay had a protector in the new
Governor, who was promoted to be the first Viceroy of La
Plata, in Madrid Ricardo Wall, who had succeeded Carvajal
in 1756, was both anti-religious and anti-Jesuit. As the treaty
was about to be repealed, he complained cynically that the
Jesuit procurators, 'with maps and documents in their hands,
are able to persuade the people of what they like because
there is no one who can stand up to them in matters of
history and geography'.[13]

In the Chaco the Abipones had been scandalized at the
sight of the Spaniards turning their arms against their oldest
allies. They accused the Spaniards of having short memories
and believed the reports that the Jesuits had sold the seven
towns to the Portuguese to work the gold that had been discovered in them. Their sense of loyalty was outraged and the
Jesuits found it difficult to regain their confidence.[14] But in
the final reckoning it was the Society of Jesus in Europe that
suffered most. Since 1750 the Marqués de Pombal, a strong
supporter if not the architect of the treaty, had been appointed
chief minister of Portugal. He had seen in the treaty an
opportunity both of furthering the territorial interests of his
country and working off his own limitless hatred of the
Jesuits. While the treaty was still in force he had nominated
his brother, Francisco de Mendonca Furtado, Captain-General
of the conquered Paraguayan provinces.* His instructions
were to destroy the Jesuits in the esteem of Joseph I, King
of Portugal. On his brother's reports from the field Pombal
himself wrote *A Short Account of the Jesuit Republic*, a work
which was translated and circulated throughout Europe. His
campaign against the Jesuits was superbly orchestrated in
a hundred other books and pamphlets addressed to the
monarchs of Europe and to the Pope himself. Before the

---

* Previously, as Captain-General of Pará, he had waited for two years
(1754–6) on the Río Negro for the arrival of the Spanish Commissioner
to redraw the northern boundary in accordance with the Treaty of
Madrid.

treaty was rescinded he effected the expulsion of the Jesuits from all Portuguese territories.

Dangerous publicity was now beamed on the Paraguay Province. It was said that the Jesuits had rebelled and provoked a war to protect their empire; their plan was to conquer all America and perhaps Europe also : their puppet, Nicolás, had been proclaimed Emperor. All this confirmed the truth in Cárdenas's attacks on the Jesuits, which were now reprinted. The exclusion of Spaniards from the Reductions was once again brought forward as proof of gold mines. These and other insinuations now poured out from the presses controlled by Pombal.

Nicolás Neenguirú, who had succeeded Sepé as General of the army, had been corregidor of Concepción. 'This is the famous Nicolás,' writes Dobrizhoffer,[15] 'whom the Europeans called King of Paraguay whilst Paraguay itself had not an inkling of the matter. At the very time when the feigned majesty of the King of Paraguay employed every mouth and press in Europe, I saw this Nicolás Neenguirú, with naked feet and garments after the Indian fashion, sometimes driving cattle before the shambles, sometimes chopping wood in the market place; and . . . I could hardly refrain from laughter.'

To give species to the fiction, a Spaniard in Quito was bribed to mint coins stamped with the name of King Nicolás: the money was sent to Europe. Cevallos discovered the fraud, but too late to kill the myth.

Nicolás himself was an ignorant pawn. After the war he surrendered to the Spanish forces. 'He was quietly heard, dismissed unpunished and continued in his office as Corregidor' :[16] he was tall, good-looking, taciturn and poorly educated, scarcely the Indian the Jesuits would have chosen to lead a rebellion. Some pamphleteers made out that he was a brother in the Society.

In Europe Padre Tadeo Enis, a Bohemian from Cebanik, was made responsible for instigating the rebellion. He was said to have raised 1,000 Guaraní to attack the Portuguese fort of Santo Amaro in February 1754 and to have taken part in the following April in a skirmish at Río Pardo. In later Portuguese tracts he is made the General of the Indian army.

However, a diary Enis kept during the war shows that he explicitly refused to accompany the Indians except as chaplain and physician to the wounded. The calumny was the creation of an ex-Jesuit, Bernardo Ibáñez de Echavarria, who distorted the diary to make Enis the rebel leader.[17] Ibáñez confessed his crime on his deathbed, but the harm was already done. Enis was totally acquitted by Cevallos's tribunal. At the time of the expulsion he was cura of a Uruguayan town. He died at Puerto Santa María in 1769 after transportation to Europe.*

In August 1762 Cevallos crossed the Río Plata, laid siege to Colonia, and took it on 31 October. Two months later, on 6 January 1763, he repulsed a joint Anglo-Portuguese expedition sent from Rio de Janeiro to recapture the city and seize Montevideo and Buenos Aires. The English flagship, with the commander of the expedition, was blown up by the Spaniards.

Cevallos then advanced up the coast against the Portuguese positions in Rio Grande do Sul and recovered for Spain all the littoral usurped by the Portuguese before the Guaraní war.

The Viceroy readily acknowledged that some 6,000 troops from the Reductions were mainly responsible for his dramatic victories.

* Enis, as drawn by Ibáñez, is the inspiration of the rebellious Jesuit in *The Strong are Lonely.*

14

Pampas and Patagonia

The decades preceding and following the Guaraní war saw continued expansion. When the next crisis came, the Indian commonwealth looked as though it was reaching an extension never envisaged at the beginning of the century. The Chaco was being slowly conquered, as well as parts of Patagonia and central Paraguay.

In 1746, after many failures, San Joaquín was founded for the Tobatines on the banks of the Río Yu to the east of Asunción in the yerba forest of central Paraguay, north of the present town of Coronel Oviedo.* Four hundred of these Indians had been discovered as early as 1697 in the forest of Taruma and gathered into the town of Nuestra Señora de Santa Fe, one of the two surviving Itatín Reductions. There they remained for several years, but returned to the forest to be rediscovered in 1723. A town was built for them, but famine, smallpox, and the poor pastures sent them back once again to the woods, where they were lost for another eleven years. At last in 1745 they were once more found in the forest of Tapebo, and another town was built for them, this time on their native soil : cattle, clothes, axes, furniture and music masters were obtained. For the first eight years they had to fight off assaults from the Guaycurú, then in 1753 the town was moved seventy-five miles south to its present site. It was

* Dobrizhoffer calls these Indians who were brought into San Joaquín Itatines; they were, in fact, Tobatines, a branch of the Guaraní family. They occupied the country recently opened up by the road from Asunción to Pedro Juan Caballero and the Guairá Falls.

256

here that Dobrizhoffer worked for eight years and entertained Carlos Murphy, Governor of Paraguay, with an orchestral concert and military tattoo. The place flourished. When Dobrizhoffer left on the expulsion of the Jesuits in 1768, it numbered 2,017 Indians.

San Estanislao, another town that survives today, was an offshoot of San Joaquín, and was founded five years after it on the plain bordering the river Tapairaquary. 'Arduous was the task of persuading the Indians to leave their native woods, because being accustomed to the shade of towering trees, they shunned the exposed and sunny plains where they believed their lives and liberties were endangered.'[1] Eventually they were gathered in by Padre Sebastián de Yegros who lived for a year in the forest with them before he could bring them to make a settlement. Soon it outnumbered San Joaquín. Among the Fathers who served here was Tadeo Enis, who figured in the controversial accounts of the Guaraní wars.

These towns, remote from Asunción and the two big rivers, formed a civilized enclave in a still primitive region. For years these Tobatines had been at war with the Guaycurú : they had remained more untouched by Spaniards than any Indians with whom the Jesuits had come in contact. Dobrizhoffer explains how he won their confidence :

The first of them we discovered in the woods was a fine young man holding a bird like our pheasants, expiring in his hand. I approached the astonished youth, complimented him on his singular skill in archery and . . . presented him with a piece of roast meat. . . . This unexpected breakfast dissipated the alarm which the sudden appearance of strangers had excited. His name was Arapotiyu, or the morning: for in Guaraní *ara* signifies day, *poti* the flower and *yu* whatever is yellow or golden; so that by the golden flower of the day they express the morning. And from this *morning* we discovered that the *sun*, captain Roy, the principal cacique in the vicinity, was the boy's father. . . . Having proceeded through the woods for the space of an hour, we beheld an emaciated old man, armed with an immense knife, creeping at a snail's pace, accompanied by two youths furnished with a bundle of arrows. The Indian Christians who were with us bent their bows and the points of their arrows to the ground to testify friendship . . . and one of the more aged of my companions kissed the left cheek of the cacique as a sign of peace.[2]

The old man was surly. Dobrizhoffer proposed that, instead of standing in the mud, they should sit together on a dry log. Dobrizhoffer then offered him snuff and some roast beef, but made little impression this time. The old man, however, warned him of the perils of meeting his people. Only after a prolonged talk did he agree to lead the priest to them. It was a day's journey through swampy forest. For fear of assassination Dobrizhoffer slept in the open with his Indians. The next day—no Orpheus, as he confessed—he played to the assembled Tobatines on the viol d'amour. As he saw that the tribesmen were very few and all very old, he concluded that most had died young from the rigours of the climate. After explaining the basic truths of Christianity, he offered the savages the amenities of civilized life—a free daily distribution of beef, corn, fruit, vegetables, new clothes annually, glass beads, medicines, and the attention of skilful physicans. To add weight to his oration, he distributed trifling gifts to each, earrings, scissors and small knives. In return, the cacique gave Dobrizhoffer some loaves baked on ashes. The priest rejected them for fear of poisoning. That night he again slept in the open. The next day he slaughtered an ox he had brought with him. There was a feast. The cacique became more relaxed. He confessed that he loathed both Spaniards and Portuguese. Dobrizhoffer, like most of the missionaries who had been sent into the Chaco and the wilder parts north of Asunción, was able to reply that he was neither. Finally, to the amusement of the Indians who formed his escort, Dobrizhoffer was offered the hand of the cacique's daughter in marriage. In the end he returned to San Joaquín with the cacique's three sons and gave them liberal entertainment.

The old methods of winning the Indians still availed in the last decade of the Jesuit era. After the success of San Estanislao, a third Reduction was planned in the same area.

Letters were obtained from the governor, a priest was posted
to it, but the same difficulties were encountered as in the first
years of the Reductions. A witch-doctor killed the cacique
Roy with poisoned potatoes. Then a Spanish trader in yerba
tried to enslave the Christian Indians and use them in place
of more expensive negroes. All the Indians who had volun-
teered to form the new town burnt their hovels and fled deep
into the forest.

This was the district for gathering yerba. The foundation
of the two towns at last made comparatively safe the dangerous expeditions to the forest. The Spaniards of Asunción
were quick to seize the chance of expanding a lucrative trade.
They sent up oxen, horses and mules and made passable for
wagons the track to the Mbaevra forest, where the modern
province of Caaguazú borders on Brazil, some two hundred
and fifty miles from Asunción. Trees were felled, the branches
laid over the marshes, bridges built across more than twenty-
five rivers, enclosures constructed for animals and huts for
Spanish workers. A great expansion seemed under way. Then,
on their first encounter with the savage Indians, the Spaniards
fled.

To their final decade in Paraguay the Jesuits continued
their work of subjugation. The last Reduction founded,
though not the last contemplated, was Belén on the river
Ypanéguazú in 1760. This was country claimed by the
Guaycurú, still full of superstitions and caring only for horses
and arms, still laying waste the Spanish settlements as in the
days of Cárdenas. They were in a state of elation over their
continuing victories over the Spaniards when Padre José
Sánchez Labrador, the botanist, explorer and anthropologist,
set out from Asunción with another priest, up the Paraguay
to attempt their conversion once again. After a fortnight they
reached the point where the Paraguay is joined by the Ypané.
There Sánchez Labrador found a group of these Indians,
learned their difficult language and by sheer kindness won
over a sufficient number to form a colony. But they kept
wandering back to the woods although they remained faithful to the peace they had undertaken to observe with the
Spaniards. In their first relief from the attacks of the Guay-

curú the people of Asunción 'promised mountains of gold for
the maintenance of the colony, but when their fears subsided,
they began to supply it sparingly or at least tardily with the
things needed for town life'.³ The Fathers were reduced to
living on dates and wild animals. Sánchez Labrador's assistant, Durán, was preparing to make a settlement among a
neighbouring group of Guanas on the east bank of the
Paraguay when the Jesuits were expelled from the Spanish
dominions.

It was from Belén, yet another town surviving today, that
Sánchez Labrador set out for the Chiquitos. When he discovered this river and overland route, an anonymous Jesuit
writer wrote enthusiastically to Rome: 'Our hope for the
total subjugation of the province Paraguay has never been
so high nor the enthusiasm of the Fathers greater.'⁴ Certainly
morale was high, and there was a gaiety of spirit among the
priests that is illustrated in Dobrizhoffer's leave-taking of Don
Pedro, his parakeet. 'I had in my possession', he writes,

> a bird of this kind, which I called Don Pedro and which
> articulately pronounced many words and even whole sen-
> tences, in the Spanish, Guarany, and Abiponian languages,
> and learnt to sing a little Spanish song admirably . . .
> Whenever I travelled on foot or on horseback, he sat on
> my shoulder, always chatty, always playful. When tired of
> his noise or his weight, I gave him to one of the Indians
> to carry—he angrily bit the man's ears, and flew back to
> me . . . When about sunset, like other fowls, he felt a desire
> for rest . . . by clapping his wings, and repeatedly biting
> my ear, he admonished me to stop the journey. When I
> stayed in the town, he sometimes walked up and down a
> very long rope suspended from two pillars outside the
> house. When I entered the dining room . . . he tasted,
> snatched, and swallowed any food that he could lay hold
> of . . . Seeing me caress a smaller parrot of another species,
> filled with envy he attempted to pierce the bird with his
> beak; but softened by a little coaxing, he not only suffered
> it to sleep under his wings, but ever afterwards treated it
> as a pupil, or rather as a son. What the older bird pro-

nounced with a deep voice, the younger repeated in a slenderer one. The Guaranies tie all their tame parrots by one foot to prevent them from flying away. These chains did not please me: I therefore clipped one wing of my parrots to prevent them from flying long or far away. . . . This Don Pedro of mine, after continuing many years faithful took advantage of the circumstances of his feathers having grown a little too much, to fly away and disappear. He was sought by many, but without success. At the end of three days he saw me passing through the wood, and knew me instantly. Without delay he crept swiftly along the boughs, and flew to my shoulder, repeating the words Don Pedro. But though he lavished caresses on me, he atoned for his desertion by the mutilation of his feathers . . . When he was hungry, he cried pobre Don Pedro, poor Don Pedro, in a tone calculated to excite compassion, repeating those words again and again, till eatable roots, bread, or some other food was given him. These particulars, relative to my parrot, the memory of which is still dear to me, I have, perhaps related with too much prolixity in order to show you how great is the power of education, even upon brute animals.[5]

On his other shoulder he carried at times a cayí, a small monkey, who was a superb mimic and mischievous playmate: if let loose in the house, it would throw about glasses and ink-stands and steal everything it could lay its hands on. He had also his fawn and pet fish. He was fearless of the cayman. 'About sunset,' he writes, 'we often went out to breathe the fresh air, and in our walks met with crocodiles of every age and species, but never received any injury from them.'[6] Like many of his fellow-missionaries he seems to have won the confidence of both Indians and animals with the irresistible charm that is transparent in his writing.

Contemporary with the Reductions of central Paraguay were several foundations in the country south of Buenos Aires, where there had been no attempt to civilize the Indians since the first days of the Paraguay Province. Still earlier, the first foundation of Buenos Aires had been abandoned in the face

of attacks from the Puelches, Peguenches and other savage
tribes stretching from the outskirts of the city to Tierra del
Fuego and known to the Spaniards by the collective name of
Patagonians. Skilled horsemen, they roved over the flat tree-
less lands to the west and south of the city, living off their
horses as Lapps off their reindeer. 'The horse', wrote one
priest, 'supplies them with food, clothes, lodging, bed, arms,
medicine, thread and what not. From the hide they make
their couch, clothing, boots, tents, saddles and weapons. The
sinews of the horse they use instead of thread. They drink
melted horse-fat and wash their heads, first with the blood
of the animal and afterwards with water in the belief that it
strengthens them.'[7] At the same time they drank as much
chicha as any other primitive Indians and often brandy as
well, which they purchased from the Spaniards.

The great height of many of these Indians, especially the
Puelches, added to the terror they struck into their enemies:
many of them, as Thomas Falkner noted,[8] reached seven
and a half feet. In battle, besides sword and spear, they used
'three stone balls covered with leather and suspended from
three thongs and hurled with great dexterity':[9] a good hit
with the bola, as it was called, could bring down both horse
and horseman and shatter bones to splinters. Their traditional
tactics were to approach a place in small bodies, each of
which was designated to attack a house, farm or other building reconnoitred the previous evening. The assault came
always after midnight. The women followed close on their
menfolk and ransacked the houses. Both then retreated
quickly. The Puelches used to leave their enemies, mutilated
in both feet, writhing on the ground in torment. 'Those they
despatch quickly with a single blow they think kindly and
humanely treated.'[10]

Deliberately they burned their dying folk alive to shorten
their pains. At other times when a man was in agony they
painted his body various colours and decorated it with blue
beads. Like the Indians of the Inca Empire, they composed
the corpse so that the knees touched the chin, as though it
were entering the womb again, then led the dead man's
horses, adorned with beads, copper belts and emu feathers,

round his tent a ceremonial number of times. They did the same with his dogs. Finally they fastened the horses to stakes from which they hung all kinds of garments. They moved across the plains in groups, seldom seen and little known. On occasion they would appear on the fringe of Buenos Aires and demonstrate their prowess by thrusting an arrow down their throat into their stomach and taking it out again after several minutes.

Their religion was equally curious. The Puelches believed in a multiplicity of gods, each presiding over a single family. At death the soul went to live with its family deity 'there to enjoy eternal happiness'.[11] Among the Puelches and some other Patagonians the profession of witch-doctor was hazardous. He was held responsible for epidemics and when a cacique died he was often slain, particularly if he had quarrelled with the dead man. Women as well as men held the office. Male witch-doctors, dressed as girls, were obliged to abandon their sex and refrain from marriage.[12] As with the Guaraní, there was little fuss over their marriages. Thomas Falkner explains that at an agreed time the parents of the girl led her to her spouse's *toldo* and delivered her over; or the man went to her parents and claimed her as his property; or sometimes she would go of her own accord. 'The following morning she is visited by her relations and being found in bed with her spouse, the marriage is concluded.'[13] The women were subjected to every kind of drudgery: they fetched water, dressed the victuals, sewed the hides and spun; when the Indians moved on, they pulled down the tent poles, packed and loaded the baggage, tightened the girths of the saddles and carried the lances before their husbands. All that was expected of the man was to fight and provide food and skins.

Widows fared worse. They were obliged to mourn and fast for twelve months shut up in their tent, face and hands blackened with soot, abstaining from the flesh of horse, cow, ostrich and guanaco. If in the course of the year the widow was found to have had intercourse with a man, the relations of her dead husband would kill them both.

Expeditions against the Puelches had proved useless in the

seventeenth century. However, in 1740, the Carayhetes asked for Christian missionaries. Anxious to bring peace to the province, the Governor and Cabildo of Buenos Aires wrote to the Provincial, Padre Antonio Machoni, who was then at Santa Fe. About the same time, Machoni received letters from two of his men, a Venetian, Manuel Querini, and an Austrian, Matias Strobel, offering themselves to undertake the mission : these priests had chanced to be in Buenos Aires when the cacique had approached the governor : they saw themselves as pioneers of a mission that in time would stretch south to the Straits of Magellan.

Machoni consented. He laid down his conditions : the Indians should be free from the *servicio personal* which, a hundred and fifty years earlier, had ruined the first attempts to bring the Quilnes into towns; the nearest Reduction was to be at least a hundred and twenty miles from Buenos Aires and free from the jurisdiction of the city; Spaniards should be barred from direct contact with the Indians. In return for these concessions the Indians in time were to provide auxiliary troops.

Straight away, four leading citizens of Buenos Aires went from house to house in the city and suburbs collecting funds for the mission : seven hundred silver pesos were raised, a thousand sheep and as many cattle. The first Reduction, Concepción, was founded on 7 May 1740 on the Río Salado that flows into the bay of Samborombón. It was at this time that Strobel pulled out an Indian alive from a grave.[14] In a letter of 20 November 1742 Strobel described his situation : 'The food of these Indians consists of mares and horses and what they get from begging from Christians on estancias. Their dwellings are tents (*toldos*) made of horses' skins. With these portable houses they travel where and when they want without stopping in any place any length of time.'[15] Nevertheless Strobel and Querini succeeded in building a small settlement : the toldos were arranged into streets round a plaza where a cross was erected; a cabildo was formed by the five caciques, and with Guaraní instructors the Indians began to cut stone for a church; the priests sowed sufficient maize, trigo, calabash and vegetables for the community, which by the year 1745 numbered 227 persons or forty-five Indian families, fourteen soldiers who guarded the pueblo from hostile Indians, nine Guaraní and sixteen others employed as labourers. 'Both Fathers possessed singular dexterity in managing the minds of the Indians', but, the observer adds, 'the proximity of the settlement to Buenos Aires and the estancias greatly retarded the conversion of the Indians.'[16]

The slow progress did not prevent the Governor of Buenos Aires reporting great conquests to Madrid. Replying, the Cortes asked the Governor to congratulate the Bishop of Buenos Aires on his 'holy initiative' and exhorted him to make further foundations. The worst set-back had occurred in 1742 when smallpox carried off a hundred and sixty Indians. The priests consoled themselves that they died 'in such Christian dispositions that there was no doubt about their salvation'.[17] But catechetical instruction (children in the morning and adults in the evening) was exhausting and largely ineffective. There was also constant danger of assault from other Indians. A deep defensive trench was dug, some arms and two small cannon were acquired, and on one occasion a hundred militiamen sent south from Buenos Aires to deal with a threatened attack in force.

Still more glowing despatches were sent to Madrid in 1744: now the Governor claimed that the area of the Reduction, previously infested by jaguars, was laid out in gardens and orchards: the Indians were singing litanies in their simple church, 'honouring the passion of Christ with great devotion'; they were leading a 'political and rational life'.[18]

In fact, before the end of 1744 the Reduction had been transferred twelve miles south-east to Loma de los Negros because the first location was found subject to floods. Nusdorffer, the Provincial, was far from optimistic. On 30 August 1745 he sent the king a realistic letter. 'The results are not in proportion to the effort of the Fathers, because the Indians are nomads, inconstant, ungrateful and much given to drunkenness. The seed of the gospel has certainly fallen on rocky ground and among thorns': the Indians, after five years of instruction, were still virtually heathen; there was little hope of success while it was possible for them to ride off on their horses any time they pleased.[19]

It was an old problem in a new context. Nusdorffer was nearer the mark than the Governor of Buenos Aires. The horse gave the Pampas Indian immunity from the law, as the forest did the Guaraní. With a horse he could ride out and maintain contact with his heathen tribesmen. At the same time the Fathers were liberal: none was forced to work even on the church, those that did were paid; trading with Spaniards was not discontinued; only the purchase of alcohol was forbidden.

Soon after this change of site, an expedition was mounted by Madrid to explore the Patagonian coast: in 1745 Philip V had summoned to an audience the two procurators of the Paraguay province then in Europe and put at their disposal a frigate, *San Antonio*, commissioned to chart the seas south from Río de la Plata: if feasible a colony was to be founded in the port of San Julián and if any Indians were found in the neighbourhood, townships were to be established for them. Padre José Quiroga, a seaman and scientist, was placed in charge. On his arrival at Buenos Aires he was joined by Padre José Cardiel; Strobel was withdrawn from Concepción to join them. Soldiers brought the party up to eighty persons. The journal which Quiroga kept is the earliest detailed description of the coast. Cardiel also kept a diary of his experiences. In all places that seemed to promise well for a settlement the priests were put ashore. For long periods the *San Antonio* sailed between reefs in unknown waters. As Quiroga discovered, the winds did not blow towards land, rather only gentle short breezes. On one occasion the *pampero* drove them far into the south Atlantic. Drifting back 'we found three bays and three good ports, but the hinterland was not suitable for cultivation and could not be populated; nor were there any signs of Indians. Only in one port did we discover good water and that was three leagues from the sea.'* Cardiel continues: 'At five leagues distance we saw a sepulchre with three dead men and five dead horses packed in straw and placed on staves. . . . The hut that served as

* This was the bay of San Julián where Magellan had wintered in 1520.

a burial mound was made of brambles. Round about there was a lot of horses' dung, not new, and a track leading inland.'

On 20 February 1746 Cardiel set out from San Julián with thirty-two volunteers, and in four days covered seventy-five miles in search of Indians, looking at the same time for a site for a settlement with sufficient grass for horses and wood for fires against the cold. From some high ground on the fourth day he caught sight of a large sierra on the horizon and returned dejected. No Indian had been encountered, but only emus, a few guanacos and 'a whitish dog barking at his men which soon ran away, hastening, as might be believed, to his master'.[20] All that the expedition established was that Indians lived a great distance from the sea, and that along the coast there was no suitable site for a Reduction. On 4 April the *San Antonio* was back in Buenos Aires. Immediately the indefatigable Cardiel set out once more across the pampas, this time on horseback. He failed again after being reduced to feeding on grass.

Meanwhile Serranos Indians and other Patagonians had visited Concepción. In turn they too asked for a town for themselves. Cardiel, after his experience at Concepción, was not hopeful. When the proposal came before the Provincial, his advisers were divided. Eventually a second Reduction was agreed on. Thomas Falkner, who had already reconnoitred the country as far south as the Río Negro, was appointed to accompany Cardiel : he was chosen for his skill in medicine which would give him authority over the witch-doctors. At the end of August 1747 the two Fathers entered the Sierra del Volcán and selected a site by the Laguna de los Cabrillos, now the Laguna de los Padres, fifteen miles inland from Cape Corrientes and two hundred and fifty miles south of Buenos Aires.* It was a fine site. In a country where the pools and lakes dried up in the summer, the Laguna de los Cabrillos, flanked by willows, was always filled with clear water. Two caciques with twenty-five toldos became the founders of

---

* The lake lies behind the modern resort of Mar del Plata, where the memory of the two priests is preserved in names of streets.

Nuestra Señora del Pilar. The Indians stayed all the time that the yerba maté and tobacco lasted—they bought it in exchange for ostrich plumes, ponchos, seal skins and bridles: when these were exhausted in February 1748 they took up their toldos, leaving behind a few Guaraní workers and others from Buenos Aires. The priests then got in a fresh supply of yerba and the caciques returned. This time they brought only nine toldos and stayed only four months. There was a further setback when some Serranos Indians on their way to Buenos Aires were arrested on suspicion of murder. The Serranos still at Pilar abandoned the Reduction through distrust of the Spaniards. Only on the release of the prisoners was it re-formed by Strobel, who joined Falkner in place of Cardiel late in 1748. 'One of the Fathers', wrote a contemporary,[21] 'goes out every day with a bell to summon the Indians and bring them to church. Once gathered, they start by reciting prayers and then go through the catechism questions according to the Council of Lima. After the catechism the priest gives an exhortation on the mysteries of the faith.' Before the Indians dispersed, a small present was given to everyone, usually yerba to the adults, a fig or small piece of biscuit to the children. Difficulties peculiar to Patagonia continued. Although by the end of 1748 there were thirty-seven toldos at Pilar, the number fell again when Strobel had again exhausted his treasure of yerba and trinkets. All the priests in Patagonia found it difficult to reduce the Indians even to a primitive form of settled life or to teach them so much as the sign of the cross.

The last foundation, Nuestra Señora de los Desamparados, twelve miles from Pilar, gave some prospect of stability. It was formed by three caciques with eighty horsemen. These Patagonians were honest and more docile, but hopes of large-scale conversions were dashed by Cangapol, the most powerful cacique in Patagonia and the hereditary *apo* or commander-in-chief of five southern tribes. In August 1750 he appeared before Pilar and Desamparados. Both Reductions had been alerted and made ready for defence. Cangapol withdrew to establish alliances before launching his attack. According to Falkner the *apo* was full seven feet in height, cruel, robust, perverse and astute; 'a kind of petty monarch', he fought fiercely and often escaped with his followers by swimming rivers his enemies were unable to cross, leaving behind their women and children to be butchered. On his orders his men, the Leuvuches, a small tribe decimated in skirmishes, marched, encamped, settled, moved on and made war. His eloquence matched and enhanced his standing. His chosen pastime was to show guests great heaps of skulls and bones of his slaughtered enemies. For the title page of his *Description of Patagonia*, Falkner sketched him and his wife Hueni. He is shown with bared head, his hair tied up and bound behind with a girdle of dyed material. In his tent he wore a mantle of skins, otter, fox or yaguane (a kind of pole-cat), sewn together and coming down to the ground. He is carrying all the offensive weapons of these Indians, the short bow with arrows usually tipped with bone, a lance four or five yards in length pointed with iron and made of solid cane with joints about five inches apart. His sword is stolen from a dead Spaniard. The rounded stones about his waist were twirled round the head and then hurled in the air with the attached thong which curled itself round the neck of a man or horse. Cangapol's wife is also bareheaded. She wears earrings of square brass plates, strings of beads round her neck, wrists and ankles. Her mantle is like her husband's, but fastened in front with a pin and gathered in round the waist. The apron, tied round the middle under the mantle, covered only her front.*

In 1750 Cangapol had been provoked by the Spaniards, who in a punitive expedition against some troublesome Indians had made an attempt on his son's life and slaughtered a kinsman and some allies. Though Cangapol was at this time over seventy, he took the field. He feared that the newly-formed friendship of the Serranos with the Spaniards would mean the end both of Indian freedom and his own power. In alliance with other savages he raised a large army, variously reckoned between one and four thousand.[22] Strobel was promised a force of seventy Spanish cavalry but it never

---

* In the background of Falkner's sketch is the volcano of Villa Rica, near which the fabulous lost city of Los Cesares was supposed to lie. Falkner considered that his explorations showed that it did not exist.

arrived. He was compelled to abandon Desamparados, then soon after, on 3 February 1753, Concepción. Buenos Aires lay wide open to a land attack. The citadel protected the port, but to the south there was no wall, ditch or fortification of any kind. Cangapol, by skilfully dividing his troops, was able in one day and night to attack estancias within six miles of the city, the district of Magdalena that supplied the city's wheat, and the bay of Barragan, thirty-six miles to the southeast, a refitting yard for ships calling at the port. Many women and children were taken captive with herds of cattle and horses. Cangapol lost only one man, a straggler. The Spaniards pursued but had not the heart to attack, though they outnumbered the Indians by two to one. Wagons laden with silver from Peru were then seized and their guards massacred; men gathering salt from the pits south of the city were killed. It was only then that 'the Spaniards perceived the utility of the southern colonies after they had abandoned them'.[23]

The handful of Jesuits from the Paraguay Province who pioneered the Reductions of Patagonia suffered as severely as the pioneer priests of the Chaco. 'At first, before oxen were sent to their assistance, the Fathers lived on horse flesh, the daily food of those Indians. Father Thomas Falkner, who wandered over all those plains . . . having no plate of pewter or wood, made use of his hat, which at length grew so greasy that while he slept it was devoured by wild dogs with which the plains were overrun.'[24]

The Provincial, Padre José Barreda, ascribed the failure of the Patagonian Reductions to the refusal of the Spanish authorities to send sufficient troops for their defence: to him it was a repetition of the story of Guairá. But although this was true, the cause was more complex. Cardiel put it down to the proximity of Buenos Aires, where the Indians learnt 'all the bad ways of the lower classes, negroes, mestizos, mulattos and urbanized Indians'; Sánchez Labrador blamed the 'natural restlessness of the Indians': for years the scarcity of food had set them in perpetual motion: when the lakes dried up in summer, they would ride as far south as the Río Negro to obtain water. Falkner agreed: 'of all nations on earth

there is no account of any so restless who have such a disposition to roving as these people, for neither extreme old
age, blindness or any other distemper prevents them from
indulging this inclination to wander'.[25]

Although peace was eventually made, the Jesuits had been
expelled from South America before the Reductions could
be rebuilt. Slowly, in the course of the nineteenth century,
the Patagonian Indians were exterminated.

15

The End

In the middle sixties of the eighteenth century, the final subjugation of the South American Indians from Charcas
through the Chaco to Patagonia seemed a prospect that
might be realized in the lifetime of the younger members of
the Jesuit Province of Paraguay. Fresh priests were on their
way across the Atlantic; the ravages of the Guaraní war had
been largely repaired; the way was now open from Asunción
to Chiquitos via Belén and the upper Paraguay; with San
Joaquín and San Estanislao well established, there was a good
chance of civilizing the tribes to the north as far as the Mato
Grosso; the line of Chaco missions on the Río Salado had
stood firm; a second attempt on Patagonia was being
prepared.

Then the blow fell. No matter what might happen or had
happened to their brethren in the Portuguese and French
dominions, the Jesuits in Spanish South America felt secure.*
Their missions marked and guarded the frontier from Panama
to Patagonia; their Superiors in Rome, first Ignacio Visconti
and then Lorenzo Ricci, had gone as far as their consciences
allowed to retain the friendship of the Spanish Crown. But
when Charles III succeeded his brother Ferdinand in 1759,
he retained as his adviser Bernardo Tanucci, a lawyer in
whom he had confided as King of Naples. Tanucci, along
with the Count of Aranda, son of Charles's principal coun-
sellor, was in league with Sebastián José de Carvalho, better

* The Jesuits had been expelled from Portugal and her possessions in
1758 and from France in 1764.

known as the Marqués de Pombal, in Lisbon, and the Duc de Choiseul in Paris. Together they aimed to destroy completely the influence of the Church, which they considered the main obstacle to the total supremacy of the civil power. Working for the same ends as these ministers were the university-educated Catholics of the day, 'intellectualist, progressive, abstract and contemptuous of traditional values which under their dusty overgrowth were biologically sound'.[1] Charles III, well-meaning but no intellectual match for the progressives, had still to be won over. The ministers proceeded by calculated stages. First, Charles's mind was poisoned against the Jesuits by a long series of calumnies, insinuations and lies, a process that was eventually uncovered in the confessions of Pombal, made in a juridical process instituted against him after his downfall.[2] The central point of the intrigue was to convince Charles III that, for mysterious reasons, the Jesuits had resolved to remove him from the throne and replace him by his younger brother. Round this alleged conspiracy Tanucci wove a web of lies with the skill of a Titus Oates. At the right moment the Jesuits would reveal to the world that Charles was the illegitimate offspring of his mother, who had always confided in the Jesuits. If the king offered resistance, then the Jesuits were prepared to sanction his assassination and that of his family.

Proofs of the conspiracy were then offered. First, a pamphlet in which the whole plot was set out in detail. It was printed in secret and held in readiness for the moment of revelation. With it went a supposed autograph letter of the Jesuit General, Ricci, in which the same ideas were exposed and their propagation urged among the Spanish Jesuits.* The proof touched the Paraguay Jesuits. The Guaraní war was something concrete to which the enemies of the Jesuits could fasten. Coins were produced, said to have been minted in Paraguay, carrying the head of the king-emperor, Dobrizhoffer's friend, Nicolás I. It was given out that they had been slipped into packages sent from Paraguay to Ricci in

* Later Pombal confessed that he was the author of both the pamphlet and the letter.

Rome, and that at the Roman Customs the packages had been seized by officials who swore to their contents. The attestations had been placed before Charles III.

The populace had already been prepared for these revelations. Pombal's *Short Relation*,* first published in 1757, had now been translated into every European language. In place of Christian doctrine it was stated that the Indians in the Jesuit missions received instruction in military architecture and firearms. There was proof of this in the papers found on a Guaraní prisoner from San Juan, although even as printed in Pombal's version they amounted to no more than a pious rule of life. To corroborate this find, a letter was produced from the cura of San Javier, written on 5 January 1756, to the corregidor of the same town giving him a 'daily prayer for wisdom and success', which was assumed, of course, to apply to success in battle. This was a situation the king could not tolerate, especially as the Indians were so subservient to the Fathers. A letter from Freire was cited : he had seen the cura of San Miguel order Indians to throw themselves on the ground and receive twenty-five azotes, then get up, thank the priest and kiss his hand. Here was proof of the power of the Jesuits.† 'These poor families live under more rigorous obedience and in a harsher slavery than negroes who work in the mines.'[3]

A Short Relation had come out in the same year as *Nicholas I, King of Paraguay and Emperor of the Mamelucos*. Professedly printed at the Jesuit press at São Paulo, it was another of Pombal's products. It gave such a vivid account of the kingdom the Jesuits were setting up in South America that when the Viceroy, Cevallos, put in at Buenos Aires, he made enquiries before landing whether the city was in

---

* The full title is : *A Short Relation of the Republic established by the Jesuits in the Dominions of Spain and Portugal in the new world and of the war waged by them against the armies of the two Crowns.*
† The suggestion that the Jesuits kept the Indians in subjection under the lash is scarcely worth refuting. Nevertheless it is interesting to note that Prince Edward, created Duke of Kent in 1799, when in command of the 7th Royal Fusiliers in Gibraltar, awarded 500 lashes for offences which today would be considered trivial. Cf. *Daily Telegraph*, 'Peterborough', 19 February 1973.

Nicolás's hands. It took much longer for Europeans to discover the truth.

Now that the stage was set, there was need only to en'ct
the drama before the eyes of the disturbed king.

Agents acting under instructions from the Count of Aranda
used for the purpose an uprising in Madrid known as *El
Motín de Aranjuez.* It occurred on Palm Sunday 1766.
Squilacci, the King's Neapolitan Minister of Finance, in an
attempt to clean up the city at night, had installed 5,000
lamps and forbidden the use of the fashionable broad-
brimmed hats and long cloaks which might conceal the
assassin's dagger. The lamps were paid for by additional
taxes, which were the immediate occasion of the riot. For
dramatic effect, the king was persuaded to seek safety at
Aranjuez, some fifty miles south of Madrid. The Duke of
Alba, a devotee of the French philosophers, confessed on his
deathbed that the discontent had deliberately been fanned
into a riot in order to frighten the king into taking action
against the Jesuits, who were blamed for it. Even without
this confession there were sufficient grounds to suspect a
contrivance. For after the king's flight, the riot had subsided,
and then unaccountably 'for forty-eight hours a curiously
controlled populace roared, shot volleys and blank musketry,
barked furiously, hardly biting at all and making much noise
with little destruction'.[4] The nobles threatened with assassination remained strangely calm and the people lacked no
funds or food. The Count of Aranda now became President
of the Council and virtual dictator of Spain. Conditions were
right for him : the Spanish army and navy had been greatly
reduced by the country's poverty and now the first expressions
of the desire for independence in the colonies were reaching
Europe. Clearly the military power of the Reductions was a
menace to the Spanish Crown.

Charles III at last acted. He declared he was moved by
compelling reasons which he kept locked up in his breast.
Sealed orders to be opened at a certain hour on a certain
day were sent to all the governors of the provinces that
comprised the Spanish dominions : they had been written
out in secrecy by children who had been employed to copy

documents they could not understand. The date chosen for
the seizure of the Jesuits was 2 April 1767, but it was anticipated by five days in Madrid. All their houses were to be
surrounded, their inmates herded into designated depots, and
from there transported out of the country by sea : they were
to be allowed no communication with outsiders or, as far as
possible, with one another; the death penalty was threatened
on the executors of the decree if a single Jesuit, even sick or
dying, was left behind. Their buildings were then to be
searched, all their property seized and inventories made of it.
Meanwhile the Jesuits themselves were to be put ashore in
the Papal States.

With the exception of Tanucci's collaborator, Roda, the
Minister of Justice, the conspirators did not come from the
people, but from the upper classes whose education had been
mainly in the hands of the Jesuits. As soon as the Spanish
Jesuits had been landed in the Papal States, Choiseul wrote to
Roda: 'We have killed the son. All that remains now is for us
to do the same with the mother, the holy Roman Church.'[5]

The Marqués Francisco de Paula Bucareli y Ursua was
appointed to carry out the decree in the recently-formed
Viceroyalty of Buenos Aires. A capable hypocrite, he sent the
king endless long-winded reports exaggerating the dangers
and difficulties of his commission.

The first stage of the expulsion of the Paraguay Jesuits was
scheduled for 2.30 a.m. on 3 July 1767. At that hour pre-
cisely, the Jesuits in Buenos Aires were made prisoners. On
12 July the Jesuits of Córdoba, the hub of the Province
with its church, university, novitiate and house of studies,
were herded into the refectory of the main residence while
an inventory was made of their treasures. Notices were posted
in the town forbidding under severe penalties any person
from communicating with the prisoners. Angry crowds formed
in the streets. As a gesture of sympathy the Prior of the
Dominicans held a public service of intercession in defiance
of Bucareli's orders. Only 5,900 pesos was found to the credit
of all the Jesuit institutions in the city, and this was largely
cancelled by the later discovery of a debt of 4,000 pesos to
the Dean and Chapter of the Cathedral.

For ten days a hundred and thirty-five Jesuits remained in confinement under the low ceiling of the vaulted refectory in their Córdoba residence. From there they were taken to Buenos Aires. No belongings were allowed them except a breviary and a change of clothes: they took no books, manuscripts or sheets of writing paper. Their fine libraries were scattered with their records of exploration, maps, notes on languages, ethnical studies of Chaco and other tribes, and Zipoli's music.* Those who felt and expressed their sorrow most overtly were the negro slaves of the Jesuits. When Santa Catalina, Jesús María and other estancias that supported the Jesuit establishments in Córdoba were confiscated, the negroes attached to them fled.

The secrecy was so closely kept that the Jesuit recruits from Europe destined for the novitiate at Córdoba arrived in the Plata estuary unaware of the expulsion order. As with their predecessors, their passage had been subsidized by the king. The voyage had lasted six months. Four of the party had died at sea. Of the thirty-six who reached Montevideo, some were so weak that the captain hoisted the distress signal as he approached the port. And they had no provisions. For twenty-four hours nothing was done. Then the governor of the city came aboard with a detachment of troops and read the decree of expulsion. The ship's captain insisted that his passengers should be landed. Under protest the governor consented and crowded them into the small Jesuit house, where a fifth recruit soon died. After five weeks he despatched them back to Europe. These were the young men destined to complete the pacification of the Chaco and re-establish the Patagonian towns.

Bucareli waited another year before proceeding against the Guaraní and Chaco Reductions. Knowing neither the Jesuits nor the Guaraní, he feared a rising. Also he had to find replacements for some hundred and forty priests in these towns. But the situation was very different from 1754. Now obedience presented no problem of conscience to the Jesuits. To avert a second Guaraní war which he believed

---

* These books were later sent to the estancia of Santa Catalina to be catalogued, but most were lost before the catalogue was complete.

imminent, Bucareli acted in a Machiavellian manner. He first summoned to Buenos Aires the corregidores of the Guaraní towns. In the cabildo built by Primoli he received them like foreign potentates. Then crossing the square to the cathedral, he attended with them a solemn High Mass. In the banquet that followed he made them flattering promises: on the expulsion of the Jesuits the Indians were to be totally independent; a university denied them by the Fathers was to be established at Candelaria, the Guaraní capital; there they would be educated in all the western arts and sciences; no longer would they be held in subjection by the Jesuits.* Bucareli then dressed the thirty caciques in Spanish costume to mark the improvement in their status. Finally he got them to sign a letter to Charles III which bears the unmistakable marks of his dictation: the king is thanked for sending Bucareli to carry out 'all the just orders of your Majesty'. With the letter was enclosed a report which resurrected all Cárdenas's charges against the Paraguay Jesuits: they were inordinately rich, kept the Indians in slavery and would not permit Spaniards to enter their towns or the Indians to learn Spanish.

The priests were still kept waiting more than a year. Bucareli could not move against them until he had found others to take their place. The Bishop of Buenos Aires reckoned that he could scarcely raise ten surplus clergy, and men at that with such disgust for the assignment that they made every effort to excuse themselves.⁶ Then he turned to the Orders. The Dominicans, Franciscans and Fathers of Mercy all protested that they had not priests to spare. Bucareli was then compelled to seek help from Europe. A party of thirty from a miscellany of religious orders was assembled for embarkation at Cadiz when panic seized them and they fled in every direction.⁷ It was then that Bucareli fell back

* This is the probable origin of the criticism propagated today by some Jesuit writers that their system of government was too paternalistic to outlast the expulsion: such a notion would have been repugnant to the Swiss, German and Czech Fathers, as well as the Spanish, who struggled to the limit of their patience to give the Guaraní a rudimentary sense of responsibility. It is also in complete conflict with the experience of present-day writers who have lived in close contact with the Guaraní.

once more on the main orders already established in the
Viceroyalty. Their representatives insisted that each Order
was to have its own territorial grouping of towns. Bucareli
conceded this but refused their request for temporal as well
as spiritual jurisdiction such as the Jesuits had enjoyed.
Instead Bucareli appointed an independent civic officer in
each pueblo.

By early April 1768 Bucareli had assembled his replacements for the Jesuits. On 24 May he began his march up the
Uruguay with three companies of Grenadiers and sixty
dragoons, a force of 1,500 in all.

The thirty Guaraní Reductions were ideally situated for
defence. Separated by hundreds of leagues from Buenos Aires,
they were surrounded by virgin forest and by marshes
impassable to troops trained in Europe. They possessed the
largest army in South America. Their armouries contained
some long English mounted guns, not heavy pieces but
accurate enough at a fair range. A word from the mission
Superior was enough to bring into the field 'clouds of horsemen, badly armed but knowing every foot of marsh and
forest, all the deep-beaten tracks which wind in the red earth
across the lonely plains, the passes of the rivers, springs,
natural fastnesses'.[8] But the Guaraní, who had been taught by
the Jesuits to obey the Spanish authorities, put their trust in
Bucareli's promises.

The Viceroy disembarked his force at the falls of the
Uruguay below Yapeyú. There he divided it into three: he
sent one detachment against the Paraná Reductions, the
second against the seven ill-fated towns on the east bank of
the Uruguay; with the third he himself marched upriver to
Yapeyú. From there he posted prolix and boastful despatches
to the Count of Aranda, revised and dated at Buenos Aires:[9]
the weather had been phenomenally bad, the rain incessant,
provisions scarce, 'savage Indians' had surprised an outpost
of his men. He continued for sixteen pages making the most
of commonplace difficulties. At Yapeyú he embarked for
Candelaria. The winds were against him and he did not reach
the capital until 27 August 1768.

On his arrival in each Reduction the priests surrendered

their keys and quietly became the prisoners of the Spanish
Crown. The expedition was over in less than four months.
'Nothing would have been easier', writes Cunninghame
Graham,[10] 'depleted as the Viceroy was of troops than to
have defied the forces which Bucareli had at his disposal and
to have set up a Jesuit State which would have taxed to the
utmost the resources of the Spanish Crown to overcome.'

In September the Jesuits from the Paraná and Uruguay
were sent down river to Buenos Aires. Bucareli in his report
expressed hypocritical shock at the dress of the Indian women
in the Jesuit towns : it was impossible, he wrote, to enlarge
on the matter without failing in modesty.* To protect his
men from temptation he had issued the Indian women with
Spanish garments to replace their graceful *tupoi.*

In the Chaco and in the towns north of Asunción the fear
of an Indian rising was real enough. When Sánchez Labrador
proposed to leave Belén immediately, he was implored by the
Commission to stay on in order to explain the reasons for his
departure. To save his own skin the Commissioner had to
promise these Guaycurú that their priest would return in time.
It was the same in other towns. When Padre Klein was taken
off from San Fernando, his faithful Abipones burnt their
Reduction, and the cacique rode to Santa Fe to demand an
explanation and Klein's immediate return. Padre Paucke had
the greatest difficulty in dissuading the Mocobíes from attacking Santa Fe in their old fashion. 'Had I not with God's help
succeeded in pacifying my Indians, in a short time they would
have made Santa Fe a heap of rubble : this would have
happened if I had not come out firmly against their design.'

Armed pro-Jesuit risings did occur in Potosí. As a result,
the Spanish authorities in the province of Charcas were forced
temporarily to replace the Jesuits in their Colleges. This was
made the excuse for still longer delays in removing the priests
from the Chiquitos towns. Remote from Santa Cruz, they lay
in the heart of territory today still largely unknown. The
tracks that led to these towns were tortuous. For eighty years
the tribes had been submissive to the Jesuits. They had known
no other masters, and if they lost them now it was feared they

---

* *Es imposibile demonstralo sin faltar a la modestia.*

would revolt.

But there was no resistance. Many of the Fathers here were old, and found it difficult to believe that they would not be left in the forest which they had made their own land. Padre Ignacio Chomé, the great authority on the languages of the Chiquitos group, was now seventy and bedridden. Carried on a hammock by two Indians under orders of a Spanish official, he was taken into the eastern Andes without even stopping as he passed through Cochabamba. At the mountain village of Oruro he died. His linguistic manuscripts were never recovered. Padre Juan Mesner from San Rafael, an asthmatic man of seventy-seven, was kept five months in Santa Cruz because his escort considered the Andes impassable for him. Then he was compelled to continue on muleback, suffering acutely in the thin mountain air. At the highest point of the pass to Lima, the animals were rested. He begged to be left to die. Instead he was hoisted once more on to his mule with a man at his side to prevent him falling. Twenty-four hours later his guard found himself supporting a corpse. Martin Schmid, the Swiss architect of several of the surviving Chiquitos churches, was younger and tougher. At first he was unable to believe the inhumanity of the king's orders. 'I am seventy-three and I shall remain,' he had written to Europe. He spent, in fact, five months on muleback. When he reached Panama he had already left eleven of his companions dead on the trail.

The Jesuits assembled in Buenos Aires had sailed in three groups: the first, in September 1767, made up mainly of men from the Colleges; the second, on 14 January 1768, priests principally from the Guaraní towns; and the final party, nearly all Chaco missionaries, including Brigniel, Paucke, Dobrizhoffer and Sánchez Labrador, in the following March. Before this last party embarked, they had to undergo sudden searchings and minute registration of the few articles they were permitted to carry. All that was ever discovered on them was a little money left over from what friends had given them to cover incidental expenses of their overland journey of nearly 1,500 miles to Buenos Aires. In spite of rat-infested quarters, all but two of these hardy missionaries survived the four-month voyage. On their arrival in Cadiz, they learned of the death of sixteen of the hundred and thirty-two who had sailed in January. The foreigners re-embarked in March 1769 for Ostend and from there travelled overland to their own countries. From Ostend Dobrizhoffer made his way to Vienna, where he entertained the Empress Maria Theresa with tales of his days in Paraguay, and at her suggestion wrote them down for the diversion of a larger audience. With sadness he learned that of the 2,017 Abipones at Rosario at the time of the expulsion, none remained. The work of his fellow Bohemian, José Klein, whom he named *El Impávido*, endured. His foundation of San Fernando for other Abipones developed into the city of Resistencia. Klein had seen the riches of the forest, and to support the mission had developed a timber industry. The mission barge, the *botecito*, with a capacity of twenty tons, was well known on the Paraná all the way down to Buenos Aires. On its return voyages it used to carry a miscellaneous freight for the towns up river. Dobrizhoffer's other friend, Padre Paucke, spent his last days in the monastery of Zwettl, where he wrote and illustrated his book on the Mocobíes. Sometimes he would be seen sneaking furtively into the kitchen to prepare a dinner of *boeuf à la mode sauvage* as a treat for the community. Thomas Falkner joined the English Province of the Society and served as chaplain to Robert Berkeley of Spetchley Park, near Worcester, then the Berringtons of Winsley, Herefordshire, and finally the Plowdens of Plowden Hall, Shropshire. There he died on 30 January 1784 in his seventy-seventh year. Thomas Pennant, who edited his book, wrote that 'by his long intercourse with the inhabitants of Patagonia he seemed to have lost all European guile and to have acquired all the simplicity and honest impetuosity of the people he had been so long conversant with'.[11] In his retirement he is said to have written three other works, including a *Treatise of American Distempers Cured by American Drugs*, which were all lost.

The Spanish priests from Paraguay, along with Jesuits from other Spanish dominions, were later dumped without leave in the Papal States. They were destitute. The Pope declined to receive them. The Cardinal Secretary wrote : 'If they are

good men the King has no right to banish them; if they are
criminals, he has no business to commit their punishment to
the Holy Father.' Repulsed from Città Vecchia, they were
carried to Corsica and left to the kindness of its people.
Eventually forced to leave by the French, they sought refuge
in Genoa. The Pope then offered his help. Faenza became
their centre. Several obtained posts as chaplains and professors;
others gave their time to writing. They pooled their earnings
and their trifling pensions from the Spanish Crown.

The difficulties of Bucareli began only after the *Esmeralda*,
with the last of the missionaries, sailed out of the Plata estuary
into the south Atlantic. The Viceroy had been faced with the
immediate need of instituting some form of government for
the Indian towns. Before leaving Candelaria he had issued on
23 August 1768 a set of instructions for the two captains who
had gone up with him.[12] Almost slavishly he followed the
Jesuit system that he had so severely criticized. And as though
the Jesuits had neglected Christian instruction, he ordered the
captains to see that 'true knowledge of the holy faith' was
taught the Indians; he also alleged that the Fathers had not
cared for the sick and dying. In a letter sent after his return
to Buenos Aires on 20 October 1768 he instructed his men
to 'find out from what quarter the Indians of these towns
extract the pieces of precious metal which they sometimes
bring to their priests'. And there were other echoes of
Cárdenas's fables.

For two years Bucareli continued to use Reduction troops
to repel Chaco Indians from the Spanish towns and to defend
the island of Chiloe, to the far south, where the English were
believed to be mounting an attack. On 15 January 1770 he
indited a long declaration of Nicolás Neenguirú and other
Indians purporting to be an account of their part in the
Guaraní war.[13] When the Jesuits were gone, Nicolás had
turned against them : at least he stated all that Bucareli asked
of him. From this statement it appears that Nicolás came
from a family that had been well known since Cárdenas's
time. Now he was the corregidor of Concepción and respected
by his fellow Indians, who held his stirrup when he mounted
his horse. These were the grounds which Bucareli gave why

credence should be given to Nicolás when he testified that he had done everything at the orders of the Jesuit, Enis: he himself was only a simple Indian who did what he was told. Nicolás ended by thanking the king for rescuing him from the hands of the Jesuits.

On 14 August 1770 Bucareli sailed for Europe. His work was completed. All the Jesuits were now expelled except one, the herbalist and physician Padre Segismundo Aperger, who had been born at Insrun in Hungary in 1687. Perhaps his reputation as the Hippocrates of South America helped his wretched case: prostrate and bed-ridden, crippled and incapable of movement and seemingly moribund, he lived on for another ten years at Apóstoles to the age of ninety-one. He was the last of the Paraguay Jesuits, 'the adventurers of the seventeenth and eighteenth centuries', 'successors of the conquistadores', as Professor Herbert E. Bolton called them. Their story was one of Homeric quality. They had

> travelled vast distances, coped with rugged nature and the fickle savage, performed astounding physical feats, won amazing victories over mountains, rivers, hunger, cold and thirst. Missionary life demanded the highest qualities of manhood—character, intelligence, courage, resourcefulness, health and endurance. They went among the heathen without escorts, into places where soldiers dared not tread. They were liable at any time to hear the blood-curdling warwhoop or to see the destroying fire by night. They were ever at the mercy of the whims of sensitive Indians or of jealous and vengeful medicine men. Even to baptize a child was often perilous, for if it died, the death might be charged to the 'bad medicine' of the padre. Martyrdom was always a distinct possibility. Most Black Robes came to America hoping to win this glorious crown, most still coveted it after seeing real Indians, and when martyrdom stared them in the face they met it with transcendent heroism.[14]

If this encomium is exaggerated, there is no doubt that the Jesuits made brave efforts. While it took the Spaniards a few decades to conquer the Inca kingdom, it took them several centuries, in spite of steel, horse and gunpowder, to subdue the Indians of the interior. The work was incomplete when the colonies rose in the next century against the dominion of Madrid. In the judgement of Métraux, the eminent ethnologist, the Jesuits, had they been left to continue their work, 'would probably have extended their rule throughout the Chaco. . . . When they left the regions pacified by them were partly lost to the white man and some areas remained *terra incognita* down to the present.'[15]

In Europe the sufferings of the exiled priests were consummated with the decree of Clement XIV in July 1773, suppressing the Society of Jesus throughout the world. Ricci, the Jesuit General elected in the same year as Clement's predecessor, was imprisoned in Castel S. Angelo : a pathetic seminary professor cruelly sinned against by the Jesuit Congregation that elected him, a man without a day's experience of government, to rule his brethren at a moment when they needed a man to match Pombal and Choiseul. Untried and uncondemned, Ricci survived into the reign of Pius VI. On 24 November 1775, before receiving viaticum, he read a protestation : it ran : 'Believing that the time has come when I must stand before the tribunal of infallible truth and justice . . . I declare and protest that the suppressed Society of Jesus gave no grounds whatever for its suppression. I declare and protest this with the moral certainty that a Superior can have who was well-informed as to the state of his Order.'

Pius VI was distressed that Ricci had died when the hour of his vindication was near. Ricci's body was taken across the Ponte S. Angelo to the Chiesa dei Florentini and buried there. It was later transferred to the Gesù to rest alongside the remains of his predecessors.

16

Epilogue

A modern author, concluding a short study of the Jesuit State of Paraguay, writes that 'it was signalized by a fervent spiritual life. Economically it was, already in the eighteenth century, an industrialized state organized on the co-operative principle. If it had survived, Latin America would have advanced nearly a century. From the social and political viewpoint it provided a model of unquestionable democracy and, what's more, a democracy for a coloured people.'[1]

On the other hand, some modern Jesuits hold it against the priests of the Paraguay Province that they organized their towns like extended religious communities : paternalism was the only form of government the Jesuits knew : the entire education they gave the Indians was directed to breaking their spirit in order to obtain their submission : all they did was to form a perpetual proletariat without any sense of private ownership : since the Indians had nothing to hold them to the towns, they quickly slipped back to the forest from which they came : they had been untrained to take their place in the civilized society that surrounded them : consequently the system built up by the Jesuits collapsed on their departure : all that the Indians received was a veneer of civilization. This is also a view made popular in some standard works on South America.*

* E.g. Professor Clarence H. Haring in *The Spanish Empire in America* (Oxford, 1947), 200–1. The statement that the Reduction Indians returned to the forest is perhaps explained by the discovery in the mid-nineteenth century of some isolated Guaraní communities in the dense forest where they still kept to the practice of the Christian faith although they had no priests.

What, in point of fact, did occur on the expulsion of the Jesuits? Certainly the Spanish Government strove its utmost to maintain the Jesuit system. On his return to Spain Bucareli, instructed by Charles III, sent his successor, Juan José Vertiz, a long Constitution for the former Jesuit towns.[2] Almost to the last paragraph it followed the governmental forms and customs that had allegedly kept the Indians in a state of tutelage. The differences were few. All the co-operative features of the regime were retained, as well as the restrictions on commerce. The progressive sections of the programme were to prove impracticable.

There is a reliable picture of Reduction life given some eighteen years after the expulsion of the Jesuits in a report of Don Gonzalo de Doblas, the Governor of the Guaraní towns, dated Concepción 27 September 1785.[3] A man of integrity, he tried to carry through Bucareli's promise of a university, but found it premature. Instead he proposed that there should be an academy of arts and letters at Candelaria taking pupils up to but not including 'theology, jurisprudence and the scholastic sciences'. As in Jesuit days, the sons of caciques were to be chosen for the experiment. Each town was to send four boys and two girls to be boarded at Candelaria. All the mission libraries were to be collected there except for the few books the priests needed for everyday use. From Candelaria the old and valuable works were to be sent to Buenos Aires and sold there to raise money for the children's text books. The books, in fact, were sold but no central school was established.

In the province, Doblas reported, there were many quarries of building stone easy to work and durable that had fallen into disuse; it was the same with the slate and copper mines in the neighbourhood of Candelaria and Santa Ana. It was a rich and fertile land. In visiting the towns he had not met a single Indian who was lame, insane or handicapped. The people used their old herbal remedies prescribed by the Jesuits and suffered no chronic diseases.

The commonplace of historians that the Indians returned to the forest and barbarism is an unproved assumption. Even before life in the Reductions became oppressive under the new regime, a large number of Guaraní were already integrated into the Spanish cities. In Buenos Aires, Montevideo, Santa Fe and Corrientes, many Indians had found employment as *oficios mecánicos* or technicians in the crafts in which they had been trained by the Jesuits. Those who had no skills found employment as *peones* or labourers on the estancias of the countryside. Also a large number, especially from the seven towns on the east bank of the Uruguay, sought refuge in Brazil. At the time of the Guaraní war, Portugal had made capital of Spain's betrayal of the Guaraní. Portuguese captains had worked hard to gain Indian sympathy. When Gomes Freire withdrew from Santo Angel in 1657, he took with him a considerable number of Reduction Indians. He installed them first on the outskirts of Río Pardo, then transferred them to Nossa Senhora dos Anjos. The generous treatment of this nucleus did much to heal the ancient enmity between Guaraní and Portuguese. When the Jesuits were later expelled, it was not difficult to entice other Guaraní across the frontier from the new and oppressive regime. In their worsening relations with Spain, the Portuguese sought to absorb as many Spanish subjects as possible who might be of service to them in future wars. The Treaty of San Idelfonso on 1 October 1777, ending the South American war, brought the Portuguese still nearer to the seven towns.* As the Portuguese in their traditional colonial manner planted settlements close to the new frontier, the exodus from the seven towns still on the Spanish side became easier.[4] The more enterprising Guaraní were encouraged to join the military, others, like those who left for the Spanish towns, got jobs as technicians or peones. The migration continued at increasing pace until the end of the eighteenth century. In 1799 the Cabildo of San Juan, Sepp's foundation, begged for aid from Buenos Aires 'before the process of expatriation of our subjects is complete through scarcity of food and clothing'.[5]

---

* By this treaty Colonia was ceded to Spain and Santa Catarina, captured by Cevallos with Guaraní troops, returned to Portugal. The new frontier followed the west shore of Lagoa Mirim westwards to skirt the sources of the Río Ibicuí, then north to bisect the Uruguay at its Pepirí-Guazú tributary.

But all attempts to enforce the law forbidding the Indians to leave were futile. Repeatedly, new officials demanded the return of fugitives, but the Spaniards were anxious to keep their newly-acquired labour and the authorities could do nothing. Even before the end of the eighteenth century Manuel Genaro de Villota, Protector of the Indians, had to admit this. By a decree of 14 June 1802 the existing whereabouts of fugitive Reduction Indians became legal : only those responsible for the support of their family were to be compelled to return. Three years earlier Félix de Azara had foreseen as a possibility the total dispersal of the thirty Guaraní towns. He did not judge this a grave loss because the Indian population was being incorporated with the Spanish and injecting a fresh vitality into an old stock. It can be argued, therefore, that at the time of the expulsion the Jesuits had achieved their aim of making Guaraní savages capable of entering civilized society.

In spite of the Portuguese effort to cultivate friendship with the Guaraní of the seven towns, it was these ill-fated Reductions that were the first to suffer almost total destruction at their hands early in the next century. The outbreak of the Spanish colonial revolt gave the Portuguese their chance to seize the whole of the Banda Oriental. In 1810 José Gervasio Artigas, an ex-Spanish soldier, a gaucho and the first of the South American guerrillas, raised the banner of free Uruguay, including the whole of the Banda Oriental, over which he held authority for three years. In 1817 the Portuguese came down against him from the north. The seven towns fell to the Portuguese, as well as several on the west bank over which Artigas had asserted his claims. In a despatch Brigadier General Francisco de Chagas, the Portuguese officer in charge of the operation, wrote : 'We have destroyed and pillaged the seven towns, and on the west bank we have merely plundered the towns of Apóstoles, San José and San Carlos.' He had transported fifty quarters of silver and church ornaments across the river, many 'excellent bells, 3,000 horses, as many mares and 1,300,000 coined reis'. In another despatch he claimed that the silver he obtained from the Christian villages weighed eighty quarters. The church ornaments were taken to Porto Alegre and later to Rio de Janeiro.

In the remainder of the Guaraní towns, the process of disintegration was slower. It might never have occurred but for the division of authority between priests and civic officers on which Bucareli. had insisted. It was under protest against this alteration of the Jesuit system that the new priests took over and for this reason it would be unfair to blame them for the slow run-down of the Reductions. Bucareli had been convinced that gold was to be found in the thirty towns, and was determined that it should not fall into the hands of the Church. Oppression, jealousies and confusion resulted from this divided rule. Priests would order the Indians to do one thing, the officers another and the Indians would be punished for obeying one rather than the other. Both cura and officer lived in the same house, often in declared emnity, each dependent on the other.[6] The community of goods which had proved the right means of caring for the temporal interests of the Guaraní in the time of the Jesuits became an instrument of repression; what had been a near ideal society was made to serve the personal gain of officials. Many Indians, to escape taxation, left the Reduction in which they had been born and christened for another where they were unknown and would be more free. Those that remained went out to work for pay and soon became demoralized by alcohol. As the population dwindled, Spaniards invaded the Reductions, robbed the Indians of their land and destroyed the maté plantations. Fields were abandoned, handicrafts lost for lack of teachers. But it was another thirty years before the desolation was near complete. There is an interesting picture of Candelaria drawn by a Scottish traveller, W. P. Robertson, in the 1830s. He writes:

Candelaria under the Jesuits had three thousand and sixty-four inhabitants; they were now reduced to seven hundred. . . . The church was in a state of dilapidation; the rain was pouring in through many apertures of the roof; the walls were bare and even the altar was uncovered by a cloth. Not having been whitewashed for years the walls

were not only bare but black. From the damp parts of
them, at not distant intervals, there oozed out a green
mould, forming a soil, from which depended nettles and
other noxious weeds. The college was pretty much in the
same state; and what had once been a brick-laid patio or
quadrangle was so completely covered with grass and weeds
that no trace of the original foundation was discoverable.
As for the unweeded garden 'things rank and gross in
nature possessed it merely'. Every fruit tree had been hewn
down for firewood. Of the original huts and cottages
scarcely a third of the number was standing; and of those
that did remain there was no line so little observable as
the perpendicular. They were awry, some leaning to one
side, some inclining to another; and all indicating a speedy
intention of laying their bones and dust in the lap of
mother earth and by the side of tenements that had already
mouldered to decay.[7]

Robertson remarked that there was no traffic across the
Paraná between Candelaria and Itapua : formerly, balsa rafts
had carried Indiahs daily across the mile and a quarter of
river to work on the Paraguayan bank. The rafts were now
destroyed and there was no need to construct others. A canoe
was used instead. The corregidores of the Jesuit times had

nothing to distinguish them from their barefooted and
ponchoed fellow-citizens but their wands of office and some
tawdry piece of finery which they would have been better
without except that it pleased them. Some wore ribbons
round their hats in the style in which recruits are equipped
before they join their regiment; others had on a bad fit of
a sergeant's coat terribly the worse for wear. . . . Everything was falling into decay—the church, the college, the
huts. . . . Weeds and briars were everywhere springing up
. . . and it was with difficulty that the two *curas* could
scrape together enough from the labour of the whole community scantily to feed and badly to clothe the members
of it.[8]

One aspect of Reduction life remained unchanged, the religious practices and ceremonial: Sodalities still flourished, the churches were crowded, Holy Week services went on as in the days of Roque González, the Corpus Christi processions were as grand as ever: Doblas, in his account, adds some details which are not recorded by Jesuit writers, the weapons, looms, tools, infants, all placed on the processional route to be blessed by the passing priest, and altars loaded with rice, mandioca, suet, dried meat and vegetables.[9]* It was the same thirty years later with secular celebrations. Robertson happened to witness a fiesta at Candelaria on his visit. He was astonished by 'the processions of dancing horses, tilts and tournaments according to Indian fashion. There were bullfights, sham fights among the Tapes themselves and feats of horsemanship of marvellous dexterity and address. In the afternoon an image of the Virgin Mary, to which the Indians paid devout adoration, was carried round the square and at night some rockets were let off in honour of the saint.'[10]

On the Paraguayan bank of the Paraná, José Francia, the first President and virtual Dictator of the newly-formed nation, in his attempt to complete the isolation of Paraguay from the rest of the world, ordered the destruction of the four missions closest to the river. Many Guaraní carrying their church treasures settled in small groups often near their old towns. Francia died in 1840. His successor, Carlos Antonio López, finally suppressed Bucareli's regime and forced the Guaraní who lived on in the remaining Reductions, some 6,000, to join the rest of the population: nine-tenths of them, with the same proportion of all males, were slain in the hopeless war that Paraguay waged for six years against the com-

---

* Many religious observances, apart from processions, are held today in the remote Chiquitos missions as they were in Jesuit times: for instance, in San Rafael on Maunday Thursday the cura, now a Franciscan, eats a ceremonial meal with twelve caciques in the courtyard of the priest's house. During the course of the meal one of the twelve, representing Judas, leaves the table to betray the Lord. On Good Friday another cacique preaches the sermon on the Passion. While at Mass in San Ignacio in Chiquitos, a cacique came in from the forest bearing a wooden cross and knelt behind me absorbed in prayer for a long time, the successor of the Indians who, unable in earlier times to attend Mass, came bearing the prayers of their people to the nearest church.

bined armies of Brazil, Uruguay and Argentina. When it ended in 1870, the last traces of the Jesuit Republic were gone.

Encarnación, now the third largest city in Paraguay, has only its site in common with Itapúa. Ignacio Guazú, the first of all the Guaraní Reductions, Santiago, Santa Rosa and Santa María, the northern towns, are today fair-sized centres of population in a rural area. Cosme, Trinidad and Jesús, made derelict by Francia, are being restored by the present government as the best tourist attraction a poor country has to offer. Between the Paraná and Uruguay the forest has taken over. Candelaria has gone, unless Posadas is considered its successor. Only Ignacio Miní of these fifteen towns has been reclaimed and partially rebuilt. Loreto waits the same fortune. But there is only masonry entwined with yatais marking the other sites. On the east side of the Uruguay, the façade of the church of San Miguel commands a hilltop like a beacon, by which a plane flying in from San Borja can get its bearings on Santo Angel, now a flourishing provincial capital but unrecognizable as one of the seven towns.

In the Chaco the tribes returned to their nomad life. In the middle of the nineteenth century the fires of the Guaycurú were once again seen across the river from Asunción as in the days of Cárdenas. Only San Fernando of the Chaco Reductions, on the opposite bank of the Paraná from Corrientes, remained to become Resistencia. The Chiquitos towns were saved by their remoteness in the tropical forest bordering on the Mato Grosso. 'Towards the end of the eighteenth century', *The South American Handbook* puts it, 'this was a populous land of plenty. The Jesuits controlled the area and guided it into a prosperous security. A symbol of their great effort is the Cathedral of San José de Chiquitos, a gem of elegance and dignity. But the Jesuits were expelled. Two hundred years of maladministration, despoliation and corruption reduced' it to lethargy.'

In pre-Columban days the Guaraní in the search for a terrestrial paradise had wandered from the spurs of the Andes to the coast of Brazil and along the whole length of the rivers Paraná and Uruguay,[11] until by their music the Jesuits had enticed them from the forest into permanent dwellings. The insistence of the Jesuits on the study of language was perhaps the key to their success, together with the total dedication demanded by Padre José de Acosta in his treatise, *De Procuranda Indianorum Salute*, used as a missionary handbook by the Paraguay Jesuits on its publication in 1608. For the Jesuits, the Guaraní language was not merely an instrument of evangelization but a means of forming an Indian culture and shaping a nation out of a multiplicity of subtribes that had a roughly similar speech in common. The Laws of the Indies had laid it down that natives were to be taught Castilian, but a later decree allowed them to retain their own languages. The Jesuits were quick to seize on this relaxation.[12] In the Guaraní language formed by the Jesuits many dialects were intermingled, from Guairá where Montoya had worked, from Tape and Iguazú, new words and abstract notions introduced, some borrowed from neighbouring tribes. Eventually, uniform usage gave a sense of nationhood, though in the process some smaller groupings lost their identity with their dialect. It could be maintained that on his visit to Madrid as procurator of the Paraguay Province in 1636, Montoya did as much for the Indians by printing his Guaraní grammar, dictionary and other works as he did by getting permission for them to use firearms. His works show in the course of creation a language which was developed in a classical form through the works that came from the printing presses in the Jesuit missions between the Paraná and Uruguay. The preservation of the Guaraní culture in modern Paraguay is largely the work of Montoya's successors.

It was the Indians' attachment to Reduction life that kept the towns in existence so long. When Nusdorffer was mission Superior, a group of Indians recently brought in from the woods left the Jesuit towns and made their own foundation near Corrientes. There they continued the ways they had been taught. They had objected to the Jesuits' insistence on monogamy, but held to all the other features of Reduction life. Eventually, they took to thieving and were exterminated by the Spaniards. Again, when the Guaraní crossed into Portuguese territory from the seven towns, they asked to live their old style of life in their own town. Their request was granted and Nossa Senhora dos Anjos was laid out for them on the Jesuit pattern. Later still, about 1818, some Guanas who had been living at Corpus made a foundation of their own where they tried to keep their faith pure and even led a number of other Indians to join them. Their sacristan and caciques acted as priests and their old folk remembered well enough the Guaraní prayers taught them by the Jesuits.[13]

In reading the masses of letters and studies written by the Paraguay Jesuits it is clear that all, no matter their nationality, had a great pride in their Province. With this went a spirit peculiar to it, though not unique among the Jesuits. It is illustrated by the regulation of the Customs Book which demanded the sanction of the mission Superior at Candelaria for all innovations a new cura might want to introduce in spiritual affairs or administration, especially in the running of the estancias, farms and even gardens. Men with no experience had done much harm in the early days of the Reductions. Yet even in their solidly established towns on the Paraná the Jesuits were never satisfied with their achievement or even with their system. Always they were looking to adjust, improve and expand. There is no evidence to support the view of some modern writers[14] that by the end of the seventeenth century their best work had been done. The curas were under instruction to seek peace by every means with the heathen Indians bordering on their towns.[15] In the last decade before the expulsion, the Superior at Candelaria was looking towards the upper Uruguay both to complete the line of defence and bring into Jesuit domain the still heathen Indians of the area.[16] Although the boundaries of the missions had been drawn in under pressure from the Mamelucos, the vision of the pioneer missionaries had never been lost. In the south it was the same. While the Chaco Jesuits were waiting embarkation at Buenos Aires, they looked with regret on a ship that sailed out of the Plata estuary for Tierra del Fuego with two priests aboard. Some shipwrecked Spanish seamen had reported on the island the existence of friendly natives whom they dubbed the *Rascabarriagas* or belly-rubbers because they approached across the hills rubbing their bellies in sign of friendship. The expedition, in fact, returned with nothing accomplished. Dobrizhoffer blamed no one, but he writes : 'I heard the groans of noble Spaniards who earnestly desired the Jesuits for this momentous expedition; they, however, God knows why, were recalled that same year to Europe.'[17]

References

Except in the first instance, references are given in the shortest convenient form. Full details of the books and articles cited are to be found in the Bibliography.

INTRODUCTION

1. *Essai sur Moeurs* (1878), vol. 12, p. 423.
2. *De la Destruction des Jésuites en France.* (1765), p. 126 f.
3. *Esprit des Lois*, Book IV, chapter 6.
4. *Histoire philosophique et politique*, vol. IV (ed. 1786), p. 233.

CHAPTER 1 — THE SCENE

1. Ruiz Díaz de Guzmán in Cunninghame Graham, *A Vanished Arcadia*, p. 33.
2. Ruiz de Montoya, *Conquista Espiritual*, f. 51.
3. *Doctrina Christiana, Confessario y Tercero Catechismo . . . por sermones.* Cf. Bartolomé Meliá, 'La Création d'une langue Chrétien dans les Réductions des Guaranís au Paraguay' (unpub. thesis 1969), *passim.*
4. Aubrey Gwynn, 'Father Thomas Fahilly' in *The Irish Way*, pp. 163–4.
5. Charlevoix, *History of Paraguay*, vol. i, p. 226.
6. Gwynn, op. cit.
7. Charlevoix, vol. i, p. 236.
8. O'Neill, *Golden Years of Paraguay*, p. 12.
9. Ibid., loc. cit.
10. Charlevoix, vol. i, p. 239.

11. O'Neill, p. 20.

CHAPTER 2 — THE TRIPLE ADVENTURE

1. Cunninghame Graham, *A Vanished Arcadia*, p. 49.
2. Del Techo, *Historia Provinciae Paraquariae* in Churchill, *Voyages*, vol. vi, p. 42.
3. Ibid., loc. cit.
4. Furneaux, *The Amazon*, pp. 58–9.
5. Del Techo, loc. cit.
6. Ibid., pp. 37–8.
7. *Conquista Espiritual*, Introducción, f. 1.
8. J. E. Groh, 'Antonio Ruiz de Montoya and the Early Reductions' in *Catholic Historical Review*, vol. 56, p. 509.
9. Charlevoix, *History of Paraguay*, vol. i, p. 249.
10. Del Techo, pp. 85–6.
11. Ibid., p. 32.
12. Meliá, *La Création d'une langue Chrétien*, pp. 98–9.
13. Ibid., p. 49.
14. Del Techo, p. 45.
15. Mörner, *The Jesuits in the La Plata Region*, p. 73.

CHAPTER 3 — THE GREAT EXODUS

1. Del Techo, p. 41.
2. Ibid., loc. cit.
3. Ibid., loc. cit.
4. Pastells, *Historia de la Compañía de Jesús en la Provincia del Paraguay*, vol. i, pp. 391–4.
5. Sepp in Churchill, *Voyages*, vol. v, pp. 391–4.
6. Del Techo, p. 50.
7. Ibid., p. 60.
8. Ibid., p. 59.
9. Muratori, *Relation of the Missions of Paraguay*, p. 53.
10. Dobrizhoffer, *Account of the Abipones*, vol. i, p. 159.
11. Muratori, op cit.
12. Del Techo, p. 75.
13. Ibid., p. 76.
14. Muratori, p. 106.
15. Lamalle, 'Jésuites wallons, flammands . . . au Paraguay' in *Archivum Historicum S.J.* (1947), p. 130.

16. Del Techo, p. 82.
17. Añuas (1615–37): *Documentos para la Historia Argentina*, vol. xx, pp. 726–7.
18. Del Techo, p. 82.
19. F. de Azara, *Descripción y Historia del Paraguay*, vol. i, p. 40.
20. Del Techo, p. 83.
21. Ibid., loc. cit.
22. Ibid., loc. cit.
23. Ibid., loc. cit.
24. Alden, *Royal Government in Colonial Brazil*, p. 463.

CHAPTER 4 — DEFEAT OF THE MAMELUCOS
1. Del Techo, p. 86.
2. Ibid., loc. cit.
3. Ibid., p. 87.
4. Ibid., loc. cit.
5. Hernández, *Organización Social*, vol. i, p. 12.
6. Del Techo, p. 96.
7. Ibid., loc. cit.
8. Dobrizhoffer, vol. iii, p. 411.
9. Del Techo, p. 100.
10. Ibid., p. 101.
11. Ibid., loc. cit.
12. Ibid., p. 102.
13. Ibid., loc. cit.
14. Ibid., loc. cit.
15. Hernández, vol. ii, p. 65.
16. Del Techo, p. 109.
17. Sepp in Churchill, *Voyages*, vol. v, p. 685.
18. *Sciences Ecclésiastiques*, vol. vii (October 1955), p. 308.

CHAPTER 5 — JESUIT MINES
1. Mörner, *The Jesuits in the La Plata Region*, p. 115.
2. Charlevoix, vol. i, p. 478.
3. Dobrizhoffer, vol. iii, p. 385.
4. Cunninghame Graham, *A Vanished Arcadia*, p. 139.
5. Ibid., p. 143.
6. Del Techo, p. 113.

7. Ibid., loc. cit.

CHAPTER 6 — DEFENCE AND INDEPENDENCE
1. Dobrizhoffer, vol. i, p. 101.
2. Furlong, *Misiones*, p. 385.
3. P. M. Dunne, 'Visitor to Paraguay' in *Mid-America*, vol. 27 (April 1945), p. 99.
4. Dobrizhoffer, vol. iii, p. 26.
5. Furlong, *Misiones*, pp. 391–6.
6. H. E. Bolton, 'The Mission as a Frontier Institution' in *American Historical Review*, vol. 23 (October 1917), p. 47.
7. Pastells, vol. i, p. 366.
8. Ibid., p. 395.
9. *Libro de Consultas* (1731–47).
10. *Sciences Ecclésiastiques*, vol. xiii (1911), pp. 401–7.
11. E.g. Eberhard Gothein, *Lo Stato christiano-social dei Gesuiti nel Paraguay* (Venice, 1928); Clovis Lugon, *La République communiste chrétienne des Guaranís* (Paris, 1949).
12. Furlong, *Misiones*, pp. 183–5.
13. Cf. Two articles by M. Mörner, 'Diego M. Cumargo and the Segregation Policy of the Spanish Crown' in *Hispanic-American Review*, vol. 42 (1962), p. 561 f., and 'The Guaraní Missions and the Segregation Policy of the Spanish Crown' in *Archivum Historicum S.J.* (July–December 1961).
14. Cardiel, *Declaración*, p. 219.
15. Brabo, *Documentos*, p. 320.

CHAPTER 7 — ECONOMY
1. Dobrizhoffer, vol. i, p. 110.
2. Sepp in *Estudios*, vol. 28 (1925), p. 55 f.
3. Peramás, *La República de Platón*, p. 50.
4. Ibid., p. 53.
5. Ibid., p. 54.
6. Steward, *Handbook of South American Indians*, vol. v, p. 351 f.
7. Customs Book.

8. Sepp in *Voyages*, vol. v, p. 293.
9. Dobrizhoffer, vol. i, p. 221.
10. Sepp, op. cit., loc. cit.
11. Dobrizhoffer, vol. i, p. 218.
12. Lacombe, 'Trois Documents' in *Revue d'Histoire Economique*, vol. 42 (1964), p. 53.
13. Dobrizhoffer, op. cit., loc. cit.
14. Furlong, *Misiones*, p. 429.
15. Charlevoix, vol. ii, p. 94.
16. Ibid., p. 361.
17. Furlong, *Misiones*, p. 413.
18. Del Techo, p. 13.
19. Cardiel, *Breve Relación*, p. 45.
20. Dobrizhoffer, vol. i, p. 106.
21. Ibid., p. 102.
22. Furlong, *Misiones*, p. 418.
23. Cardiel, loc. cit., ibid.
24. Dobrizhoffer, vol. i, p. 105.
25. Brabo, *Inventarios*, pp. 88–9.
26. Cunninghame Graham, *Vanished Arcadia*, p. 204.
27. Cardiel, *Declaración*, p. 131.
28. Brabo, *Inventarios*, p. 159.

CHAPTER 8 — REDUCTION LIFE, MEDICINE, SICKNESS AND DANGER

1. M. W. Nichols, 'Colonial Tucumán' in *Hispanic-American Review*, vol. 18 (1938), p. 481.
2. Añuas (1615–37): *Documentos para la Historia Argentina*, vol. xx, p. 727.
3. Dobrizhoffer, vol. i, p. 50.
4. Sepp in *Voyages*, vol. v, p. 688.
5. Ibid., p. 161.
6. Brabo, *Inventarios*, p. 316.
7. Ibid., p. 368.
8. Furlong, *Historia Social y Cultural del Río de la Plata*, pp. 49–50.
9. P. M. Dunne, 'Visitor to Paraguay' in *Mid-America*, vol. 27 (1945), p. 102.
10. Sepp in *Voyages*, vol. v, p. 689.

11. Ibid., p. 669.
12. Lacombe, 'Trois Documents', in *Revue d'Histoire Economique*, vol. 42 (1964), p. 52.
13. *Sciences Ecclésiastiques*, vol. vii (October 1955), p. 302.
14. F. Keller-Leazinger, *The Amazon and Madeira Rivers*, p. 68.
15. Ibid., p. 67.
16. Dobrizhoffer, vol. ii, p. 332.
17. Ibid., p. 338.
18. Customs Book.
19. Muratori, p. 99.
20. Dobrizhoffer, vol. ii, p. 202.
21. Sepp in *Voyages*, vol. v, p. 682.
22. Cunninghame Graham, *Vanished Arcadia*, p. 199.
23. *Libro de Consultas*, under 5 December 1731.
24. Sepp in *Voyages*, vol. v, p. 694.
25. Ibid., p. 692.
26. Ibid.
27. Lacombe, 'Trois Documents', p. 47.
28. Muratori, p. 102.
29. Sepp, op. cit., p. 688.
30. Dobrizhoffer, vol. ii, p. 245.
31. This figure is given by H. A. Huorder, *Catholic Encyclopedia* (ed. 1910), article on 'Reductions'; Dobrizhoffer (vol. ii, p. 240) gives the same figure, but for the year 1734.
32. Dobrizhoffer, vol. ii, p. 240.
33. Muratori, p. 270.
34. Ibid., p. 102.
35. Dobrizhoffer, vol. ii, p. 257.
36. Dobrizhoffer, vol. i, p. 305.
37. Ibid., p. 37.
38. Falkner, *Description of Patagonia*, p. 32.
39. Furlong, *Misiones*, p. 604.
40. C. Darwin, *Voyage of the Beagle, passim.*
41. Dobrizhoffer, vol. i, p. 255.
42. Ibid.
43. Dobrizhoffer, vol. i, p. 256.
44. Sepp in *Voyages*, vol. v, p. 892.

45. Muratori, p. 270.
46. Añuas (1615–37):*Documentos para la Historia Argentina*, vol. xx, p. 666.
47. Ibid.
48. Muratori, p. 276.
49. Sepp, op. cit., p. 691.
50. Dobrizhoffer, vol. i, pp. 254–5.
51. Ibid., p. 256.

CHAPTER 9 — GOVERNMENT

1. Sepp in *Voyages*, vol. v, pp. 687–8.
2. Dobrizhoffer, vol. ii, p. 58.
3. Ibid., p. 59.
4. Sepp, op. cit., p. 693.
5. Muratori, pp. 133–6.
6. Sepp, op. cit., p. 695.
7. Peramás, *La República de Platón*, p. 73.
8. Dobrizhoffer, vol. i, p. 172.
9. Customs Book.
10. 'Trois Documents', pp. 55, 63–4.
11. Peramás, op. cit., p. 95.
12. Ibid., p. 93.
13. Sepp, op. cit., loc. cit.
14. Ibid., p. 689.
15. Ibid.
16. Peramás, op. cit., p. 65.
17. Ibid., p. 88.
18. Ibid., p. 89.
19. Muratori, p. 83.
20. Sepp, op. cit., p. 684.
21. Muratori, p. 101.
22. Dobrizhoffer, vol. i, p. 222.
23. Sepp, op. cit., p. 671.
24. Muratori, p. 64.
25. Ibid., p. 16.
26. Lacombe, 'Trois Documents', p. 64.
27. Sepp, op. cit., p. 693.
28. Del Techo, p. 96.

CHAPTER 10 — CHIQUITOS

1. Jürgen Riester, 'Julian Knogler, S.J. und die Reduktionem der Chiquitano in Ostbolivien' in *Archivum Historicum S.J.* (July–December 1970), pp. 268–348.
2. Ibid., loc. cit.
3. Ibid., loc. cit.
4. Ibid., loc. cit.
5. Ibid., loc. cit.
6. 'Cartas de P. Jerónimo Herrán' in *Estudios*, vol. 21 (1921), p. 63.
7. Dobrizhoffer, vol. i, p. 46.
8. Riester, art. cit.
9. Ibid.
10. José Chantre y Herrera, *Historia de las Misiones en la Marañon Español.*
11. Añuas, 1756. Arch. S.J. Rome, *Para. Hist.* 1710–67, ff. 188–9.
12. *Relación de las costumbres y religión de los Indios Manasicas* (Madrid, 1901).
13. Dobrizhoffer, vol. ii, p. 84.
14. Muratori, p. 37.
15. Steward, *Handbook of South American Indians*, vol. iii, p. 392.
16. Añuas, loc. cit.
17. Dobrizhoffer, vol. iii, p. 412.
18. Sánchez Labrador, *El Paraguay Católico* (ed. 1910), vol i, pp. 13–15.
19. Peramás in *Archivum Historicum S.J.* (1938), p. 62.
20. T. Merton, quoted in E. Rice, *The Man in the Sycamore Tree* (1970), p. 111.

CHAPTER 11 — THE CHACO

1. Del Techo, p. 63.
2. Leonhardt, 'Dos Mártires del Chaco' in *Estudios*, vol. 67 (1942), pp. 297–312.
3. Del Techo, p. 107.
4. Ibid., p. 108.
5. Dobrizhoffer, vol. iii, p. 112.
6. Dobrizhoffer, vol. i, p. 130.

7. Ibid., p. 10.
8. Dobrizhoffer, vol. iii, p. 118.
9. Ibid., p. 132.
10. Ibid., loc. cit.
11. Dobrizhoffer, vol. ii, ch. 3.
12. Ibid., ch. 4.
13. Ibid., loc. cit.
14. Leonhardt, 'Padre Julian Lizardi' in *Estudios*, vol. 52 (1935), pp. 92–103.
15. Arch. S.J. Rome, *Para. Hist.* (1710–67), f. 191 f.
16. Sánchez Labrador, *El Paraguay Católico* (ed. 1910), vol. iii, ch. 19.
17. Dobrizhoffer, vol. iii, p. 59.
18. Dobrizhoffer, vol. iii, p. 265.
19. Florián Paucke, *Hacia Allá*.
20. Arch. S.J. Rome, *Para. 6, Cat. Trien.* (*1703–62*), f. 371.
21. Dobrizhoffer, vol. ii, p. 59.
22. Furlong, 'The Jesuit Contribution to Agriculture and Stock-Raising in the Argentine' in *Historical Bulletin*, St Louis University (May 1933), p. 67.
23. Paucke, *Hacia Allá*.

CHAPTER 12 — SONG, DANCE AND CHURCH

1. Furlong, 'Los Grandes Maestros de la Música Colonial Ríoplatense' in *Estudios*, vol. 67 (1942), pp. 408–29.
2. R. Fülöp-Miller, *The Power and Secret of the Jesuits* (1930), p. 285.
3. Pál Kelemen, *Baroque and Rococo in Latin America*, p. 227.
4. Enrique Peña, *Life of Francisco Céspedes*, p. 173.
5. Del Techo, p. 111.
6. Sepp in *Voyages*, vol. v, p. 685.
7. Dobrizhoffer, vol. i, p. 70.
8. F. Keller-Leazinger, *The Amazon and Madeira Rivers*, p. 160.
9. Furlong, 'Domenico Zipoli, músico eximio en Europa y América' in *Archivum Historicum S.J.* (July–December 1955), pp. 418–28.
10. Dobrizhoffer, vol. i, p. 384.

11. Añuas (1615–37): *Documentos para la Historia Argentina*, vol. xx, pp. 725–6.

12. Dobrizhoffer, vol. i, p. 384.

13. *Documentos de Arte Argentino*, vol. xx, pp. 25–6.

14. Sepp in *Voyages*, vol. v, p. 690.

15. Lamalle, 'Jésuites wallons, flammands . . . au Paraguay' in *Archivum Historicum S.J.* (1947), pp. 154–8.

16. Sepp, op. cit., p. 690.

17. Furlong, *Antonio Sepp y su 'Gobierno Temporal 1732'*.

18. Sepp, op. cit., p. 669.

19. Dobrizhoffer, vol. i, p. 313.

20. Ibid., loc. cit.

21. Customs Book.

22. Pál Kelemen, p. 196.

23. J. Buschiazzo, 'La Arquitectura de las Misiones de Mojos y Chiquitos' in *Südamerika* (Buenos Aires), November 1953.

CHAPTER 13 — THE GUARANI WAR

1. Alden, *Royal Government in Colonial Brazil*, p. 64.

2. Luis G. Jaeger, *A Expulsão da Companhia de Jesus do Brazil en 1760*; also G. Kratz, *El Tratado Hispano-Portugues de Límites de 1750*, p. 252.

3. Simancas, Estado 742, f.: copy in the Jesuit Archives of San Miguel. Cf. also Furlong, *Manuel Querini*, ch. iv.

4. O'Neill, p. 219.

5. Ibid., p. 229.

6. Dobrizhoffer, vol. i, p. 21.

7. Astraín, vol. vii, p. 653.

8. Dobrizhoffer, vol. i, p. 23.

9. *Diario del Capitán de Dragones, D. Francisco Graell* in *Colección de Documentos para la Historia de España*, vol. iv, p. 463 f.

10. Dobrizhoffer, vol. i, p. 25.

11. *Diario del Capitán de Dragones*, p. 483.

12. Arch. S.J. Rome, *Para. Hist.*, 1710–67, f. 186.

13. O'Neill, p. 235.

14. Dobrizhoffer, vol. iii, p. 195.

15. Dobrizhoffer, vol. i, p. 28.

16. Ibid.
17. Furlong in *Archivum Historicum S.J.* (January–June 1933).

CHAPTER 14 — PAMPAS AND PATAGONIA
1. Dobrizhoffer, vol. i, p. 55.
2. Ibid., pp. 63–4.
3. Ibid., p. 98.
4. Annual Letters: Arch. S.J. Rome, *Para. Hist.*, 1710–67, f. 188.
5. Dobrizhoffer, vol. i, pp. 320–3.
6. Ibid., p. 297.
7. Ibid., p. 131.
8. Falkner, *Description of Patagonia* (ed. 1935), p. 122.
9. Dobrizhoffer, vol. i, p. 132.
10. Ibid., loc. cit.
11. Falkner, p. 114.
12. Ibid., p. 117.
13. Ibid., p. 125.
14. Dobrizhoffer, vol. ii, p. 262.
15. Ibid.
16. Dobrizhoffer, vol. i, p. 138.
17. Bruno, *Historia de la Iglesia en la Argentina*, vol. v, p. 60.
18. Ibid.
19. Ibid.
20. Dobrizhoffer, vol. i, p. 148.
21. Sánchez Labrador, *Paraguay Católico*, pp. 106–7.
22. Falkner, p. 107.
23. Dobrizhoffer, vol. i, p. 144.
24. Ibid., loc. cit.
25. Falkner, p. 109.

CHAPTER 15 — THE END
1. Salvador de Madariaga, *The Fall of the Spanish-American Empire*, p. 274.
2. P. Hernández, *El Extrañamiento de los Jesuítas, passim.*
3. *A Short Relation* (Eng. ed., 1757), p. 23.
4. Madariaga, op. cit., loc. cit.

5. Ibid., p. 280.
6. Brabo, *Documentos*, p. 187.
7. Furlong, *Misiones*, p. 677.
8. Cunninghame Graham, *Vanished Arcadia*, pp. 267–8.
9. Brabo, *Documentos*, p. 185 f.
10. *Vanished Arcadia*, loc. cit.
11. Falkner, p. vii.
12. Brabo, *Documentos*, p. 200 f.
13. Ibid., p. 280.
14. Mörner, *The Expulsion of the Jesuits from Latin America*, p. 84.
15. Métraux, 'The Contribution of the Jesuits to the exploration and anthropology of South America', *Mid-America* (July 1944), p. 183.

CHAPTER 16 — EPILOGUE

1. Lacombe, in *Sciences Ecclésiastiques*, vol. vii (October 1955), p. 315.
2. Brabo, *Documentos*, pp. 320–67.
3. Gonzalo de Doblas, *Memoria Histórica*, pp. 96–7.
4. Aurelio Porto, *Historia das Missões Orientais do Uruguay*, vol. i, p. 462.
5. J. M. Mariluz Urquijo, 'Los Guaraníes después de la expulsión de los Jesuítas' in *Estudios Americanos*, no. 25, p. 326.
6. J. P. and W. P. Robertson, *Letters on Paraguay*, vol. ii, p. 109.
7. Ibid., pp. 127–9.
8. Ibid.
9. Gonzalo de Doblas, *Memoria Histórica*, p. 66.
10. *Letters on Paraguay*, vol. ii, p. 130.
11. Steward, *Handbook of South American Indians*, vol. iii, pp. 69–77.
12. Hernández, *Organización Social*, vol. i, pp. 257–8.
13. Meliá, p. 55.
14. Mörner, *Jesuits in the La Plata Region*, p. 133.
15. Customs Book.
16. Ibid.
17. Dobrizhoffer, vol. i, p. 153.

Appendices

I

The Sense of Spanish and Guaraní Words Used in the Text

abambaé	the land privately owned and cultivated by a Reduction Indian.
alcaldes	the title given to the two leading members of the town council.
aldea	a small Indian village.
alférez real	a royal standard bearer.
arroba	a unit of weight about 25 lb or 11·5 kilos.
audiencia	the high court of justice located at Charcas (now Sucre).
azote	strap or lash made from a hide or a blow with it.
Banda Oriental	area of the east bank of the Uruguay roughly co-terminous with the present Republic of Uruguay.
cabildo	the town council or town hall.
cacique	chieftain, an Arawakian word adopted by the Spaniards.
capitán general	a high military title used by certain Indian chiefs who claimed a wide area of jurisdiction.
chacra	small farm.
charquí	(Quincha) meat cut into strips and dried in the sun.
chicha	a strong beer made from fermented grain or mandioca.
compañero	the assistant priest in a Reduction.

309

corregidor	the highest official in a Reduction, roughly equivalent to a mayor.
cura	the priest in charge of a Reduction.
doctrina	parish (an ecclesiastical designation).
encomendero	the holder of an *encomienda.*
encomienda	the grant of the labour of a number of Indians to a colonist or corporation on condition that they were cared for and instructed in the Christian faith.
estancia	ranch or cattle farm.
guazú	(Guaraní) suffix signifying big.
hacienda	farm : private allotment of a Reduction Indian.
Mamelucos	half-breed Brazilian slave-hunters.
mandioca	root cultivated by the Indians from which they made meal.
matadero	slaughterhouse : park into which cattle were herded after being driven up from the estancia.
maté	drink made from *ilex paraguayensis.*
miní	(Guaraní) suffix signifying small.
mita	(Quincha) turn : requisitioned Indian labour for public works, usually in the mines.
mitayo	one who performs *mita.*
peón	labourer on an estancia.
peso	currency unit : *peso fuerte* (*corriente*) equivalent to eight *reales.*
pueblo	town, the civic designation of a Reduction.
real (*de plata*)	Spanish silver coin.
servicio personal	performance of day labour performed by Indians held in *encomienda.*
teniente	deputy, usually deputy governor or mayor.
toldo	tent carried around by Patagonian Indians.
trigo	South American wheat.

tupambaé	Reduction land cultivated and held in common by Indians for the benefit of the community.
yanacona	(Quincha) an unfree Indian, synonymous with *originario* in Paraguay.
yerba	*ilex paraguayensis* from the leaves of which maté is prepared.
yerbal	forest where the yerba grows, or artificial plantation of the yerba.

Common Words Used in a Peculiar Sense with Reference to the Jesuits

Annual Letters	A compilation made every year from reports sent in by local Superiors and together forming a general account of the work of a Province.
Assistancy	A grouping of Jesuit Provinces usually by national or geographical boundaries.
Assistant	Adviser to the Jesuit General on the affairs of the provinces making up an Assistancy.
Brother	A Jesuit not ordained, holding an administrative post or exercising a craft or peculiar skill, e.g. architect, infirmarian, military adviser.
Province	An administrative unit of the Jesuit Order determined normally by geographical or national factors.
Provincial	Priest appointed to take charge of a Province for a period of three to six years.
Consultation	A meeting of the Provincial with his advisers.
Consultor	One of four advisers of the Provincial who meet in conference once a month.
Customs Book	Excerpts from the ordinances of Provincials and Generals drawn up according to subject and forming a code for the conduct of priests on the Reductions.

General	The head of the Society of Jesus elected for life by a general Congregation.
Mission Superior	Priest in charge of all the Guaraní Reductions under the Provincial.
Novice	A candidate for admission to the Order.
Novitiate	House where the novices are trained.
Procurator	A delegate chosen by the Provincial Congregation to conduct the affairs of the Province in Europe or to represent its interests at a General Congregation.
Rector	Priest in charge of a larger Jesuit establishment.
Scholastic	A Jesuit student for the priesthood.
Visitation	Inspection carried out by a Provincial or a Visitor.
Visitor	A priest appointed to visit a Province and report on its affairs, always with specified terms of reference and authority.

II

List of Jesuit Generals
1607–1768

Claudio Acquaviva	1581–1615
Mutio Vitelleschi	1615–1645
Vincenzo Caraffa	1646–1649
Francisco Piccolomini	1649–1651
Alessandro Gottifredi	1652
Goswin Nickel	1652–1664
Giovanni Paolo Oliva	1664–1681
Charles de Noyelle	1682–1686
Tirso González	1687–1705
Michele Angelo Tamburini	1706–1730
Franz Retz	1730–1750
Ignazio Visconti	1751–1755
Luigi Centurione	1755–1757
Lorenzo Ricci	1758–1773

The Jesuits were suppressed by Pope Clement XIV on 21 July 1773. Lorenzo Ricci died a papal prisoner in Castel S. Angelo on 24 November 1775.

III

List of the Provincials of Paraguay 1607–1768

Diego de Torres del Bollo	1607
Pedro de Oñate	1615
Nicolás Durán Mastrilli	1622
Francisco Vásquez Trujillo	1628
Diego de Boroa	1634
Francisco de Zurbano	1640
J. Bapt. Ferrusino (Ferrufino)	1646
Juan Pastor	1651
Francisco Vásquez de la Mota	1655
Simón de Ojeda	1658
Francisco Jiménez	1664
Andréz de Rada	1666
Augustín de Aragon	1669
Christóbal de Gómez	1672
Diego Francisco Altamirano	1677
Tomás de Baeza	1681
Tomás Dombidas	1684
Gregorio de Orozco	1689
Lauro Núñez	1692
Simón de León	1695
Ignacio Frías	1698
Lauro Núñez	1702
Blas de Silva	1706
Antonio Garriga	1709
Luis de la Roca	1713
J. Bapt. de Zea (Cea)	1717
José Aguirre	1719
Luis de la Roca	1722

Ignacio Arteaga	1726
Jerónimo Herrán	1729
Diego Aguilar	1733
Antonio Machoni	1739
Bernardo Nusdorffer	1743
Manuel Querini	1747
José Barreda	1751
Alonso Fernández	1757
Pedro Juan Andreu	1761
Manuel Vergara	1766

IV

Reductions Staffed by the Jesuits of the Province of Paraguay at the time of their expulsion from South America

GUARANI

On the East Bank of the Uruguay
1. San Borja
2. San Nicolás
3. San Luis
4. San Lorenzo
5. San Miguel
6. San Juan
7. Santo Angel

Between the Uruguay and the Paraná
8. Yapeyú (Three Kings)
9. La Cruz
10. Santo Tomé
11. Concepción
12. San Javier
13. Santa María la Mayor
14. Mártires
15. Apóstoles
16. San José
17. San Carlos
18. Candelaria
19. Santa Ana
20. San Ignacio Miní
21. Loreto
22. Corpus

North of the Paraná
23. Itapuá
24. Trinidad
25. Jesús
26. San Cosme y Damian

27. Santiago
28. Santa Rosa

29. San Ignacio Guazú
30. Santa María de Fe

In Taruma
31. San Joaquín

32. San Estanislao

CHIQUITOS
1. San Javier
2. Concepción
3. San Rafael
4. San Miguel
5. San José

6. San Juan
7. Santiago
8. Santa Ana
9. Corazón
10. San Ignacio

THE CHACO
1. San José (Vilelas)
2. San Esteban (Lules)
3. Pilar (Pajanes)
4. Nuestra Señora de Buen Concilio (Vilelas)
5. San Juan Bautista (Toquistines)
6. Rosario de las Salinas (Chiriguanos)
7. San Ignacio de Ledesma (Tobas)

8. San Fernando (Abipones)
9. San Jerónimo (Abipones)
10. San Javier (Mocobíes)
11. San Pedro (Mocobíes)
12. Concepción (Abipones)
13. Belén (Mbayá and Guaycurú)
14. Rosario (Abipones)
15. San Juan Nepomuceno (Guanas)

V

Non-Spanish Jesuits in Spanish South America

By virtue of a papal Bull of 1508 which gave the king *real patronato de las Indias,* or the right of controlling the presentation and removal of ecclesiastics in his overseas possessions, the Crown was able strictly to regulate the appointment of all priests and students for the priesthood in South America. In practice, the Crown decided the number of Jesuits sent overseas and the nature of their work.

However, Spain soon found herself unable to provide

sufficient priests for her colonies, and was compelled to adopt a fairly liberal policy. Thus, until the Cárdenas affair, priests from non-Spanish countries subject to Spain, for instance the Spanish Netherlands, Sicily, Naples, Milan and Sardinia, were given permits to work in Spanish territories. In 1647 seventy-five Jesuits (nearly all of them non-Spaniards), assembled by Padre Juan Pastor, the pioneer missionary of the Chaco, were turned back from Sevilla and Cadiz where they were waiting to embark for South America. Cárdenas had charged foreign Jesuits in Paraguay with violation of the *real patronato* by discovering mines and working them in secret. For the next twenty-five years there was no expansion of the work done by the Paraguay Jesuits.

In 1664 Spain was again forced by shortage of priests to revise her regulations. A contributory cause of the revision was the assurance given by the Governor of Paraguay, Juan Blázquez de Valverde, of the loyalty of the non-Spanish members of the Paraguay province. He did this in a letter of 15 January 1658 after completing a visitation of all the Reductions on the Paraná and Uruguay. The change of policy which he initiated was set out in a reply from the Council of the Indies addressed to Valverde's successor in 1659. Henceforth foreign Jesuits were permitted to enter Paraguay and other Spanish possessions provided they were vassals of the King of Spain or of the Austrian Emperor and that their total number did not exceed one-fourth of all the Jesuits sent to the Spanish colonies. Moreover, they had to be approved personally by the Jesuit General and had to reside for a year in the Jesuit province of Toledo before seeking the consent of the Council of the Indies to go to the Spanish possessions. Finally, they had to carry papers of identification.

In 1674, ten years later, Doña Mariana of Austria, the Queen Regent of Spain, increased the quota of foreign Jesuits to one-third and dispensed with the need for them to reside a year in the province of Toledo.

Earlier the Jesuit General, Giovanni Paolo Oliva, had pointed out to the Council of the Indies that it was impossible for the provinces of Castille, Toledo, Andalucía and Aragon to provide sufficient priests for the overseas commitments of the Jesuits. He argued also that foreign provinces, being more numerous, could be more stringent in their choice of men. Padre Sebastián Izquierdo, Oliva's Assistant for Spanish territories, went so far as to say that 'experience had proved that foreigners were better at learning Indian languages than Spaniards'.

In fact, between 1586, the year before the arrival of Padre Fields in Paraguay, and 1650, the year of Cárdenas's final departure from Asunción, the three German provinces (Upper Germany, the Rhine and Austria) had grown in membership from 771 to 2,829. In 1623 the Province of Austria had been divided into Austria and Bohemia, and in 1626 the Rhine Province had been divided into the Upper and Lower Rhine. In 1673 the total membership of the German Assistancy (included in it were Poland, England and Ireland) was three times that of the Spanish Assistancy, approximately 6,600 to 2,040.

However, the more liberal policy of Doña Mariana could not be fully implemented for several decades until the Atlantic sea routes had been cleared of pirates. In September 1664 Oliva wrote: 'All the ocean routes by which the missionaries are ordinarily sent have been cut off by Dutch heretics'; nor could any money be sent for the support of the missions 'without manifest risk': only the China mission benefited, for priests could reach their stations there by an overland route.

Missionary enthusiasm in the German provinces had been stimulated by St Peter Canisius, who in 1561 had sought to resign his office as Provincial in order to go to the Indies. This enthusiasm was later sustained by the fourteen volumes of missionary letters, the famous *Lettres Edifiantes et Curieuses*, published first in Paris, then in other capital cities, including London, between 1702 and 1776. These letters stressed the number of natives everywhere 'ready for the harvest', and fired the romantic imagination of students in Jesuit Colleges throughout Europe. In addition, several Jesuits on the missions wrote long letters (Sepp's are an example) to their families, who circulated them privately and sometimes had them published and even translated into other languages.

These letters stressed the horrors of the sea passage and the warm welcome the new priests received from their brethren on disembarkation.

Spanish policy remained unchanged until the beginning of the eighteenth century, by which time the Chiquitos mission had been established. The War of the Spanish Succession (1701–14) revived suspicion of all foreigners, and it was only with the signing of the Treaty of Utrecht (1715) that non-Spanish Jesuits were again allowed into South America. In that year a party of eighty priests left Europe, sixty *en route* for Paraguay, twenty for the Marañon missions: only the Kingdom of Naples and the Duchy of Milan, among the Spanish European dominions, were excluded as sources of supply. It was with the coming of these men that work in the Chaco was resumed. Foreign priests continued to enter Paraguay until 1756, when the charges against them were renewed at the time of the Guaraní war: it was then alleged that the Jesuits were setting up an independent realm in Paraguay. A Padre Och from the Upper German Province waiting embarkation at Cadiz in 1755 wrote in his diary that his sailing had been delayed because 'the mythical fool, King Nicolás, appeared on the world stage about this time'. Och never reached Paraguay. In parts of Europe it was believed that Nicolás was a German, and it was therefore thought inadvisable to send more Germans to Paraguay. The fact that non-Spanish Jesuits were frequently assigned to remote and difficult regions like the Chaco became a ground of suspicion. The reason, of course, was that they were more acceptable to Indians who in these areas had a long history of hostility to the Spaniards.

Cf. Theodore E. Treutlein, 'Non-Spanish Jesuits in Spain's American Colonies': contribution to *Greater America: Essays in Honor of Herbert Eugene Bolton* (California, 1945), pp. 219–43; W. Eugene Shiels, 'The Critical Period in Mission History' in *Mid-America* (April, 1939), vol. 21, pp. 97–109.

Bibliography

In a general work of this kind I have judged it necessary to give references only to sources from which I have taken direct quotations or on which I have based a statement or conclusion which might not immediately be accepted by scholars. The fullest and near-exhaustive bibliography of colonial Paraguay, compiled by Guillermo Furlong, S.J., in his *Misiones y sus Pueblos Guaraníes* (Buenos Aires, 1962), runs to eighteen double-column pages and does not take in the Chiquitos or Chaco Reductions. Furlong's book is now rare and difficult to obtain in Europe or the United States. More accessible to English readers are two selective bibliographies compiled by Dr Magnus Mörner, Director of the Institute of Ibero-American Studies in Stockholm: the first, in his *Political and Economic Activities of the Jesuits in the La Plata Region: the Hapsburg Era* (Stockholm, 1953), is more general than the title might suggest; the second, in the author's book of extracts illustrating *The Expulsion of the Jesuits from Latin America* (New York, 1965), is discursive, and covers mainly the last chapters of my book.

The manuscript material I have used is to be found either in Rome, in the central archives of the Jesuits, or in Buenos Aires in the Archivo General de la Nación and in the Archives of the Argentine Jesuit Province, formerly at the Colegio del Salvador and now housed in the Colegio de San Miguel outside the city. In the Roman Archives I drew on the Catalogues of the Paraguay Province, some unpublished Annual Letters and, among the documents under the heading *Paraguariae Historia* (1710–67), an important and hitherto unused report on the Chaco Reductions (f. 191 f.) on which a large part of the second half of chapter 11 is based. In the Archivo General de la Nación I took notes from the Customs Book of the Guaraní missions and from the Libro de Consultas (División Colonia, vol. 1302) containing the minutes of the conferences held regularly by the Provincial on his visitation of the Reductions. These sources seemed to me particularly valuable because they were intended for circulation only among the Jesuits of Paraguay. Also at Buenos Aires, in the Archives of the Jesuit Province at San Miguel, I found many transcripts made by Padre Carlos Leonhardt from Simancas covering the events in chapter 13.

For my purposes, sufficient government papers have been collected and published in the six volumes of Padre Pablo Pastells, *Historia de la Compañía de Jesús en la Provincia del Paraguay según los Documentos Originales del Archivo General de Indias* (Madrid, 1912–46). These volumes and the documents contained in the annotations have been particularly useful in the chapters on Guairá and Cárdenas.

Curiously, the first general history of the Reductions, del Techo's *Historia Provinciae Paraquariae* (1673), remains the most satisfactory: like P. Charlevoix's *Histoire du Paraguay*, 3 vols (Paris, 1756), it contains much material not to be found elsewhere. In English, Cunninghame Graham's *A Vanished Arcadia* is still valuable, though published in 1901. The short, enthusiastic *Golden Years on the Paraguay* (1934) by George O'Neill is a useful popularization of the work of the Spanish Jesuit, Antonio Astraín, *Historia de la Compañía de Jesús en la Asistencia de España* (Madrid, 1913–25). There is an excellent but brief survey of the Reductions in chapter 4 of Robin Furneaux's *The Amazon* (1969). A French essay, *La Vie Quotidienne au Paraguay sous les Jésuites* (Hachette, 1967), is what its title indicates and not a history of the Jesuit State.

Where they exist I have used established English translations of Jesuit sources. This applies to del Techo's *Historia* (printed in volume 4 of Awnsham and J. Churchill's *Collections of Voyages* (1704–32)), Martin Dobrizhoffer's *Historia de Abiponibus* (tr. Sara Coleridge, 3 vols (London, 1822)), Charlevoix's *Histoire du Paraguay* (published in London in two volumes in 1759) and Antonio Sepp's earlier letters (printed in translation in volume 5 of Awnsham and J. Churchill's *Voyages*): the later letters can be found in several other places, e.g. *Estudios*, vol. 28 (1925). Nothing perhaps can compare in importance with G. Furlong's *Misiones y sus Pueblos Guaraníes*, an encylopedic work drawing on an immense range of sources.

In addition to the above-mentioned papers I have used the following books and articles.

Books

Astraín, A., *Historia de la Compañía de Jesús en la Asistencia de España* (Madrid, 1913–25).

Alden, Dauril, *Royal Government in Colonial Brazil* (California University Press, 1968).

Brabo, Francisco Xavier, *Colección de Documentos relativos a la expulsión de los Jesuítas de la República Argentina y del Paraguay* (Madrid, 1872).

Brabo, Francisco Xavier, *Inventarios de los bienes hallados a la expulsión de los Jesuítas* (Madrid, 1872).

Bruno, Cayetano, *Historia de la Iglesia en la Argentina* (Buenos Aires, 1969), volume 5.

Cardiel, José, *Breve Relación de las Misiones del Paraguay* in Hernández, *Organización*, vol. ii, pp. 514–614.

Cardiel, José, *Declaración de la Verdad* (ed. Buenos Aires, 1900).

Charlevoix, P., *Histoire du Paraguay*, 3 vols (Paris, 1756).

Chantre y Herrera, José, *Historia de las Misiones en la Marañon* (ed. Madrid, 1901).

Doblas, Gonzaguo de, *Memoria sobre la provincia de Misiones de Indios Guaraníes* (Buenos Aires, 1836).

Documentos para la Historia Argentina, vol. 20 (Buenos Aires, 1929).

Documentos de Arte Argentino: Cuaderno XIX, Las Misiones Guaraníes: Arquitectura (Buenos Aires, 1946); *Cuaderno XX: Escultura, Pintura, Grabados y Artes Menores* (Buenos Aires, 1946).

Edmundson, George, *The Journals of Father Fritz* (Hakluyt Society, 1922).

Falkner, Thomas, *A Description of Patagonia and the Adjoining Parts of South America* (Hereford, 1774; reprint, Chicago, 1935).

Fernández, J. Patricio, *Historica Relatio de Missionibus Patrum S.J. apud Chiquitos* (Madrid, 1733; Spanish ed. Madrid, 1895).

Fülöp-Miller, R., *The Power and Secret of the Jesuits* (London, 1930).

Furlong, G., *Antonio Ruiz de Montoya y su Carta a Comental* (Buenos Aires, 1964).

Furlong, G., *Misiones y sus Pueblos Guaraníes* (Buenos Aires, 1962).

Furlong, G., *Antonio Sepp y su Gobierno Temporal* (Buenos Aires, 1962).

Furlong, G., *Bernardo Nusdorffer y su Novena Parte* (Buenos Aires, 1971).

Furlong, G., *Historia Social y Cultural del Río de la Plata: El Transplante Cultural* (Buenos Aires, 1969).

Furlong, G., *Ladislao Oroz y su Nicolás del Techo* (Buenos Aires, 1966).

Furlong, G., *Los Jesuítas y la Cultura Ríoplatense* (Montevideo, 1933).

Furlong, G., *Thomas Falkner y su Acerca de los Patagones* (Buenos Aires, 1954).

Furneaux, Robin, *The Amazon* (1969).

Grahame, Cunninghame, *A Vanished Arcadia* (1901).

Hanke, Lewis, *Aristotle and the South American Indians* (Indiana University Press, 1959).

Hanke, Lewis (ed.), *History of Latin American Civilisation: Sources and Interpretation*, vol. 1 (Methuen, 1969).

Hernández, Pablo, *El Extrañamiento de los Jesuítas del Río de la Plata* (Madrid, 1908).

Hernández, Pablo, *Organización Social de las Doctrinas Guaraníes*, 2 vols (Barcelona, 1913).

Ibáñez de Echavarría, Bernardo, *El Reyno Jesuítico del Paraguay* (Madrid, 1770).

Jaeger, Luis Gonzaga, *A Expulsão da Companhia de Jesus do Brazil en 1760* (Porto Alegre, 1960).

Kelemen, Pál, *Baroque and Rococo in Latin America* (New York, 1951).

Keller-Leazinger, F., *The Amazon and Madeira Rivers* (London, 1874).

Kratz, G., *El Tratado Hispano-Portugués de Límites de 1750 y sus Consecuencias* (Rome, 1954).

Madariaga, S. de, *The Fall of the Spanish-American Empire* (London, 1947).

Manuale ad usum Patrum S.J. qui in Reductionibus Paraguariae versantur (printed at the Reduction of Loreto).

Meliá, Bartolomé, 'La Création d'un langue Chrétien dans les Réductions des Guaranís au Paraguay', unpublished doctorate thesis, University of Strasbourg, 2 vols (1969).

Mörner, Dr M., *The Expulsion of the Jesuits from Latin America* (New York, 1965).

Mörner, Dr M., *Political and Economic Activities of the Jesuits in the La Plata Region: The Hapsburg Era* (Stockholm, 1955).

Muratori, L., *A Relation of the Missions of Paraguay* (London, 1759).

O'Neill, George, *Golden Years on the Paraguay* (1934).

Pastells, P. P., *Historia de la Compañía de Jesús en la Provincia del Paraguay según los Documentos Originales del Archivo General de Indias* (Madrid, 1912–46).

Paucke, Florián, *Hacia Allá y Para Acá: Una Estada Entre los Indios Mocobíes*, 3 vols (Buenos Aires, 1942–4).

Peramás, J. E., *La República de Platón y los Guaraníes* (ed. Buenos Aires, 1947).

Peramás, J. E., *Vita Sex Sacerdotum Paraguaycorum* (1791).

Peramás, J. E., *Vita XIII Virorum Paraguaycorum* (1793).

Plattner, Felix Alfred, *Genie im Urwald: Das Werk des Auslandschweizers Martin Schmid* (Zurich, 1959).

Plattner, Felix Alfred, *Deutsche Meister des Barock in Südamerika* (Basel, 1960).

Popescu, Oreste, *Sistema Económico en las Misiones Jesuíticas* (Barcelona, 1967).

Porto, Aurelio, *Historia das Missões do Uruguay*, vol. i (Porto Alegre, 1955).

Ruiz de Montoya, Antonio, *Conquista Espiritual* (1639, Madrid, University Microfilms, Inc., Ann Arbor).

Sánchez Labrador, José, *El Paraguay Católico*, 3 vols (Buenos Aires, 1910–17).

Steward, Julian H. (ed.), *Handbook of the South American Indians*, vols i, iii and v (Washington D.C., 1946–8).

Sierra, Vicente D., *Los Jesuítas Germanos en la conquista espiritual de Hispano-América* (Buenos Aires, 1944).

Service, Elman R., *Spanish-Guaraní Relations in early Colonial Paraguay* (Ann Arbor, 1954).

Techo, del, *Historia Provinciae Paraquariae* (1673).

Articles

The Americas (Washington, D.C.)

Habig, Marion A., vol. 2, no. 4 (April 1946), 'The Franciscan Provinces of South America: IX: Provincia de la Asunción'

Anales de la Real Academia de Farmacia (Instituto de España)

Cignoli, Francisco, no. 1 (1953), 'Médicos y boticarios misioneros'

Archivum Historicum Societatis Jesu (AHSJ) (Rome)

Delattre, Pierre, and Lamalle, Edmond (Jan.–Dec. 1947), pp. 98–176, 'Jésuites wallons, flammands, français missionaires au Paraguay 1608–1767'

Furlong, G. (Jan–Dec. 1938), pp. 54–79, 'De la Asunción a los Chiquitos por el Río Paraguay'

Furlong, G. (July–Dec. 1955), pp. 418–28, 'Domenico Zipoli, músico eximio en Europa y América'

Mörner, Magnus (July–Dec. 1961), pp. 376–83, 'The Guaraní Missions and the Segregation Policy of the Spanish Crown'

Riester, Jurgen (July–Dec. 1970), pp. 268–348, 'Julian Knogler, S.J. und die Reduktionen der Chiquitano in Ostbolivien'

Estudios (Buenos Aires)

Vol. 20 (1921), vol. 21 (1921), *passim*, 'La guerra de los siete pueblos'

Vol. 27 (1924), vol. 28 (1925), *passim*, 'El Padre Antonio Sepp'

Blanco, José, vol. 22 (1922), pp. 91–6, 'Un escultor y arquitecto colonial'

Blanco, José, vol. 50 (1934), pp. 263–71, 'Procesiones Eucharísticas'

Furlong, G., vol. 57 (1937), pp. 81–100, 'La Arquitectura en las Misiones Guaraníes'

Furlong, G., vol. 67 (1942), pp. 408–29, 'Los Grandes Maestros de la Música Colonial Ríoplatense'

Leonhardt, C., vol. 26 (1924), 'Datos Históricos sobre el teatro misional en la Compañía de Jesús del Paraguay'

Leonhardt, C., vol. 36 (1928), pp. 92–9, 193–208, 'El Padre Roque González y compañeros, mártires S. J. según documentos contemporáneos'

Leonhardt, C., vol. 52 (1935), pp. 92–9, 'El Padre Julián Lizardi'

Leonhardt, C., vol. 57 (1937), pp. 102–18, 'Los Jesuítas y la Medicina en el Río de la Plata'

Leonhardt, C., vol. 63 (1940), pp. 297–312, 'Roque González de Santa Cruz'

Leonhardt, C., vol. 67 (1942), pp. 297–312, 'Dos Mártires del Chaco, Gaspar Osorio y Antonio Ripario'

Estudios Americanos (Seville)

Urquijo, José M., vol. 6, no. 25 (Oct. 1953), pp. 324–30, 'Los Guaraníes después de la expulsión de los Jesuítas'

Hispanic-American Review (Durham)

Mörner, Magnus, vol. 42 (1962), 'Diego M. Cumargo and the Segregation Policy of the Spanish Crown'

Service, Elman R., vol. 31 (1951), '"The encomienda in Paraguay'

Historical Bulletin (St Louis)

Furlong, G. (May 1933), pp. 66–68, 'The Jesuit Contribution to Agriculture and Stock-raising in the Argentine'

Mid-America (Chicago)

Blankenburg, Angela, vol. 29 (1947) nos. 1 & 2, 'German Missionary Writers in Paraguay'

Dunne, Peter M., vol. 27 (1945), no. 1, 'The Jesuit Archives at Buenos Aires'

Dunne, Peter M., vol. 27 (1945), no. 2, 'Visitor to Paraguay in 1714'

Jacobsen, Jerome V., vol. 29 (1947), no. 2, 'Dobrizhoffer, Abipon Missionary'

Métraux, Alfred, vol. 26 (1944), no. 3, 'The contribution of the Jesuits to the exploration and anthropology of South America'

Month (London)

Bury, J. B. (June 1953), 'The Jesuit Contribution to Brazil'

Revista de Arquitectura (Buenos Aires)

Furlong, G. (July 1944), 'Jesuítas y Arquitectos'

Revue d'Histoire Economique et Sociale (Paris)

Lacombe, Robert, vol. 42 (1964), no. 1, pp. 27–73, 'Trois Documents Français du début du xviii siècle sur les Jésuites du Paraguay'

Revue de Paris

Métraux, Alfred (June 1952), pp. 102–13, 'Jésuites et Indiens en Amerique du Sud'

Sciences Ecclésiastiques (Montreal)

Armani, A. and Lacombe, Robert, vol. 13 (Oct. 1961), pp. 401–7, 'Les Institutions politiques et sociales dans les Réductions au Paraguay'

Lacombe, Robert, vol. 7 (Oct. 1955), pp. 293–318, 'Sur la terre comme au ciel: l'expérience économique des Jésuites au Paraguay'

Studies (Dublin)

Gwynn, Aubrey (1924), 'Fr. Thomas Fields'

Gwynn, Aubrey (1932), 'The Dispersion of the Spanish Jesuits'

Südamerika (Buenos Aires)

Buschiazzo, Mario, J. (Nov. 1953), 'La Arquitectura de las Misiones de Mojos y Chiquitos'

PARÁ

MATO GROSSO

BAHIA (SALVADOR)

LIMA

MACHUPICHU
CUZCO
JULI
LAKE TITICACA
LA PAZ
ALTIPLANO
SANTA CRUZ DE LA SIERRA
SUCRE (CHARCAS)
POTOSÍ
TARIJA
CHIQUITOS
FUERTE OLIMPO
CONCEPCIÓN
ITATÍN
JUJUY
SALTA
CHACO
ASUNCIÓN
GUAIRÁ
RIO DE JANEIRO
SÃO PAULO
TUCUMÁN
SANTIAGO DEL ESTERO
CORRIENTES
RIOJA
PORTO ALEGRE
TAPE
CÓRDOBA
SANTA FE
SANTIAGO DE CHILE
PAMPAS
BUENOS AIRES
MONTEVIDEO
ATLANTIC
OCEAN
BAHÍA BLANCA
PATAGONIA
COLONIA
SAN JULIÁN

SOUTH
AMERICA
SOUTH OF 10°S

0   300 Miles

Map 1

325

GUAIRÁ
REDUCTIONS
1610-1630

TROPIC OF CAPRICORN
ASUNCION
SAO PAULO

RÍO PARANAPANEMA
LORETO
S.IGNACIO
S.JOSÉ
TROPIC OF CAPRICORN
SAO PAULO
RÍO PARANÁ
VILLARRICA
SANTOS
CIUDAD REAL
S.JAVIER
S.PABLO
S.TOMÉ
ENCARNACIÓN
S.MIGUEL
JESUS MARIA
S.ANTONIO
CONCEPCIÓN
RÍO IGUAZÚ
S.PEDRO
ATLANTIC OCEAN
DEMARCATION LINE OF TREATY OF TORDESILLAS

■ SPANISH TOWNS
● INDIAN TOWNS

0   50 Miles

Map 2

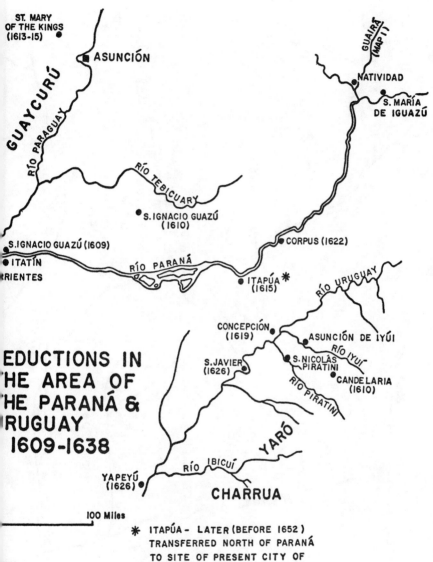

ST. MARY
OF THE KINGS
(1613-15)

ASUNCIÓN

GUAYCURÚ

RÍO PARAGUAY

RÍO TEBICUARY

S. IGNACIO GUAZÚ
(1610)

S. IGNACIO GUAZÚ (1609)

ITATÍN

RRIENTES

RÍO PARANÁ

ITAPÚA
(1615)

CORPUS (1622)

GUAIRÁ
(MAP 1)

NATIVIDAD

S. MARÍA
DE IGUAZÚ

RÍO URUGUAY

CONCEPCIÓN
(1619)

ASUNCIÓN DE IYÚI

S. JAVIER
(1626)

S. NICOLÁS
PIRATINI

RÍO IYÚI

CANDELARIA
(1610)

RÍO PIRATINI

YARÓ

EDUCTIONS IN
HE AREA OF
HE PARANÁ &
RUGUAY
1609-1638

YAPEYÚ
(1626)

RÍO IBICUÍ

CHARRUA

100 Miles

 ITAPÚA – LATER (BEFORE 1652)
TRANSFERRED NORTH OF PARANÁ
TO SITE OF PRESENT CITY OF
ENCARNACIÓN

Map 3

327

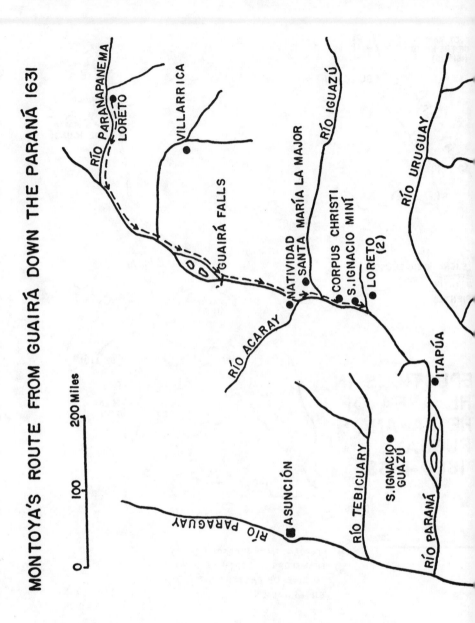

MONTOYA'S ROUTE FROM GUAIRÁ DOWN THE PARANÁ 1631

Map 4

328

ITATÍN 1631-1669

ÁNGELES
S.JOSÉ
— 20°S
SANTA MARÍA
DE FE
S.BENITO
NATIVIDAD
ANDIRAPUCÁ
YATEBU
TEPOTÍ
S.IGNACIO DE CAAGUAZÚ (1)

RÍO JUJUY
S.IGNACIO
DE CAAGUAZÚ (2)

ASUNCIÓN
— 25°S

RÍO PARAGUAY
RÍO TEBICUARY
SANTA MARÍA DE FE
SANTIAGO
RÍO PARANÁ

0   100 Miles

Map 5

1632 Four towns founded: Angeles, San José, San Benito and Natividad.
1633 Invasion of the Mamelucos: the remnants of these four towns gathered into two new towns: Andirapucá and Tepotí.
1634 These two towns gathered into one: Yatebu.
1635–47 Yatebu is divided into two: Santa María de Fé and San Ignacio de Caaguazú.
1648 Santa María de Fé moved south and called Nuestra Señora de Fé.
1651 San Ignacio de Caaguazú moved south.
1659 Santa María de Fé and San Ignacio de Caaguazú moved south of Asunción and the Río Tebicuary to their present sites of Santa María de Fé and Santiago.

329

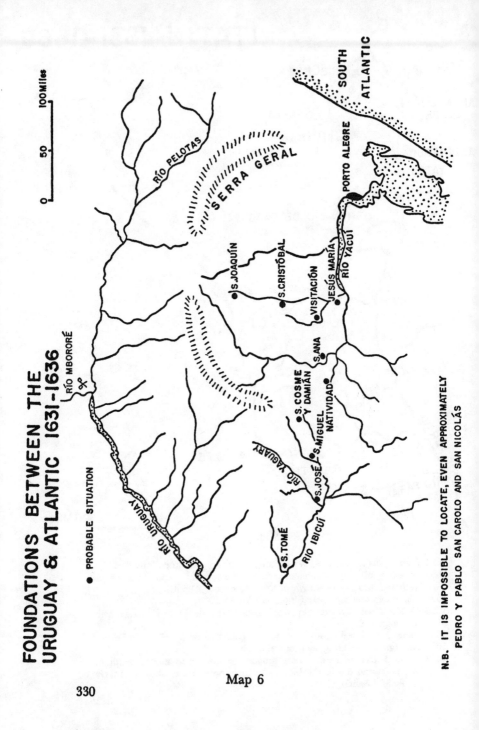

FOUNDATIONS BETWEEN THE
URUGUAY & ATLANTIC 1631-1636

● PROBABLE SITUATION

N.B. IT IS IMPOSSIBLE TO LOCATE, EVEN APPROXIMATELY
PEDRO Y PABLO SAN CAROLO AND SAN NICOLÁS

Map 6

330

GROUPS OF JESUIT REDUCTIONS HOLDING
THE SPANISH SOUTH AMERICAN FRONTIER

Map 7

THE THIRTY GUARANÍ
REDUCTIONS WITH THE
TERRITORY BELONGING
TO THEM IN THE MID-
EIGHTEENTH CENTURY

▬ CULTIVATED YERBAL
BELONGING TO
NEARBY REDUCTION

▨ NATURAL YERBAL

0   50 Miles

1. STA MARÍA DE FE	11. LORETO	21. STO. TOMÉ
2. S. IGNACIO GUAZÚ	12. STA. ANA	22. S. BORJA
3. STA. ROSA	13. CANDELARIA	23. S. NICOLÁS
4. SANTIAGO	14. S. CARLOS	24. S. LUIS
5. S. COSME	15. MÁRTIRES	25. S. LORENZO
6. ITAPÚA.	16. S. JOSÉ	26. S. JUAN
7. TRINIDAD	17. STA. MARÍA	27. STO. ÁNGEL
8. JESÚS	18. S. JAVIER	28. S. MIGUEL
9. CORPUS	19. APÓSTOLES	29. LA CRUZ
10. S. IGNACIO MINÍ	20. CONCEPCIÓN	30. YAPEYÚ

Map 8

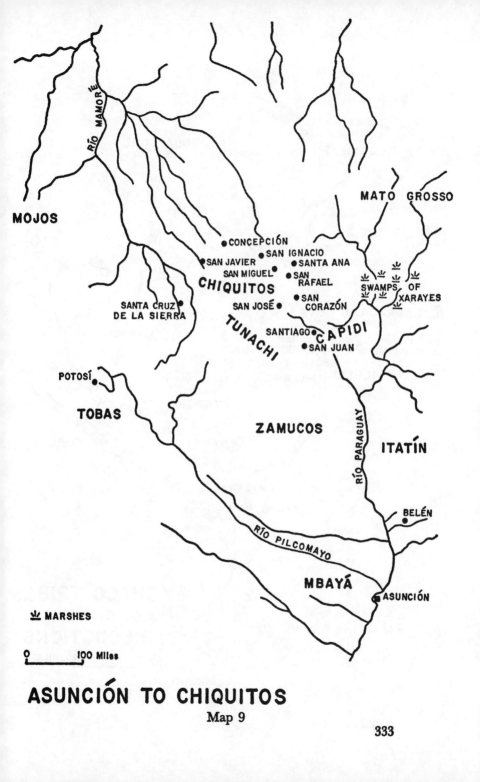

MATO GROSSO

MOJOS

RÍO MAMORE

CHIQUITOS

● CONCEPCIÓN

● SAN IGNACIO

● SAN JAVIER

● SANTA ANA

SAN MIGUEL ●

● SAN RAFAEL

SWAMPS OF XARAYES

SANTA CRUZ ●
DE LA SIERRA

SAN JOSÉ ●

● SAN CORAZÓN

TUNACHI

SANTIAGO ● CAPIDI

● SAN JUAN

POTOSÍ ●

TOBAS

ZAMUCOS

ITATÍN

RÍO PARAGUAY

BELÉN ●

RÍO PILCOMAYO

MBAYÁ

● ASUNCIÓN

⚘ MARSHES

0 ⊢────── 100 Miles

ASUNCIÓN TO CHIQUITOS
Map 9

333

LAGUNA

GUAYCURÚ

CHIRIGUANOS

S. JUAN
NEPOMUCENO

MBAYÁ

RÍO PARAGUAY

TARIJA

ROSARIO DE
LAS SALINAS

TOBAS

BELÉN   RÍO YPANÉ

RÍO PILCOMAYO

JUJUY

LADRADILLO

SALTA

RÍO BERMEJO

LULES

TOBAS

ASUNCIÓN

RÍO PARANÁ

CALCHAQUÍ

N.S. DE
BUEN CONSEJO

S. ESTEBAN

S. JUAN BAUTISTA

TOQUISITINES

N.S. DEL PILAR

CONCEPCIÓN

VILELAS

PAJANES

MOCOBÍES

TUCUMÁN

S. JOSÉ

S. FERNANDO

YARÓ

CORRIENTES

SANTIAGO
DEL ESTERO

RÍO SALADO

MATARÁ

ABIPONES

RÍO URUGUAY

YARÓ

ARROYO DEL REY

S. JERÓNIMO

S. PEDRO Y PABLO

MOCOBÍES

CÓRDOBA

S. JAVIER

CHARRUA

CALCHAQUÍ

SANTA FE

CHACO TRIBES
AND
REDUCTIONS

0   250 MILES

■ SPANISH TOWNS

♦ REDUCTIONS

Map 10

334

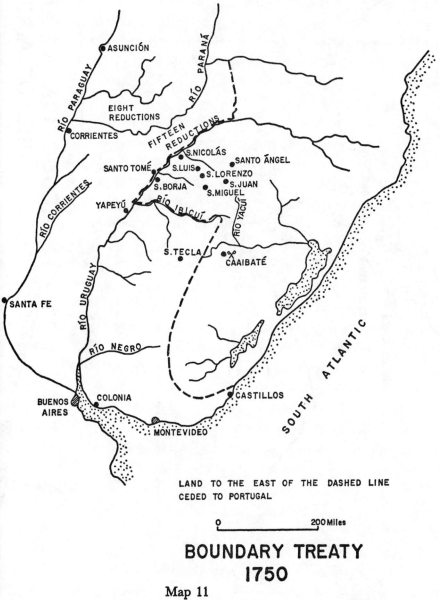

LAND TO THE EAST OF THE DASHED LINE
CEDED TO PORTUGAL

0   200 Miles

BOUNDARY TREATY
1750

Map 11

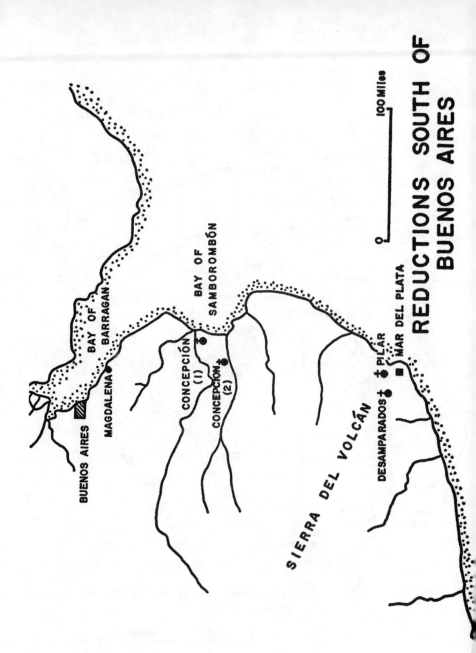

REDUCTIONS SOUTH OF
BUENOS AIRES

100 Miles

BUENOS AIRES

MAGDALENA

BARRAGAN

BAY OF

BAY OF
SAMBOROMBÓN

CONCEPCIÓN
(1)

CONCEPCIÓN
(2)

SIERRA DEL VOLCÁN

DESAMPARADOS

PILAR

MAR DEL PLATA

Map 12

Index

337